Royal Manchester Children's Hospital

"Pendlebury"

1829 - 1999

incorporating
Booth Hall,
Duchess of York
and
St Mary's Children's Unit

Pamela Barnes

CHURNET VALLEY BOOKS

ISBN 1 897949 42 1

Dedication

For my Mother, my sons and grandchildren,
and in loving memory of my husband (1933-1993)
and my father (1909-1980)

Acknowledgements

This has been a daunting undertaking. I have been greatly encouraged by Professor Robert Boyd, Professor Joe Moore and the late Dr Geoffrey Watson; by my sons Andrew and Nicholas, and many others, during the three years it has taken to get this history down.

I am most grateful to all the staff past and present who have rallied to my assistance with information and old photographs.

I acknowledge the great assistance of local history units especially that at Salford, and the Department of History of Medicine at Manchester University. I also must thank the Disley Local History Society and the Portico Library.

I have a special debt of gratitude to my tutors John Pickstone and Joan Mottram for their patience and understanding and to my son Nicholas for his critical assessment of my work.

Finally it is impossible to thank the many individuals who have helped in the collection of this information and I hope they will accept my collective thanks for their role in this homage to one hundred and seventy years of service to children.

Printed in Malta by Interprint Limited

FOREWORD

"There can be few more emotive subjects than that of sick children. With the advent of the 21st century, the Royal Manchester Children's Hospital will move into a new purpose built building and surroundings. As a tribute to all who have contributed to the well being and care of the thousands of children who have passed through this revered institution since 1829, it is fitting that the history is written. The true spirit of a hospital is to restore health and make advances in its methods and expertise. The writing of a history, not only honours the past, but highlights the purpose for the future; that children deserve the very best that can be offered to them, especially in time of sickness.

May the hospital continue to serve children in the future as it has in the past."

Sir Harry Secombe C.B.E.

GENERAL HOSPITAL FOR SICK CHILDREN, PENDLEBURY

(From a Photograph by Dr. H. R. Hutton.)

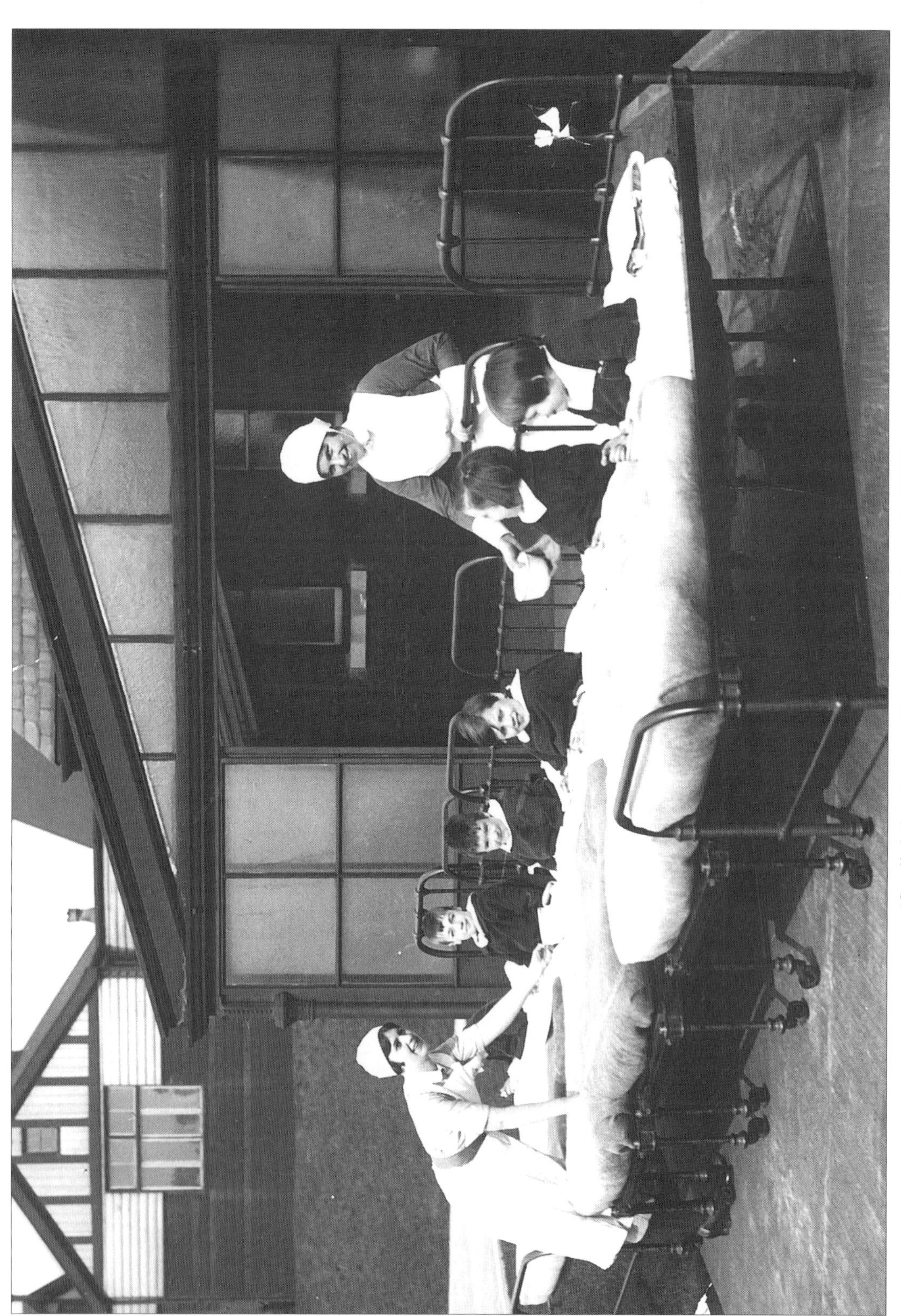

'Sunlight' and open-air treatment in the early 1920s.

Preface

This book is first and foremost about those who have believed in and become involved in the care of sick children here in the environs of Manchester and Salford over the past 170 years. It is the story of human endeavour to relieve the pain and suffering of children, through which was built up a service for children second to none in this country or the world. It is a quality service for children and their families.

Being involved in the care of very sick children is one of the most demanding responsibilities that can be given to anyone. Every single member of a hospital community has a very important role to play in the care of a sick child. Everyone shares in the many triumphs - and in the occasional tragedies. When a child is struck down by serious illness or injury, the family, and all hospital staff members, are not only attempting to treat the child' illness but to come to terms with the intolerable. A children's hospital is like no other.

The story of The Royal Manchester Children's Hospital - and the other children's hospitals in Manchester and Salford - is about the courage, compassion and understanding of all concerned. It is also the story of those who believed in the rights and needs of children, and it is the story of a developing speciality in medicine.

The Royal Manchester Children's Hospital was opened in 1829 as a General Dispensary for the Children of Salford and Manchester, in Back King Street, Manchester. The establishment of the dispensary, entirely for children, was part of a broader scene, enabling children's medicine to extend, and to achieve the level of expertise it has in this community today. When Booth Hall Children's Hospital and The Duchess of York Hospital for Babies opened in this century, the service for children was again greatly enhanced.

In the present climate of imminent change in the services for children in the Manchester and Salford area, I felt a history had to be written, otherwise not only will much interesting material be lost, but important contacts would vanish. It is unthinkable that the enthusiasm, determination and energy that went into establishing these hospitals should go unrecorded.

The history of the Children's Hospitals in Manchester and Salford is one of many dedicated people working tirelessly, philanthropists, professionals and others, joined together in an effort to improve the care of sick children. Hand in hand with the hospital's history we see the progress over the years in the treatment of the diseases of childhood. Medicine was at the forefront of the changes in society. Christopher Lawrence says in his book *Medicine in the Making of Modern Britain, "By the 1920s, treatment in hospital, especially of the acutely ill young, using scientifically informed potent therapy, had become the object of much admiration"* and therefore was " *an instrument for social betterment"*.

Many historians have attempted to document the way in which clinical medicine became so important during the late 19th and early 20th centuries. Perhaps in a small way this history will add to the greater picture. So much has happened in the field of child health in Manchester and Salford since the opening of the General Dispensary for Children in 1829.

Finally, it is as a parent of a former patient treated in The Royal Manchester Children's Hospital, and also presently a member of the Board of Trustees for The Children's Trust, that I am attempting to put this history together. I intend it as a tribute to all who have contributed to the story, but I hope that, at the centre of every aspect, can be seen the issue of a child and family in crisis.

PENDLEBURY CHILDREN'S HOSPITAL. Engraving 1879.

Contents

Acknowledgments		
Foreword		
Preface		
Introduction		p. 9
Chapter 1	1829: The establishment of health care for the children of Manchester and Salford	p. 13
Chapter 2	The green slopes of Pendlebury - from city centre to the suburbs. Pendlebury - the first forty years	p. 21
Chapter 3	Victorian philanthropy and money raising	p. 43
Chapter 4	I 1829-1900. Pioneers in paediatrics - 1829-1900	p. 51
	II 1900 onwards. The World stage	p. 56
	The Convalescent Home, Lytham St Annes	p. 59
	Gartside Street Dispensary	p. 61
	Public health in Manchester and Salford	p. 66
Chapter 5	Nursing	p. 71
Chapter 6	Charities, royals and visiting celebrities	p.101
Chapter 7	The impact of two world wars on children's services	p.117
	Zachery Merton Convalescent Home, Pendlebury	p.126
	Outside influences on growing and learning, education, play and health	p.128
Chapter 8	The National Health Service	p.149
Chapter 9	Manchester Paediatric Club & the future of paediatrics	p.167
Chapter 10	Coming together - The Childrens Trust	p.175
	Booth Hall Children's Hospital	p.175
	Duchess of York Hospital for Babies	p.180
Chapter 11	Looking Back, Looking Forward	p.183
Appendices	1. MILESTONES AT A GLANCE	p.187
	2. HISTORY OF EPONYMOUS DEPARTMENTS	p.189
	3. BIBLIOGRAPHY AND REFERENCES	p.190
THE UNIVERSITY OF SALFORD SCHOOL OF NURSING		p.191
ROYAL MANCHESTER CHILDREN'S HOSPITAL LEAGUE OF FRIENDS		p.192

Etching of Manchester - the Cathedral and the River Irwell, 1815.
(Courtesy of Cannon Denby, Manchester Cathedral)

Introduction

The story of the Royal Manchester Children's Hospital and the growth of a health service for children in Manchester, Salford and beyond, is also a story of the people themselves. When the Royal Manchester Children's Hospital was inaugurated, Manchester was emerging as the first great industrial city. The growth of Manchester, particularly between 1780 and 1850 is an important part of the story of a people and their special culture.

Manchester has been inhabited for over two thousand years. At the time of the Roman Empire, Mancunium was a small settlement and frontier post. After the collapse of the Roman Empire in the 5th century, Manchester is not noted again until the Norman Conquest in 1066, and it was not considered a town of any importance until well into the 1700s.

At the time of the Norman Conquest it was part of the Salford Hundred, which slowly dwindled away under the Norman Earl to whom it was bequeathed, and the administrative separation of Manchester and Salford was achieved. Manchester became a manor land ruled by the Grelley family for over two centuries. Although small during the medieval period, it was a centre of craft industries and was beginning to be wealthy. It was important enough to gain its charter in 1301, at which time it covered about 60 square miles, including Stockport, Urmston, Flixton, Eccles, Prestwich, Oldham and Ashton. A collegiate was granted in 1421 to St Mary's and this eventually became the Cheetham's Hospital School and Free Public Library.

In 1590 the Mosleys took over the manor and lands and held them until they were purchased by the Corporation of Manchester in 1846. Salford itself was incorporated into the Duchy of Lancaster in 1399 and has remained thus ever since.

During the 16th and 17th centuries the town of Manchester developed into the regional capital of South East Lancashire. Long before the industrial revolution Manchester was evolving as a market centre for woollens and linens. Its economy was built on diversity as it fast became a merchant town. Raw materials were imported and this attracted immigrant workers; *"Its population rose from an estimated 2,300 in 1543 to around 43,000 in 1773"*. Cotton was not added to established production until the 1690s.

During the 18th century Manchester really began to emerge as a town of significance. A system of trade and manufacturing had produced many successful families, and a well established business community. The advent of a transportation system centred in Manchester, of packhorse paths, roads and canals, with the final completion of the canal route from Manchester to Liverpool in 1736, sealed Manchester's importance. The scene was set for the most historic explosion to be witnessed in the industrial world. Manchester, alongside the City of Salford, became the greatest trading city created by the industrial revolution.

Salford was also an ancient town with a charter dating back to 1230. This 'ancient and royal borough' was partially divided from Manchester by the River Irwell. During the industrial revolution it grew rapidly with factories, engineering works and collieries, and acquired city status. The Manchester Ship Canal had a great influence on Salford as it became the main docks for the area. It was to become the 'gateway to south-east Lancashire'.

The industrial character of the city was to cause the same social difficulties as it did in Manchester. It shared the same appalling housing conditions for most of its population, giving rise to much chronic illness and disease, great infant mortality and much reduced life expectancy in the population as a whole. Yet this population of 'workers' was much needed for the ever increasing number of factories, warehouses and transportation services.

So alongside this picture of quick profit and fortunes, and the need for an enormous workforce, there were the squalid conditions of industrial urbanisation of most inhabitants of Manchester and Salford. Manchester was at the turn of the century *"one of the most overcrowded and unhealthy places in the whole of England"*. (Howarth *Boomtown Manchester)* Against this background, the story of the Sick Children of Manchester and Salford is told.

The industrial revolution saw a huge increase in the birth rate and children were indeed seen as a splendid economic resource to enable the wheels of industry to turn. The effects of polluted water, vile housing conditions, abysmal ventilation, festering rubbish heaps and poor drains made Manchester the prey of recurrent epidemics of disease. Work kept the whole family outside the home and children were increasingly under the control of those who were profiting through their labours. No longer were they working within the family circle of a close-knit society. But as well as those whose ambition fueled the economic necessity of child labour, and the atrocious conditions in which children and families lived with a terrible child death rate - "50% of children under 5" - some *"medical missionaries"* began to care about the health needs of the population, and especially children.

Gradually public concern was expressed. Another contributory factor was the end of the Napoleonic Wars, which was followed by a severe depression in trading. The picture for most children in Manchester and Salford was one of wretchedness, and destitution. The Poor Law dating from 1600 had always given inadequate care. The New Poor Law Amendment of 1834 had a utilitarian agenda seeking to reduce the weight and expense of poverty on the parishes. It also promoted vaccination. Society as a whole mistrusted the agenda of this new poor law.

During the late 18th century there had been the emergence of 'enlightened thought' - the 'Age of Reason' - with the professional and educated classes promoting good citizenship. Local industrialists and aspiring philanthropists began to see the need for 'institutions' to provide care for the *'deserving'*. Throughout the Country there was an explosion of hospitals and dispensaries - and these were fueled by the failures of the Poor Laws. The amended Poor Law of 1834 again showed a society wanting to distinguish between the *'deserving'* and *'undeserving'* poor.

As far back as 1796 a Board of Health was set up by local medical practitioners in Manchester, to try to slow the raging tide of various epidemics such as typhus fever, scarlet fever and small pox. This led to the establishment of the House of Recovery for adults in Portland Street. Sir Robert Peel, president of this new fever hospital, was able to use the evidence from Manchester doctors, regarding children, to support his 1802 legislation protecting apprentices, with the Restriction of Hours of Work Bill. This was followed in 1819 by the Bill to *"Prohibit the employment of children under 9 and nightwork of children in cotton factories."*

Alongside this legislation the effects on the health of the children of vaccination was beginning to be appreciated. But even these small advances were overtaken by the steep rise in other serious diseases, especially infectious diseases such as measles which were encouraged by the new urban overcrowding. *"John Roberton found that during the period 1821-1825 measles was twice as fatal to young children as smallpox"*.

At this time small charities were emerging for the relief of the poor married woman in child labour, known as Lying in Charities. These charity committees began to support dispensaries, persuading them to allow their apothecaries to help the Lying in Charities, for a fee. But more was needed. The birth rate was increasing, more women in labour were needing assistance - and many children born into this scene of squalor had little chance with disease. Childhood mortality was rising sharply. The terrible conditions in the factories, where children were employed from very early ages, were also responsible not only for an increase in disease but horrendous accidents, leaving children maimed and mutilated.

Perhaps the first step in recognising the health needs of children, was the establishment of the Foundling Hospital in 1742 in London by the distinguished philanthropist Captain Thomas Coram, *"for the maintenance and education of exposed and deserted young children."* An orphanage was also founded in 1751 in Paris and reorganised into a hospital in 1802. By 1815 this institution, Enfants Trouvés, was caring primarily for sick babies, but with a death rate of 93%. Despite this high rate of mortality, there were still those that perceived the need for special services for children; through charitable institutions, local citizens could fulfil the most *"humanitarian requisite of providing helpless children with medical and nursing care unavailable in their own homes."*

The *"dispensary for children movement"* began in 1816 in this country when John Brunnell Davis founded the Universal Dispensary in London. The mission of this dispensary was to enable sick children to receive treatment, to teach parents about child care and to enable physicians to learn about childhood diseases. In the forefront of this humanitarian movement were some citizens of Manchester and Salford, who set about founding a General Dispensary for Children and on 14th January 1829 the following news item appeared:

GENERAL DISPENSARY FOR CHILDREN.
—7, Chapel Walks, January 14, 1829.—At a GENERAL MEETING of the COMMITTEE, holden this day,—JAMES OUGHTON, Esq., in the chair:

It was resolved,—That the degree of public support with which this institution has already been favoured, and the additional aid which its projectors are promised, appear to this meeting to authorise the completion of the necessary arrangements for the commencement of its charitable designs.

That this meeting acknowledges with gratitude the kindness of the very Reverend the Warden of Manchester, in consenting to become the President of the institution.

That the premises situate No. 25, in Back King street, Manchester, being from their situation and extent, well adapted, to the purposes of the institution, the same be now taken and opened for the general objects of the Dispensary on the first Monday in February.

That an adequate number of recommendations for out and home-patients, according to the form now submitted, be immediately printed, and distributed for use amongst the subscribers.—By order of the Committee,

THOMAS WHEELER, Honorary Secretary.

This was the birth of hospital services for children in Manchester and Salford, and it would continue, without interruption, from January 1829 for a total of 170 years to today. The history of the Manchester Children's Hospital Service is the history of the oldest continuous service for sick children in this country.

Monday morning out-patients in the Dispensary about 1870.

CHAPTER 1

1829 - THE ESTABLISHMENT OF HEALTH CARE FOR THE CHILDREN OF MANCHESTER AND SALFORD

British children's hospitals were much slower to develop than their counterparts in Europe. Children's Hospitals had already been established in countries such as Austria, Belgium, Denmark, Germany, Italy, Russia and Turkey at least fifty years before they were founded in Britain. In 1802, a previously existing establishment for children in Paris was changed into a hospital for children, but there was no development in Britain until 1816, in London, and this was discontinued after a few years. Hospitals established at this time were intended for the worthy only - and children were not necessarily thought worthy - indeed other peoples' children were rarely considered so. Their severe illnesses were mainly infectious fevers like measles, scarlartina and diphtheria, and it was risky to admit them to hospital. It was felt that most children's illnesses were not cureable anyway.

The establishment of the General Dispensary for Sick Children in Manchester in 1829, places the Royal Manchester Children's Hospital as the first continuous service for children in the country. It was also to become *"the first paediatric teaching establishment in Great Britain"*. At last there were those who were beginning to take children's health seriously.

The services for children now moved forward encouraged by articles like that by Dr Kay, a small dissertation regarding *The Moral & Physical Conditions of the Working Classes Employed in the Cotton Manufacture in Manchester,* written in 1832. He recognised that public welfare could only be promoted by communicating the poor conditions of the population to the middle class and gentry of England. He highlighted the situation of a family: The Browns lived in furnished apartments, in a couple of rooms up two flights of stairs, in a house where there were two other sets of lodgers. There were eight children and the total income for the family was that earned by the eldest boy of sixteen years of age.

He wrote that the *"united exertions of the individual members of society were required, to procure a moral and physical change in the community."* He explained that the political safety of the wealthy *"was in danger of collapsing through ignorance of the poor."* He was certain that only by improving the conditions of the poor and teaching them about health and hygiene could the health of the population as a whole move forward. He maintained that legislation to ensure that this happened would be necessary.

From the *Illustrated London News* 1862, the *"Dwellings of Manchester Operatives"*.

The rationale behind setting up the General Dispensary is somewhat unclear. Was it because children were excluded from voluntary hospitals; was it the relevant medical men, excluded from voluntary hospital appointments seeking to promote their own expertise, or was there a genuine desire to alleviate the plight of the many poor and destitute children in the community? It was generally agreed that *"strong children were needed to produce a healthy adult labour force"*, a thought which may have underlaid some of the philanthropy of entrepreneurs. It would seem from all the literature available, including the annual reports, that it was a combination of all these aspects.

The first committee of the Dispensary, elected on 27th November 1828, included:

Hugh Beaver - Spinner & Manufacturer. The Temple, Cheetham Hill.
William Townsend - Merchant. Ardwick Place, Ardwick.
James Lees - Merchant. Adelphi, Salford.
William Crossley - General Agent. York Street, Manchester.
William Hurst - Cotton Merchant. Ardwick Green.
Asshetor Clegg
John Crossley (John Crossley & Sons) - Cotton Worsted Spinners. 5 Cromford Court.
John Dixon
Wainwright Belhouse
John Gould - Manufacturer. Leigh Place, Ardwick.
Thomas Wheeler - Attorney. 7 Chapel Walks.
John Shaw - Gentleman. Gratrix Street, Hulme.
Thomas Cash - Merchant. Gorsefield, Bolton.
Thomas Bent - Ale Brewer. 1 Broughton Road, Salford.
James Collyer Harter - Dry Salter. Broughton Hall Broughton Nr. Preston.

The new clinic would depend entirely upon voluntary contributions from subscribers. Daniel Grant, said to have been the basis for one of the Cheeryble brothers immortalised by Charles Dickens, was one of the first subscribers and a most generous benefactor, giving over two thirds of the first year's income, £42. From this list of intitial subscribers it is clear that it was the emerging merchants and manufacturers who had the greatest desire to support children. There seems little evidence at first of any medical impetus.

It was a very small dispensary that was first set up in Back King Street, Ridgefield, treating sick children gratuitously. Resources were small and the income in the first year barely reached £60. Upwards of 1,500 sick children were treated annually through voluntary subscriptions and the medical staff stayed the same until 1854. Dr Alexander, a physician, served the Dispensary for 25 years, leaving Manchester in 1854, but the reason for his departure is not given in the reports. Mr Walton Barton Stott MRCS was a subscriber, as well as the surgeon, and served the Dispensary for 28 years. He left part of his estate to the Dispensary on his death and is buried at St. Mary's The Virgin Churchyard, Disley, where he lived for many years. These doctors probably gave their services for free. It would help them to enhance their own private reputation and gain recognition while making a very evident contribution to society.

Daniel Grant

In 1833 the President of the Dispensary for Sick Children was the Very Rev. T. Calvert DD, Warden of Christ's College, Manchester (later the Cathedral). The committee included the Rev Wray, Daniel Grant Esq, Benjamin Heywood MP and Thomas Houldsworth MP. The medical officers were Dr

Alexander and W. Barton Stott Esq, the Apothecary was Mr Hollowell. By 1833 the Dispensary was beginning to attract other significant names who felt they would benefit from the association wth the children's Dispensary. Daniel Grant Esq. who had given an initial subscription of £42 in 1829, continued to subscribe £10 annually.

In 1833 the medical report established that:

Total	1105	children were admitted
	208	were still on books at commencement of year
	1313	Of these during the year -
	942	discharged as cured.
	56	discharged as relieved
	34	discharged as incurable
	95	discharged for non attendance
	82	Died
leaving	104	children remaining on the books.

The budget of expenditure in 1833 was £154 16s 5d.

"And what compact so holy and so binding as that which, resulting from recollection of kindness rendered by the rich to the poor in their affliction, connects the gift with the giver, the gratitudes with the receiver?" Extract from the 1833 Annual Report.

This extract from the report shows how association with the institution was felt to be advantageous. The following extracts further support the belief that there was at last a genuine desire to offer and promote the cause of the sick and needy children in Manchester and Salford.

"The unnaturalness - the strange anomaly of a child's death - is seldom reflected upon as it deserves. We are too ready to acquiesce in the premature extinction of infant lives as if it were a law of Nature - So careful of the type she seems, So careless of the single life; - when the fault really lies at our own doors.

"A dying child," says the Rev. Charles Kingsley, "is to me one of the most dreadful sights in the world.

"I believe it to be a priceless boon to the child to have lived a week or a day; but oh! What has God given to this thankless earth, and what has the earth thrown away; and in nine cases out of ten, from its own neglect and carelessness."

Extracts from Report of Medical Officers of the Dispensary 1863.

1833 saw the Factory Act to prohibit children under 9 years of age working in factories and allowing those between 9-13 years to work only 9 hours per day. Many parents though, needing the money, lied about the ages of their children. Sunday was the only day that some of these children would see sunlight. Rotting garbage strewed the streets and sanitation was non-existent. Housing was poor, often a damp dark cellar, as was nutrition.

There was very little administrative change until 1843 when the rules of Governors were altered - *"That any sick child (wherever residing) recommended by a subscriber, be admissible to this charity as an Out Patient; and that all children (under the age of 14) residing within Manchester and Salford be considered (upon such recommendation) entitled to be visited as a Home Patient if case require it"*. The medical staff was increased by a further surgeon, Mr Hancock. The rules of government were amended to say that medical officers could be increased according to need and in 1849 Mr Nadin became a further medical officer working alongside Mr Stott and Mr Hancock, with Dr Alexander the Consulting Physician. The medical officers may have been salaried in a form of internship to gain experience under a leading physician.

By 1850 the General Dispensary for Children had moved to 126 Cross Street from Back King Street. The numbers of children admitted remained the same, approximately 1500, with fewer deaths during this year.

1851-52 saw a drop in the numbers of children treated as a direct result of a lack of funding. Only 1,000 were admitted and the death rate rose to 66. However, by 1854, when the Dispensary moved to North Parade, St. Mary's, subscriptions had again increased and so had the number of admissions. In 1854 The Right Rev Lord Bishop of Manchester became the patron, with the Dean of the new Cathedral, becoming the president. The name of Dr Louis Borchardt appears as the Consulting Physician, whilst the medical officers remain as Mr Stott, Mr Hancock and Mr Nadin. Dr Louis Borchardt was a political refugee from Berlin, a specialist in children's diseases, with considerable knowledge and an experience of hospital administration.

Dr Louis Borchardt

In 1855, 1555 cases were treated, 156 died and 215 were visited at home. The cases were treated at an average cost of 1s 6d per head. This was at a time when 50% of the children in Manchester and Salford died under the age of 10. Dr Borchardt had persuaded the governing body to offer 6 beds for in-patients on a trial basis. There was fortunately a big upturn in subscribers, a name now appearing being that of the wife of Sir Charles Hallé, of Hallé Orchestra fame. Daniel Grant continued his subscription of £10 annually.

The in-patient beds were opened in May 1855 and were deemed to be a great success. By 1858 it was agreed to extend to 25 beds, and the objects of the institution were to be:

I. The medical and surgical treatment of poor children.

II. The attainment and Diffusion of Knowledge regarding the Disease of Children.

The patron of the Dispensary, in 1858, continued to be the Lord Bishop of Manchester, together now with the Mayor of Salford. The president was Robert N. Phillips Esq. The name also appears of Mr H.M. Steinthal as a member of the committee. He was honorary secretary from 1880 to 1899.

Although the increase from 6 to 25 in-patient beds was agreed in 1856, there were still only 6 in-patient beds in 1858. During the year, 2561 children were treated in the Dispensary, 54 in-patients were treated, 47 were cured and 3 died. The most common diseases that required attention and treatment were those of the "*respiratory organs*", which probably had much to do with poor clothing, and the filthy and polluted air in the two cities.

Mr H.M. Steinthal

The following year 1859 saw the Dispensary move to 16 Bridge Street. R.N. Phillips Esq., a new Manchester MP, became the president of the governing body. Dr Louis Borchardt was working at the Dispensary every day and of the 1858 children treated 48% were diagnosed with infections of mucous membranes. There was a severe outbreak of scarletina in Mancheser and Salford but with fewer deaths than previous outbreaks.

The subscription system allowed for examination and admission of children to the Children's Hospital through recommendation by subscribers. This was common practice throughout hospitals and was locally called the 'Governors ticket'. When the subscription list was published in 1859, with the annual general report, it could be seen that an anonymous friend and the Mayor of Manchester had both given £100 each, a considerable amount. A proposition was made to the governing committee to amalgamate the children's institution with St Mary's Hospital. The committee felt there to be strong and unanswerable objections to this proposal and minuted "*treatment of the very different diseases of children and women should ever be kept apart and distinct*".

Dr Louis Borchardt was not alone as a European doctor to influence the early history of services for sick children in Manchester and Salford. A professor of medicine from Budapest, Dr Schoepf Merei, received support from Mr Salis Schwabe Esq. to set up a dispensary for children in Stevenson Square in 1853. In 1856 it was a considerable dispensary for children with 2 in-patient beds. Dr Merei died in 1858 and in 1876 the establishment moved to Cheetham Hill, where there were 24 beds initially. These beds for children were moved at a much later date, 1934, into the Northern Hospital on Cheetham Hill Road, Manchester.

Dr Schoepf Merei

Dr Merei founded a School for the Instruction in Diseases of Children, and the study of "*proper development*". He published a book in 1855 which was called *On the Disorders of Infantile Development and Rickets*. His pioneering work with children will have had much influence on the Children's Dispensary. At the time of Dr Merei's work in Stevenson Square, the Dispensary was run by Dr Louis Borchardt. Both of these European doctors believed in the importance of paediatric services and there is some evidence of cooperation between them, but the death of Dr Merei in 1856 probably allowed the Dispensary to gain greater prestige under the guidance of Dr Borchardt.

The Schwabe family who supported Dr Merei owned, in 1839, a silk mill in Portland St, Manchester. The silk was spun, thrown and dyed on the premises, and the Jacquard loom was used to produce splendid silks for mansions and royal palaces, some being sold at 7 guineas a yard. In the 1860s the Schwabe family also supported the Children's Dispensary extensively. It is noted that Mrs Adolph Schwabe, in 1867 at Christmas time, gave every child in the hospital clothes and toys. They also donated a Schwabe family cot.

By 1864 the success of the Children's Dispensary and Hospital run by Dr Borchardt began to be obvious. The governing body had increased - there were now three patrons: the Bishop of Manchester, the Mayor of Manchester and R.N. Phillips Esq. M.P., Oliver Heywood Esq., had been elected president and there was a formidable Ladies Committee now established with nine members, including Mrs R.N. Phillips and Mrs Charles Souchay, wives of two of the Board of Governors. Dr Louis Borchardt was the Consulting Physician, W.B. Stott the Consulting Surgeon, J.E.K. Nadin has become an Honorary Surgeon and Mr Robert B. Smart, Mr John Lang and Dr John Roberts were Medical Officers. Mr James Gwyther was the House Surgeon and Miss Thompson the Matron.

An extremely interesting letter in 1864 in the Manchester Guardian on infant mortality in Manchester, encapsulated the situation as seen by E.M. Stoehr, Esq., a wealthy merchant from Fallowfield, supplying comparative figures. It demonstrates the enormously high mortality rate of the children in Manchester and districts, said to be the highest in the country:

Sir, - My statement in a former letter addressed to you, respecting infant mortality in Manchester, I took from a paper by John Snow, M.D., F.R.S., published in the Medical Times and Gazette, May 28, 1853, and re-printed in the "Half-yearly Abstract of Medical Sciences." Dr Snow says:- "In Liverpool and Manchester, half the children born die before they are five years of age, the numbers being 52 and 51 per cent. In Birmingham, 48 per cent of the deaths occur before this age; and in London rather more than 40 per cent, but in Wiltshire and Surrey only 31 per cent."

I might rest satisfied with this extent, shielding myself with such an eminent authority. My purpose was to arouse sympathy of the benevolent towards the Children's Hospital, in Bridge Street, and kindred institutions, and I used the statement only as an auxiliary to prove the great necessity for them in this city. If it can be shown that the mortality of infants is greater in Manchester than in other large towns, my argument will stand unimpaired, even if my figures were not quite correct.

Your correspondent, "J. Whitehead, M.D.," takes the whole district, Chorlton and Salford included, and gives an average of deaths, under five years, for the three years, 1859-61, as 32 per cent. To show how the case stands for Manchester alone, I have extracted from the Registrar-General's report the following figures:-

	Births in Manchester	Deaths under Five years of age	%
1854	9,395	3,852	41%
1855	9,166	3,354	37%
1856	8,979	3,942	43%
1857	9,076	3,690	40%
1858	8,741	3,852	44%
1859	9,083	3,237	35%
1860	9,087	2,908	32%
1861	9,320	3,575	38%
Total	72,847	28,410	

The average death rate under five years of age for the last eight years is therefore, 39 per cent of all the children born in Manchester.

The Registrar-General's report gives the births and deaths, but not the infants' deaths, in the several districts which form the Manchester Union. From the general death rate of these districts we may, however, I think, draw a conclusion as to the proportion of children's deaths.

I will take the five districts, Ancoats, Deansgate, London Road, Market Street, and St George's, which form the inner town, and contained in 1860, on 1,480 acres, a population of 185,410, and compare them with the five districts, Newton, Cheetham, Failsworth, Blackley, and Prestwich, the outer town, which are on an area of 11,148 acres, inhabited by 58,578.

In the eight years, 1854-61, the figures are as follows:-

	Total Births	Total Deaths	Proportion of Deaths to Births
Inner town	57,787	49,991	86%
Outer town	14,960	9,248	below 62%

> Or, in other words, to every 100 births there are, annually rather more than 86 deaths in the inner town, and less than 62 in the outskirts.
> If the total proportion is so highly favourable to the town districts, which are inhabited by the working classes and the poor, and who furnish almost exclusively the applicants to such institutions as the Children's Hospital, it may be presumed that the death rate of infants bears a similar unfavourable proportion, and that Dr Snow's estimate may, after all, not be far from the truth."
> *'Infant Mortality in Manchester' - letter to The Editor, Manchester Guardian, E.M. Stoehr. 1864.*

Mrs Stoer, the wife of the above, was a member of the Ladies committee.

With the recession in 1865 came stoppages in the cotton mills; entire families were out of work. The annual report of 1865 documents a change of direction in the policy of the Dispensary, that of greater visiting of sick children in their homes. The report claimed *"much lasting good for children and parents alike"*. The policy followed recommendations of medical officers of health who had highlighted the poor nutrition of children and the inability of mothers to understand and cope with the problem. The Hospital and Dispensary encouraged the mothers to be with their children on the ward. The Governors saw this as an opportunity to educate them in the needs of their children. This policy for parents to be with their children gradually decreased in the years following, ceasing altogether in the early 20th century. Not until after research in the 1940s and 1950s did it again become a part of the care of children in hospital.

By 1867 the governing body, in a clear and confident statement, decided to uproot from their position in Bridge Street and move to the spacious fields of Pendlebury. They now had a well established and notable board of governors and an ambitious and motivated medical team. The Dispensary in Bridge Street had become indispensable but they needed more accommodation for in-patients. At the annual meeting of 1867 the momentous decision was made to relocate and build a new Children's Hospital and Dispensary. The Committee determined, because of the extreme overcrowding of the present building, to build a larger hospital in the suburbs and to erect a new dispensary within the city for the constantly growing number of applicants requiring medical relief. Gartside Street Dispensary, which was later to become the Out-patients' Department for the Royal Manchester Children's Hospital, was commissioned to be built. On 18th September 1868, the Bishop of Manchester laid the foundation stone for this new Dispensary within the city.

At this time there were 3 Patrons and 21 Vice Presidents, with Oliver Heywood Esq. as the president. Oliver Heywood was the second son of Sir Benjamin Heywood. Born in 1825, he was educated at Eton and conducted the affairs of the family bank until 1874. He became chairman of many local charities and was a particularly well-loved and well-known figure in Manchester, continuing to drive his white horse between his business and home for many years. He became the first freeman of Manchester in 1888.

The number of cases treated in the old Bridge Street premises of the Dispensary had risen to 7,000, with 350 admitted to hospital. The new Gartside Street Dispensary would accommodate all the out-patients, whilst in-patients would go out to Pendlebury. The new Gartside Street would remain, with some alteration, an out-patient provision until it closed in 1991 when it moved into the Old Nurses Home, Colwyn House, at Pendlebury (RMCH).

A suitable green field site of nearly six acres was secured at Pendlebury. The cost of this new site was £450 per acre, and the hospital was to be built on the new pavilion system, so favoured by Miss Florence Nightingale.

The Royal Manchester Children's Hospital.

CHAPTER 2

THE GREEN SLOPES OF PENDLEBURY - FROM CITY CENTRE TO THE SUBURBS

The new site chosen by the governing body was considered a *"bright and airy spot"* and was four miles from Manchester city centre. Land, of course, was considerably cheaper here in Salford and the site bought for the new hospital on a hillside in the green fields of Pendlebury, was well suited for the purposes. Although called the Manchester Children's Hospital, even after the distinction of 'Royal' was conferred on it by King George V in 1923, the Hospital has always been known affectionately as 'Pendlebury'. I will refer to it as such in this book.

The decision to build was taken at the AGM in 1867, but the committee had long beleved in the need for a separate children's establishment for the treatment of childhood diseases. As far back as 1855 the committee had minuted that children must be treated in an institution solely for that purpose and they quoted testimonies from two men of high repute within the medical profession to substantiate their beliefs:

"The establishment of a Children's Hospital, while proving an inestimable boon to themselves and their distressed parents, must also greatly tend to the advancement of science in the important department of infantile diseases." Sir John Forbes.

"It is a truth which deserves publicity, that the imperfection of our knowledge in Children's diseases is mainly owing to the want of Hospitals dedicated to the reception of sick children." Dr Watson.

The quotations are also a clear statement of rising professional careerism - the emergence of an independent hospital is driven not only by need but also by professional ambition. This was a time of emerging new disciplines in medicine, eg ear, nose and throat (E.N.T.) and ophthalmology specialities, both of which are reflected in the growth of the Children's Hospitals. The governing body of the hospital endorsed these opinions:

It is the wish of the Committee, with God's blessing, to forward these several ends. To attain them will demand a considerable increase of income; but in this important particular they confess they are very hopeful. Their past experience will not suffer them to mistrust, in this good cause, the sense of duty, the intelligence, humanity, and liberality, of their fellow-citizens.

When at the 38th meeting of subscribers in 1867 the general report was read for the previous year, it was stated that 7,014 cases had been treated, 4,702 were cured and 478 relieved. There had been 326 children admitted of whom 217 were deemed cured and 59 relieved. The Board acknowledged the dedication to their duties of Dr Borchardt and Dr Gwyther, and also the huge increase in their work and the overcrowding of the facilities. The total expenditure for the year had been £1,743. 2s. 2d. Subscriptions had fallen below the expenditure. The average cost of treating a child in the Dispensary had gone up to 3s 1d., and to £2 12s 3d for those admitted. The death rate for children in Manchester and Salford was still running at approximately 50% under five, and the committee found that 25 beds were inadequate to cope with the needs of sick children.

So despite the financial shortfall, a proposal was made to build a new hospital and dispensary. The committee considered the character of the new buildings *"meticulously"* and decided upon the Pavilion System for the Hospital. There were to be 3 wards of 26 beds each. The relocation of the dispensary would cost £3,000 and the hospital building would cost approximately £12,000, making a total of £15,000 required. The President, Mr Oliver

Heywood already had promises of £10,000. The meeting of the Governors, on March 27th 1867, in the Mayor's Parlour of Manchester Town Hall, passed the proposal for a new hospital.

Heywoods Bank in St Annes Square. Oliver Heywood, of the Heywood banking family, and a director of the bank, was the second President of the Hospital (1865-92).

There now began a large increase in home visits. Typhus and diphtheria continued to be deadly diseases of childhood, but the largest group was still amongst those suffering from respiratory disorders. The medical report continued to point out strongly the poor sanitary conditions in Manchester and that these conditions led to the high mortality rate of children. It was minuted that Manchester should appoint an officer of health to combat this situation, but a huge argument ensued between the medical men and the council over this issue, and the minutes show that compromises were reached and they moved on to the main business of *"contributions for the new building"*.

The building fund was inaugurated with the large donation of £1,000 from J.&N. Phillips & Co, followed by £750 each from Mr H. M. Steinthal and Mr Adolph Schwabe, £500 from Oliver Heywood and other large amounts from other subscribers.

At the meeting of subscribers in 1871, the planning of the new hospital was well under way. A small building committee was set up consisting of Mr Steinthal, Mr J.H. Agnew and Drs Borchardt, Barton and Gwyther. Bankers to the New Hospital Fund were Heywood Bros & Co. St Annes Square.

The designs of Pennington & Bridger, Architects of Manchester, were chosen by the building committee and were exhibited in the Free Trade Hall and the gallery of Messrs. Agnew in Exchange St. The plans showed arrangements for 6 pavilions, containing 160 beds, together with administrative buildings. There would be 3 pavilions with 82 beds in the first phase. The builders were to be the company of a Mr Sentheim.

The plans showed the resident officers and lady superintendent's rooms near to the entrance hall. The corridor leading to the wards was to be light, twelve feet wide and to traverse the entire building. All wards were to resemble each other and be accessible from the

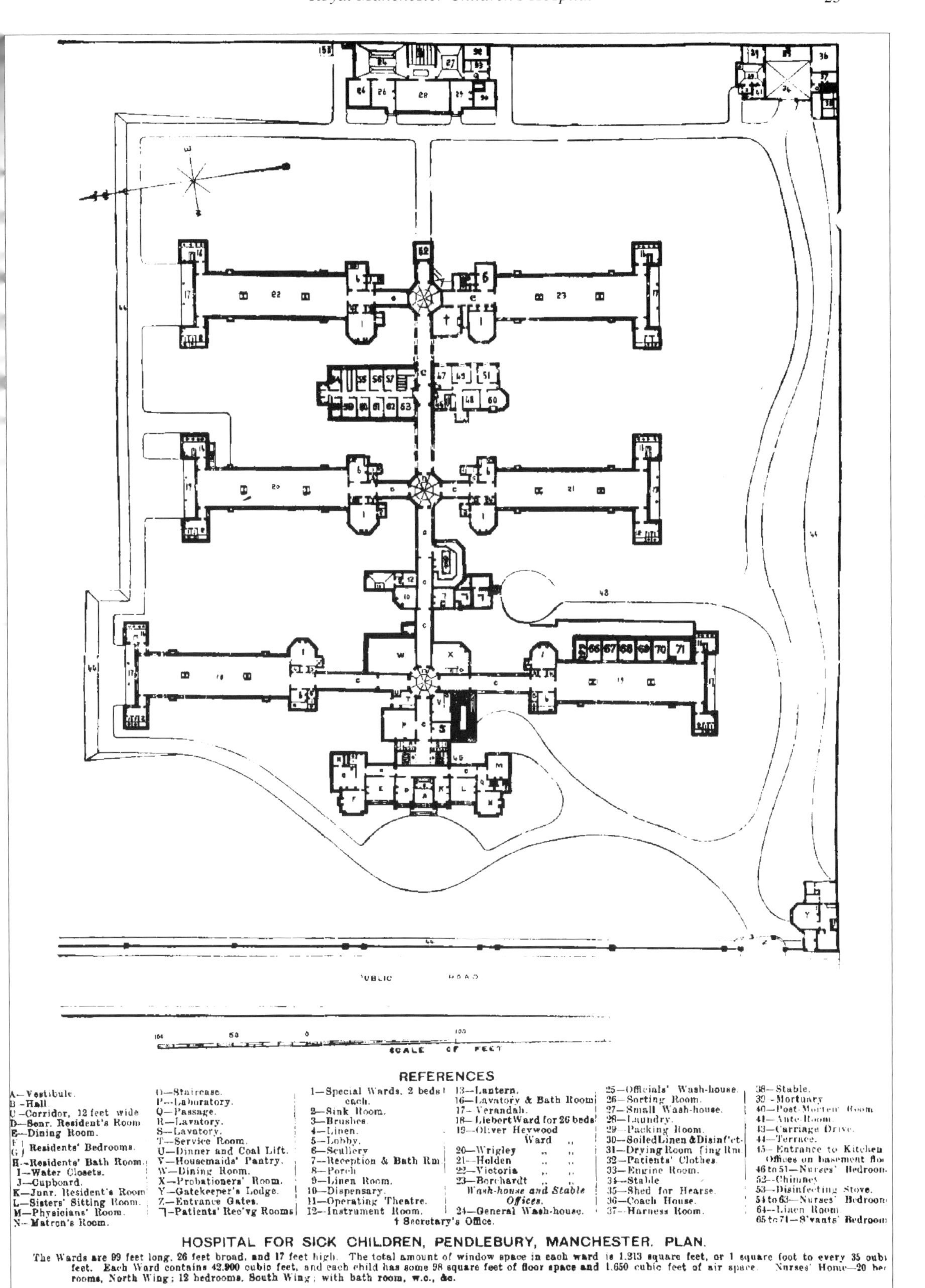

The plan of the original six pavilion wards and administration block.

main corridor - except for the fever ward. Each ward was to be under the care of a head nurse, assisted by 5 nurses. The building was identical in design to the new St Thomas's Hospital in London, built in 1870, and this is possibly why Florence Nightingale was to take such an interest in the new Manchester Childrens Hospital at Pendlebury.

At 1pm on 9th January 1873, in the new Fever Ward, the keys were handed over by Mr Steinthall, the Chairman of the Building Committee, to the Trustees Board of Governors, amidst a small gathering of invited guests. Amongst those present were the Lord Bishop of Manchester, the Lord Mayor of Manchester and Mrs Borchardt with Miss Borchardt and Master Borchardt. After looking around the new hospital the gathering sat down to a luncheon.

The floors of the wards were of shiny oak with four open tiled fireplaces in the centre of each ward, built back to back. Nurses accommodation was on the first floor above the administration block and the servants slept on this floor also, but they used a different staircase.

The designs for the new hospital were exhibited in the Free Trade Hall. The Grand Bazaar held here, in 1875, raised £24,000 over 3 days for the hospital building - an enormous sum at the time.

With the move to Pendlebury the annual number of *"in-patients rose from about 320 to about 550, and the expenditure was doubled by 1875 and doubled again by 1880"*. (J.V. Pickstone, *Medicine and Industrial Society,* 1985)

It had been argued that parents would not allow their children to be treated so far away from their homes in Pendlebury but the increase of patients belied this issue and Dr Louis Borchardt was able to claim that his doctors spent more than five hours a week in the Children's Hospital, far more than was spent by medics in other hospitals per week. The advent of the telephone was also believed to play an important part in the success of the venture. There was a direct line between Pendlebury and Gartside Street, allowing if necessary resident medical officers to communicate with the physician and surgeon.

Very soon the pressure on the institution demanded the completion of the building and the second phase to give the six planned wards. Further raising of funds was underway and the Free Trade Hall in Manchester was to see one of the largest fund raising events to take place in the country. The "bazaar" lasted for 3 days and raised over £24,000. Further generous donations from Mr Bernhard Liebert and Mr Oliver Heywood allowed full completion of the further three wards, which were formally opened on 30th January 1878.

So this institution, conceived in 1828, and moving between addresses over the next thirty years was finally commissioned as a children's specialist hospital and completed in

1878. It had a home in Salford not far from Manchester, in a high and pleasant green site, away from the filth, grime and poor air of the city. Built of "white" brick and set among its own landscaped gardens, the hospital would become home to some of the best medical and nursing expertise available to children not only in this country but internationally. The objects of the institution were reaffirmed in 1873:

I The Medical & Surgical Treatment of Young Children.

II The Attainment and Diffusion of Knowledge regarding the Diseases of Children.

These would be the basis on which a worldwide reputation in the treatment of the diseases of childhood would be achieved.

PENDLEBURY - THE FIRST FORTY YEARS (1873-1914)

The Grand Bazaar of 1875 had made the new project financially sound, and was added to by the many bequests including that from the estate of the late Mr Bernhard Liebert. The new hospital building was designed on the Pavilion System, advocated by Florence Nightingale of Crimean War fame. This Pavilion System or European model of hospital building, had a central corridor from which wards extended, allowing air and light on 3 sides, with beds facing outwards from the two long walls and high ceilings. This allowed a system of high quality nursing, as established by Florence Nightingale in nursing the Crimean troops. Pavilion wards became known as Nightingale wards throughout the country, as the system was gradually taken up everywhere.

The hospital was run by a Board of Governors who appointed the staff. A list of subscribers was published in the annual report at the Annual meeting, usually held in the Mayor's Parlour in the Town Hall of Manchester. The three patrons were to remain the Right Rev The Lord Bishop of Manchester, the Right Worshipful The Lord Mayor of Manchester, and the Right Worshipful the Mayor of Salford right up until the Hospital was incorporated into the N.H.S. in 1948.

The Board of Governance consisted of Trustees, with a President and Vice Presidents as elected, and the Board of Governors with a Chairman and Vice Chairman, with power to add to their number. The President, Honorary Physicians, and Honorary Surgeons were ex officio members of the Board. There was an elected House Committee and a Ladies Fund Committee. Rules of governance were carefully laid down and were very little altered over the years, usually then only to admit further property to their trusteeship.(See p. 40)

The Lady Superintendent (the title did not become Matron until the 1950s) was appointed by the Governors and was directly responsible to the Board. There was an interesting case testing this issue in 1937 when the then Lady Superintendent made an executive decision that was unacceptable to the Chairman of Governors. However as she was of *"Good ability in her professional skills"* she continued in her duties and the row subsided. In fact the minutes of the special meeting were wax sealed into an envelope with instructions not to be opened for 10 years. In today's climate the action of the Matron would have been considered a *"non issue"*. The Lady Superintendent (Matron) appointed was to devote her whole time to the duties of her office and make no arrangements which could interfere with the interests of the hospital. She was unable to leave the hospital without permission from the Governors.

There were several favourable aspects which coincided with the change from city centre to Pendlebury that enabled the new institution to be very successful. Firstly it was beginning to be appreciated that fresh air was beneficial for patients, particularly after the overcrowded conditions in which many of them lived. The second important issue was the development of the telegraphic communications system and installing a direct link system between the Hospital and the Dispensary (Out-patients).in Gartside Street as described earlier. The third aspect was that the reputation the hospital was rapidly gaining ground in the field of childhood disease. By the early 1900s it was considered to be a *"Mecca for physicians"*. And perhaps a fourth component was that fundraising for children, and particularly sick children, was now high on the list of Victorian philanthropy. Together, all these factors contributed to making the venture very quickly a great success story for sick children.

In 1879 the doctor who had contributed so much to all this, Dr Louis Borchardt, retired, and a new and very clever young doctor, Henry Ashby, was appointed as the Visiting Physician. He was to take the hospital forward and to increase its reputation still further, into the next century.

A letter from Florence Nightingale to the hospital in 1879, said that she considered the Children's Hospital in Manchester to be *"one of the best constructed hospitals in Europe"*.

The first three wards at Pendlebury were called the Heywood, Liebert and - on Dr Borchardt's retirement - Borchardt Wards. Oliver Heywood was the President at the time and like Bernhard Liebert a great benefactor. The new hospital was entered by a set of steps leading to an impressive colonnade and the front door. This led directly into the administration block and then onto the 12 footwide corridor from which the pavilion wards were accessed. A tall tower of over 100 feet was originally built above the administration block but this unfortunately had to be removed at a later date, due to subsidence caused by underground colliery workings. (A small compensation was paid by the colliery - £204.1s 6d - in the 1930s.)

The six pavilion wards had been completed in 1879, and in 1902 the ward used as a dormitory for nurses became available for patients. It was named Victoria Ward after the Queen who died in 1901 and the nurses were rehoused in a new block with separate bedrooms.

The hospital had a very formal ward routine. Grace was sung before meals. Children were dressed in blue and red flannel jackets with blouses and collars. Children were not allowed to be visited until they had been in for two Sundays and their visiting was then for two hours, two days per week. The Lady Superintendent visited and inspected every ward daily. One of the important duties of nurses looking after a ward was to make sure that the ward fires did not burn out. The day to day management was the responsibility of the Board of Governors. For instance the Housekeeping Committee would order all the food and other commodities and then pass on these orders to the governors.

During the late 1880s and into the 1890s hospitals throughout the country saw a major shift in emphasis. This was mostly a managerial change, but was also reflected in such areas as nurse training and conduct and these changes were evident at Pendlebury. By 1890 the hospital already had a reputation for the training of nurses. Nurses also looked after patients in their own homes, for which they received extra payment, and directions for the management of infants and young children were printed for the guidance of these nurses and parents. Every sister in charge of a ward was given "Bye Laws" from the Hospital which were not to be taken away. The Secretary of the Board was now known as the Chief Executive and conducted all business of the hospital unconnected with medical, surgical or nursing practice. He was not allowed to live further away than a five mile radius. He supervised the condition of buildings, looked after all Board Meetings and during Whit Week superintended the entire cleaning of the hospital. He worked closely with the Secretary of the Board of Governors in the Out-patients Department at Gartside Street. The Out-patients department was also cleaned during Whit Week.

Staff of the hospital were all resident, except for the honorary physicians and surgeons. This practice lasted into the second half of the twentieth century. Census returns for 1881 and 1891 throw an interesting light on the mix of staff and on the staff/patient ratios at these times. In 1881, on the night of the census, two medical officers were in residence, the Lady Superintendent, Miss Edith Elizabeth Cobb from Struck in Kent, plus 25 sisters, a housekeeper, maids, gardeners and others. It is interesting to note that the nursing sisters came from a wide variety of places - Glasgow, Norfolk, London, Leicester, Northampton, Wales, Canada, Ireland, New Zealand and Australia.

The 1891 Census showed that F.H. Westmacott, who was then 23 and went on to be the Oral Surgeon with an interest in anaesthetics. was resident that night, as was Richard Bowman, a fellow surgeon of 27 years of age. The Lady Superintendent was Hannah Maria Turner, 31, from Scotland, with six Head Sick Nurses including Jeanette Stevens, 31, who went on to become Matron at St Anne's Convalescent Home in 1897. The 15 other nurses present came from Surrey, Sussex, London, Liverpool, Cheshire, Shrewsbury, Hampshire, South Wales, Ireland and India. The 111 patients in the hospital on that night, came from as far afield as Birmingham, Chester, Derby, Ashton and Didsbury, and as close as Swinton, Pendlebury, Salford and Manchester.

During the years following the move of the hospital to Pendlebury up to the turn of the century, the ways in which children were treated and the medical conditions involved were continually widening. The great concern in the late 1860s was the very high infant mortality rate, with a large group of children suffering from diphtheria and typhus and respiratory organ

Lady Superintendent Grace Neill, her nursing staff and a doctor in 1879.

Main Corridor, Pendlebury, as designed in 1873. This is the main artery of the Hospital to this day.

Wrigley Ward showing the original fireplaces in the centre of the ward - photographed in the 1920s.

diseases. This was improving and the medical officers considered that rickets was receding, but there were still many cases of diseases relating to the digestive organs.

It should be noted that until the end of the 19th century it was still not acceptable practice amongst the middle classes to have their children admitted to hospital. Children's medicine was still strongly associated with fevers and highly infectious disease. Dr Borchardt's ward was indeed termed a 'fever ward' with a separate entrance from outside the hospital. The gradual implementation of many new procedures like Nightingale nursing and Listerian antisepsis slowly changed middle class attitudes. The following figures are available for the turn of the century:

Dispensary Figures for 1899	
New Patients	1488
Transferred as In Patients	1330
Made Home Patients	724
Deaths	224
Visits to Patients Homes	2000
Hospital Cases under treatment	1443
Discharged recovered/relieved	1213
Discharged unrelieved	29
Died	98
Remaining in Hospital	103
Surgical Operation	1067

The average number of days during which each patient remained in hospital was 32 days, and the average cost per in-patient was £5. 9s. 7d. The cost per bed was £59. 5. 0. Figures for other children's hospitals were as follows;

Great Ormond St.	£83. 0s 0d
East London	£64.15s 0d
Victoria Hospital	£87.15s 0d
Eveline	£85.10s 0d
North Eastern Hospital	£87.10s 0d
Paddington Green	£70.15s 0d
Manchester Children's Hospital	£59. 5s 0d
Birmingham Hospital	£78. 5s 0d

These figures were taken from Burdett's Hospital Annual and compare Manchester Children's Hospital very favourably with other similar institutions.

By 1900 the Dispensary was increasing further its workload, the Children's Hospital was treating a very large number of children and the Convalescent Home in St Anne's was receiving about 250 children per year. The patients came from a very wide geographical spread, as far away as Conway, St Anne's, Hayfield, Morcambe, Warrington and Wales, as well as locally from Manchester and Salford, Bury, Burnley, Rochdale and Altrincham.

The tables on the next two pages show the workload of the hospital in the way in which it was presented at the Annual Meeting, demonstrating the various conditions treated within the institutions for the children in 1899. By extracting the tables from the annual report in 1873 it demonstrates clearly the increase in workload and the variation of the pattern of disease.

This information gives a flavour of the developments from the move to Pendlebury in 1873 to the turn of the century. It would be fascinating to look at the entire pattern of changes in childhood disease in greater depth than this short history can hope to do. The doctors did not seem to think it an important issue to explain and record the medical conditions they were treating and it was not until the latter 19th century that case notes are available, reflecting again the management and practice changes at the time.

Tabular View of the Admission and Termination of Cases in the Dispensary of the General Hospital and Dispensary for Diseases of Sick Children.

DISEASE.	AGE OF PATIENT AND SEX ON ADMISSION.																				TOTAL.			MODE OF DISCHARGE OR TERMINATION.							
	6 Months.				2 Years.				5 Years.				7 Years.				12 Years.							Dead.		Cured.		Otherwise		Under Treatment	
	M.	Deaths.	F.	Deaths.	M.	Deaths.	F.	Deaths.	M.	Deaths.	F.	Deaths.	M.	Deaths.	F.	Deaths.	M.	Deaths.	F.	Deaths.	M.	F.	Total.	M.	F.	M.	F.	M.	F.	M.	F.
Typhus and Typheid	7		12	1	32		24	1	32		35	1	38		58		22		20		131	149	280	...	3	128	138	4	1	4	2
Measles and Sequelæ	14		26	1	30		32		7		11		3		6		...		1		54	76	130	...	1	36	60	1	...	17	15
Scarlatina and Sequelæ	5		8	1	27	1	30		15		22		9		17		2		3		58	80	138	1	1	52	70	4	5	1	4
Variola	1		5		1		3		1		2		2		4	1	...		...		5	14	19	...	1	4	11	...	1	...	1
Varicella	7		8		13		13		5		7		2		5		...		...		27	33	60	...	...	27	33	...	...	...	...
Febricula	7		10		11		41		13		8		18		15		6		3		55	77	132	...	...	55	77	...	...	...	...
Diphtheria	...		1		...		2		1		...		...		...		...		1		1	4	5	...	...	1	4	...	...	...	...
Erysipelas	4		1		1		2		...		4		...		1		...		...		5	8	13	...	...	5	8	...	...	...	...
Pertussis	150	4	171	2	151	3	197	2	54		76		13		20		2		2		370	466	836	7	4	353	449	6	12	4	1
Syphilis	55	5	40	3	2		7		...		...		...		...		...		...		57	47	104	5	3	37	36	2	1	13	7
Scrofula and Tuberculosis	8		6	1	13		19	1	11		21		31		30		8		11		71	87	158	...	2	48	57	11	23	12	5
Phthisis Pulmonalis	...		...		1		3		...		7		9		11		2		2		12	23	35	...	...	8	10	4	10	...	3
Tabes mesenterica	3	1	1		2		2		...		...		...		...		...		...		5	3	8	1	...	4	2	...	1	...	...
Tubercular Meningitis	6	1	1	1	4	1	5	2	1		1		1		2		...		...		12	9	21	2	3	3	1	6	5	1	...
Epilepsy and Convulsions	13	2	14		3		2		10	1	7		6		9		7		7		39	39	78	3	...	18	22	10	11	8	6
Chorea	...		...		...		1		1		9		9		17		...		2		10	29	39	...	...	10	27	...	...	...	2
Essential Paralysis	7		4		3		5		1		2		1		...		...		...		12	11	23	...	...	2	1	4	6	6	4
Neuralgia	...		...		...		1		...		...		...		...		...		...		...	1	1	...	...	...	1	...	...	...	...
Hysteria	...		...		...		...		...		...		...		4		...		8		...	12	12	...	...	...	12	...	...	...	...
Idiotcy	1		...		...		1		1		...		...		...		...		...		2	1	3	...	...	..	...	2	1	...	...
Chronic Hydrocephalus	2		...		1		...		...		...		1		...		...		...		4	...	4	...	...	.	...	4	...	...	...
Congest Cerebri	18	2	15		5		4		1		3		2		6		2		3		28	31	59	2	...	24	29	...	...	2	2
Laryngismus Stridulus	3		4		1		...		...		...		...		...		...		...		4	4	8	...	...	4	2	...	...	...	2
Catarrh	127	1	94		43		56		17		25		19		9		4		8		210	192	402	1	...	206	187	...	...	3	5
Croup	1		2		2		1		...		...		...		...		...		...		3	3	6	...	...	3	2	...	1	...	...
Laryngitis sub-acute	10		5		6		5		3		1		3		5		4		1		26	17	43	...	...	26	15	...	...	...	2
Bronchitis	275	10	249	10	123	2	141	3	62		72		56		51		13		24		529	537	1065	12	13	483	500	4	3	30	21
Pneumonia	27	2	25	2	30		22		8		12		6		6		3		1		74	66	140	2	2	66	58	3	2	3	4
Pleurisy	1		1		4		2		7		3		3		10		2		3		17	19	36	...	...	14	19	...	...	3	...
Stomatitis	44		38	1	25		38		10		10		6		4		..		4		85	94	179	...	1	82	85	...	...	3	8
Tonsillitis	3		5		3		7		3		10		7		12		4		7		20	41	61	...	...	20	38	...	...	...	3
Cancrum oris	...		...		...		...		...		...		...		...		...		...		...	...	...	...	...	...	...	...	...	...	...
Dyspepsia and Constipation	69	1	83	2	30		21		25		28		32		33		7		19		163	184	347	1	2	160	178	...	...	2	4
Diarrhœa and Dysentery	477	19	444	14	132		117	1	25		23		29		21		3		10		664	615	1279	19	15	639	587	4	9	2	4
Fistula in Ano	...		...		...		...		...		...		2		1		...		...		2	1	3	...	...	2	1	...	...	...	...
Total carried forward	1345	48	1273	39	699	7	804	10	312	1	399	1	308		357	1	91		140		2755	2973	5728	56	51	2520	2720	69	92	114	105

Tabular View of the Admission and Termination of Cases in the Dispensary of the General Hospital and Dispensary for Diseases of Sick Children—(Continued).

DISEASE.	AGE OF PATIENT AND SEX ON ADMISSION.																				TOTAL.			MODE OF DISCHARGE OR TERMINATION.							
	6 Months.				2 Years.				5 Years.				7 Years.				12 Years.							Dead.		Cured.		Otherwise		Under Treatment	
	M.	Deaths.	F.	Deaths.	M.	Deaths.	F.	Deaths.	M.	Deaths.	F.	Deaths.	M.	Deaths.	F.	Deaths.	M.	Deaths.	F.	Deaths.	M.	F.	Total.	M.	F.	M.	F.	M.	F.	M.	F.
Total brought forward	1345	48	1273	39	699	7	804	10	312	1	399	1	308		357	1	91		140		2755	2973	5728	56	51	2520	2720	69	92	114	105
Prolapsus Ani	3		4		2		5		1		...		...		...		...		...		6	9	15	...	...	6	9	...	...	...	...
Polypus Recti	...		...		...		...		2		...		...		1		...		1		2	2	4	...	...	2	2	...	...	...	...
Icterus	...		2	1	...		...		...		2		1		...		...		1		1	5	6	...	...	1	4	...	...	...	...
Enlargement of Liver	...		...		...		...		...		...		...		...		...		...		...	...	...	...	...	...	...	...	...	...	...
Calculus Versicæ	...		...		...		...		1		...		...		...		...		...		1	...	1	...	...	1	...	...	...	...	...
Incontinence of Urine	3		1		1		1		2		[illegible]		2		1		...		...		8	4	12	...	...	8	4	...	...	...	...
Chronic Bright's Disease	...		...		2		...		...		2		1		...		...		1		3	3	6	...	...	2	2	...	...	1	1
Phymosis and Paraphymosis	...		...		5		...		4		...		2		...		...		...		11	...	11	...	...	11	...	...	...	...	...
Hydrocele	...		...		...		...		...		...		...		...		...		...		...	...	...	...	...	...	...	...	...	...	...
Leucorrhœa	...		4		...		8		...		2		...		2		...		...		...	16	16	...	...	...	15	...	1	...	...
Disease of Heart	1		...		...		2		1		1		4	1	[illegible]		8		7		14	14	28	1	...	4	5	4	4	5	5
Nœvus	4		3		...		2		...		1		...		...		...		...		4	6	10	...	...	4	6	...	...	11	...
Diseases of Bones and Joints	8		7		8		15		23		16		15		10		8		5		62	53	115	...	...	55	49	2	5	5	8
Rickets	42		37	1	37	1	32	1	5		3		2		2		2		...		83	74	162	1	2	75	67	2	...	10	5
Morbus Coxæ	1		...		7		2		11		2		4		4		1		1		24	9	33	...	...	10	3	5	[illegible]	9	4
Diseases of Skin	115		98		109		95		89		67		45		43		12		19		371	322	693	...	...	360	309	...	...	4	3
Deformities and Malformations, including contraction of Tendons	12		12		7		4		1		1		3		1		1		...		24	18	42	...	...	23	18	...	...	1	...
Diseases of Eye and Ear	16		12		20		33		13		20		13		13		9		4		71	82	153	...	...	67	79	...	...	4	3
Burns and Scalds	5		3		4		7		2		1		2		...		...		1		13	12	25	...	...	13	12	...	...	...	...
Fractures and Dislocations	[illegible]		2		2		6		...		2		2		...		...		...		5	10	15	...	...	5	10	...	...	...	...
Contusions, Wounds, &c.	5		5		5		8		3		10		11		4		...		1		24	28	52	...	...	24	28	...	...	...	...
Cancer	...		...		...		...		...		...		...		...		...		...		...	...	...	...	...	...	...	...	...	...	...
Hernia	15		3		3		1		1		2		1		...		...		...		20	6	26	...	...	18	4	1	...	1	2
Abscesses and Ulcers	32		21		25		22		12		15		16		7		7		6		86	71	157	...	...	78	68	...	...	8	3
Inflamed Glands	9		12		15		8		10		14		13		11		...		...		47	45	92	...	..	44	43	2	[illegible]	2	1
Worms	7		3		21		18		14		14		[illegible]		10		1		3		47	48	95	...	...	47	48	...	...	...	...
Atrophy	39	7	45	5	7		3		...		2		1		...		...		...		47	50	97	8	5	32	39	1	1	6	5
Dentition	10		4		...		...		...		...		...		...		...		...		10	4	14	..	...	10	4	...	...	...	...
Parotitis	5		2		4		6		2		1		3		3		...		1		14	13	27	...	...	14	13	...	...	...	...
Anæmia	1		4		5		4		4		4		6		2		6		4		22	18	40	...	...	22	18	...	...	...	...
Rheumatism	1		2		1		3		11		11		14		11		7		5		34	34	68	...	...	34	34	...	...	...	...
Not Specified	20	3	17		18	1	15	1	17		9		18		11		[illegible]		8		75	60	135	...	...	72	57	...	3	...	4
Not Classified	8		11		7		13		7		11		9		7		[illegible]		6		31	48	79	...	...	20	46	...	...	5	2
Total	[illegible]	58	1567	45	101[illegible]	8	1117	12	548	1	613	1	495	1	[illegible]	[illegible]	[illegible]		211		3920	4037	7957	66	58	3588	3703	86	109	186	151

See text page 29. The tables for hospital activity in 1873 (above) and in 1899 (opposite) show the dramatic increase in work during this period.

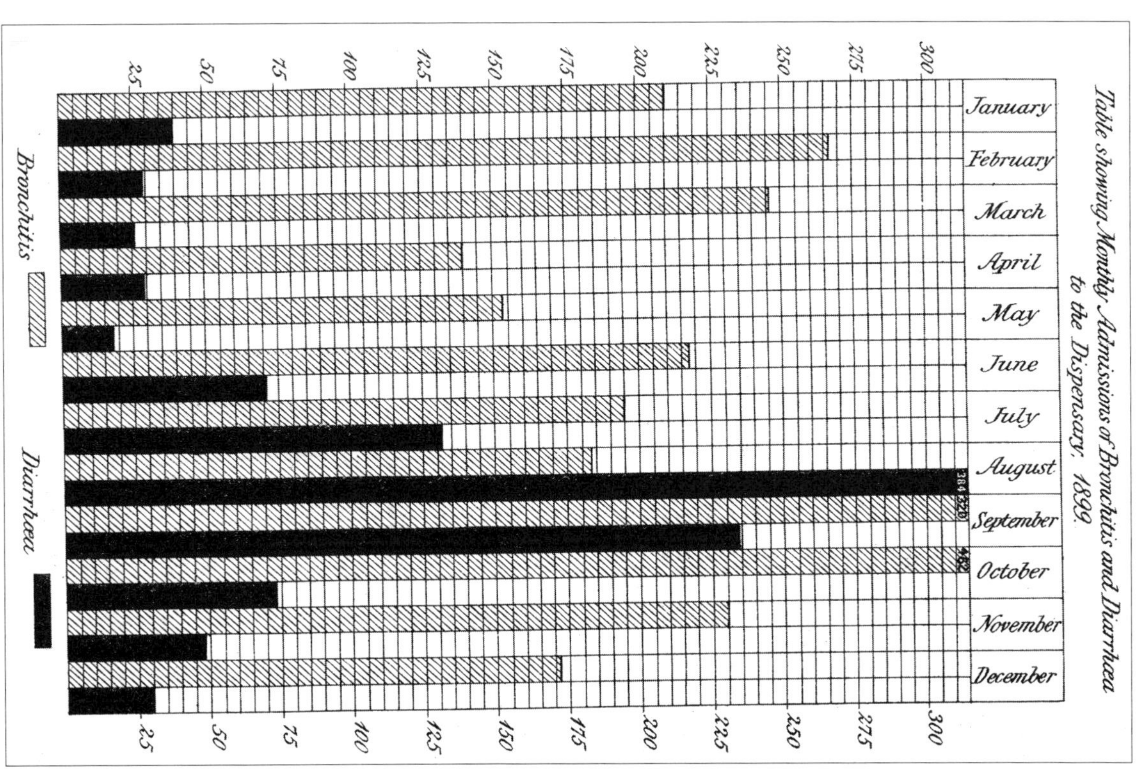
Table showing Monthly Admissions of Bronchitis and Diarrhœa to the Dispensary, 1899.
January
February
March
April
May
June
July
August
September
October
November
December
25
50
75
100
125
150
175
200
225
250
275
300
384
320
462
Bronchitis
Diarrhœa

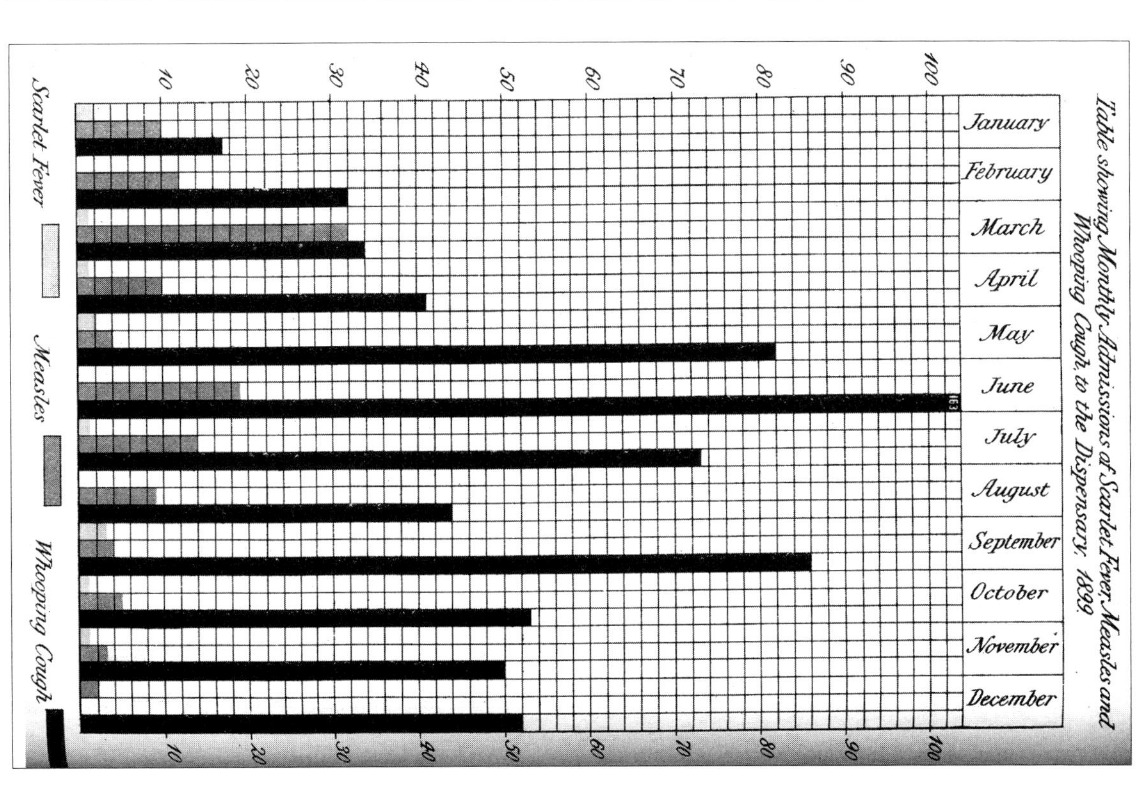
Table showing Monthly Admissions of Scarlet Fever, Measles and Whooping Cough to the Dispensary, 1899.
January
February
March
April
May
June
July
August
September
October
November
December
10
20
30
40
50
60
70
80
90
100
163
Scarlet Fever
Measles
Whooping Cough

Changes were happening in other areas, particularly in nurse training and in 'care'. Nursing, health visiting and social work were taking place more and more in the home, and a considerable degree of professional autonomy was being created for women, which provided the impetus to launch the struggle for universal suffrage at the beginning of the 20th century.

Doctors were beginning to take on specialist roles in hospitals outside the very big voluntary hospitals. In 1896 the first anaesthetist, Mr Westmacott was added to the list of officers of the charity. Mr Westmacott was also an oral surgeon.

During 1897 the fever ward at Pendlebury was closed and Manchester Corporation paid £50 p.a. for the fever cases to be directly admitted to Monsall Hospital to the north of the city. It had opened as a "House of Recovery" and "Convalescent Home" for fever patients in 1871. Children continued to be admitted to Monsall Hospital until late in the 1970s, when the beds were moved to Booth Hall Children's Hospital.

All six pavilion wards were in use by 1902. The Wards were named as follows:

BORCHARDT: After Dr Louis Borchardt, "*A gentleman with special experience in the treatment of children's diseases, and in hospital management*". Appointed Physician in 1854 and responsible for admitting the first patients to be treated by the Children's Dispensary. He gave 25 years of continuous service to the Children's Dispensary and Hospital. He died in 1883. A marble bust of Dr Borchart stands outside this ward today.

HEYWOOD: After Mr Oliver Heywood one of the Vice Presidents of the Hospital from 1860 to 1865 and then President from 1865 until his death in 1892. He gave a very generous gift towards the new hospital where he was known as a good friend and generous benefactor. He became the first Freeman of the City of Manchester in 1888.

HOLDEN: Originally named South Ward, altered to Holden in 1899, following the receipt of a donation of £10,000 from the trustees of the late Mr James Holden of Rochdale.

LIEBERT: Named after the late Mr Bernhard Liebert who gave £3,000 to the building fund in 1872 through a bequest.

VICTORIA: Named in memory of Her Majesty Queen Victoria. Originally this ward was used for nurses accommodation and was altered to a medical ward in 1902, when the nurses moved into a new building between Borchardt and Holden wards.

WRIGLEY: Originally known as North Ward, but altered to Wrigley after the late Mr Thomas Wrigley of Bury left a bequest to the hospital of £10,000 in 1881.

The new hospital with its up to date hospital architecture, the new convalescent home at the seaside and a new building for out patients in the city centre moved into the first decade of the twentieth century with an ever increasing reputation in the treatment of childhood disease. In the words of Sir Henry Burdett KCB KCVO, one of the leading authorities on hospital matters at the time, in his entry in the visitors book in 1909:

> *"It must be nearly thirty years since I last inspected this hospital, at the time of the scarlet fever trouble. Many things have happened since then and many new and up to date hospitals have been built. Still good and efficient as it was then, I am satisfied that it is even better today in all departments than ever before. To write this with assured conviction and I write it, after careful and critical inspection, entitles this hospital to claim that it is the most efficient of Children's Hospitals. If anyone wants to give money wisely to a Children's Hospital they should now know where to send it. I am sorry to miss the face of my friend the late Dr Ashby whose name should live as long as this hospital endures. The children are happy and quiet throughout the hospital, an infallible sign of good nursing and excellent management."*

Nurse receptionist 1870s.

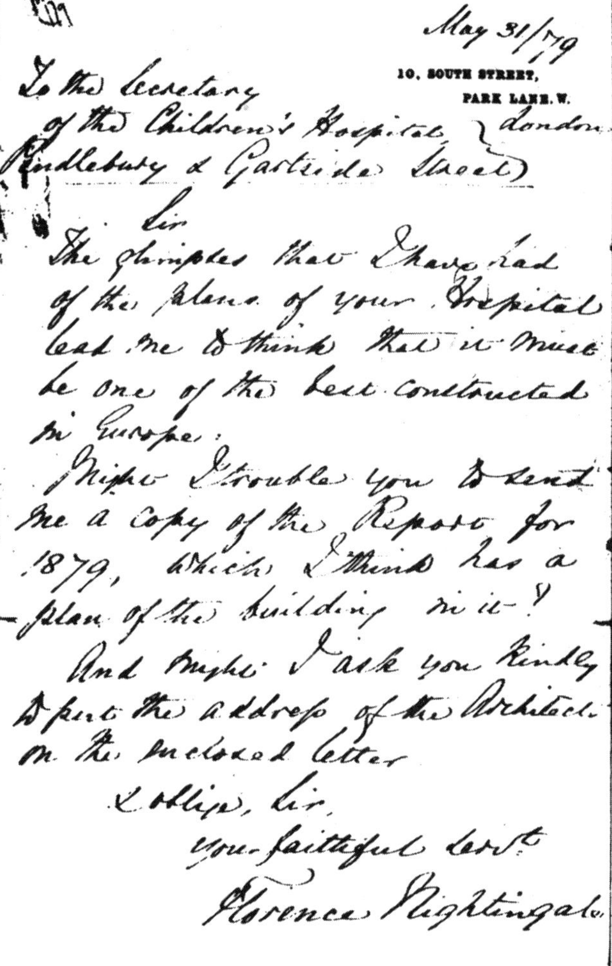

May 31/79

10, SOUTH STREET,
PARK LANE. W.

To the Secretary
of the Children's Hospital, } London
Pendlebury & Gartside Street)

Sir

The glimpses that I have had
of the plans of your Hospital
lead me to think that it must
be one of the best constructed
in Europe.

Might I trouble you to send
me a copy of the Report for
1879, which I think has a
plan of the building in it?

And might I ask you kindly
to put the address of the Architect
on the enclosed letter

& oblige, Sir,
your faithful servt.
Florence Nightingale.

The letter from Florence Nightingale congratulating the Governors on the Hospital design in 1879.

Nurse uniform 1898.

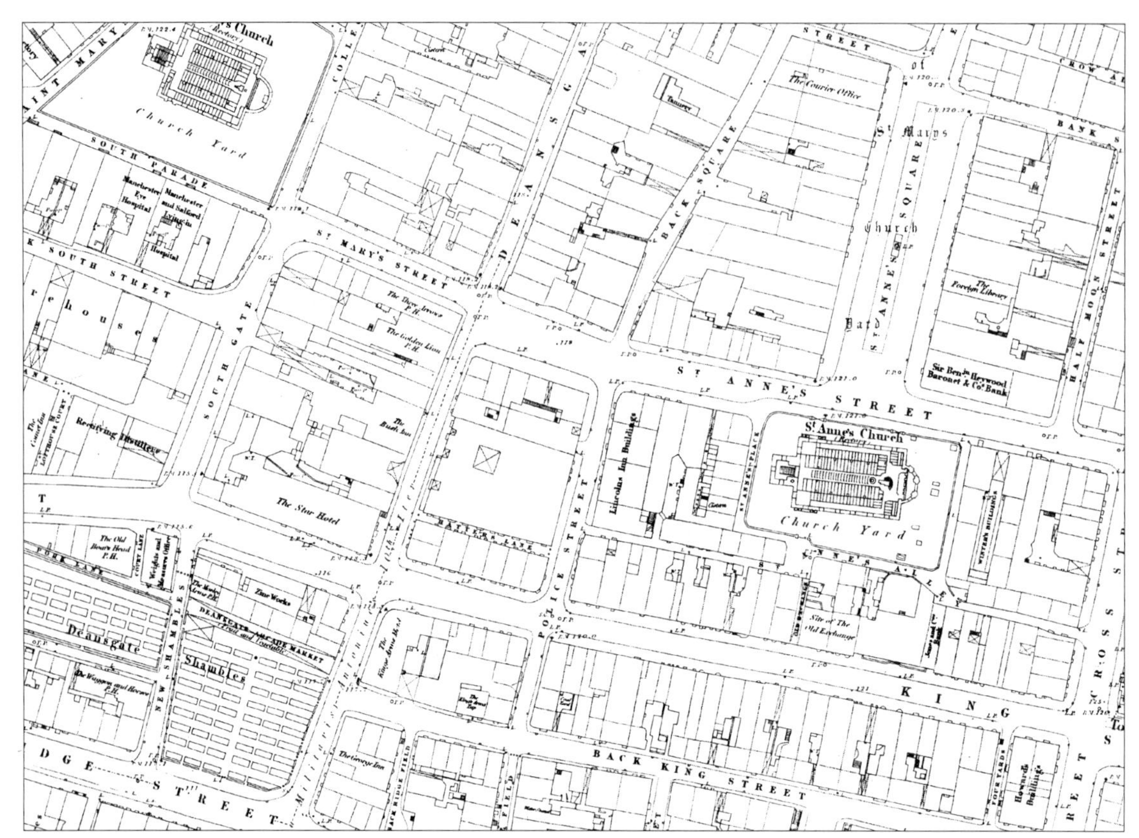

Manchester City Centre in 1849 showing Back King Street, bottom centre, Cross Street, right bottom corner (corner of Town Hall in King Street just showing) and Bridge Street, bottom left corner. Below: Pendlebury 1908.

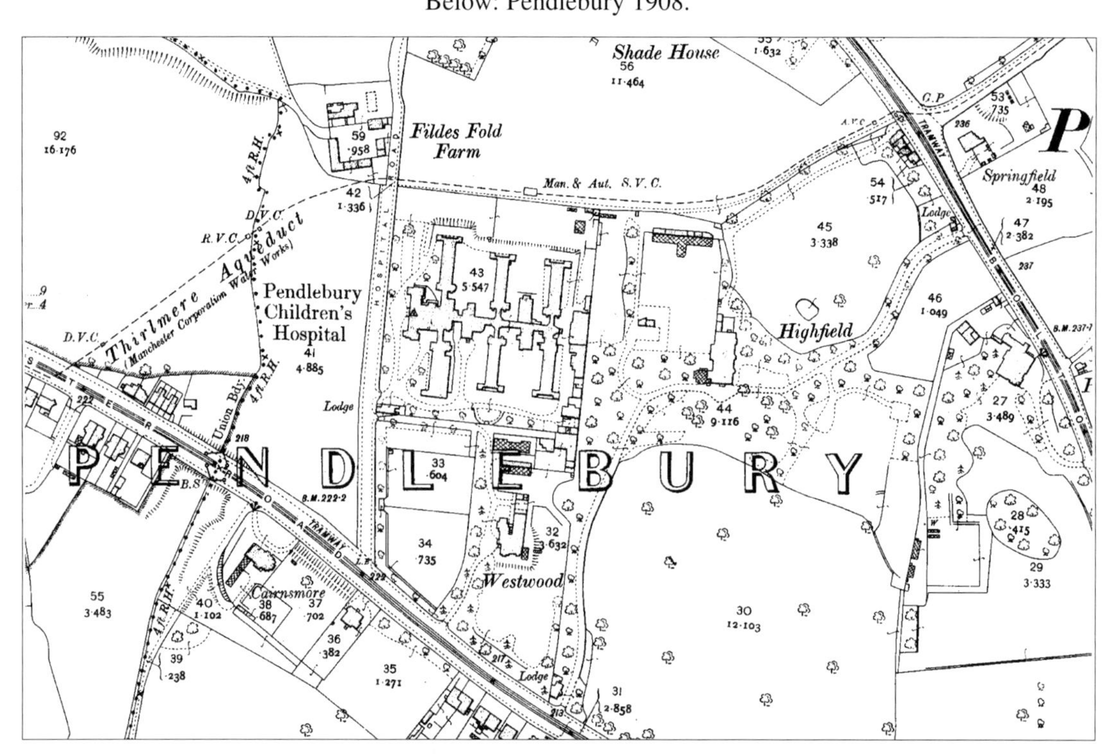

BOARD OF GOVERNORS FOR 1924.

(WITH POWER TO ADD TO THEIR NUMBER.)

Chairman—JOHN DENDY, O.B.E.

Vice-Chairman—PETER EADIE.

THE PRESIDENT, VISITING PHYSICIANS, VISITING SURGEONS, AND ORTHOPÆDIC SURGEON, *ex-officio.*

ALFRED K. ARMITAGE, J.P.	H. A. HEYWOOD.
ALFRED L. ARNOLD.	G. A. T. JESSON, M.B.E.
HAROLD BOWMAN.	P. LINDLEY.
HAROLD BRADBURN.	WILLIAM C. MACARA.
J. T. BROWNE.	SIR G. CHAS. MANDLEBERG.
W. BUCKLEY, C.B.E., J.P., C.C.	T. C. MIDWOOD.
GEORGE COMBER, J.P.	MRS. A. ORR.
MRS. ALEC. DUNN.	ALAN D. ROBERTSON.
J. FRANCIS GIBB.	FRANK H. ROBY.
A. A. GILLIES, J.P.	J. SILLAVAN.

THE HON. H. CON. SMITH.

Honorary Treasurers.

A. A. GILLIES, J.P. THE HON. H. CON. SMITH.

Honorary Secretary—G. A. T. JESSON, M.B.E.
Endsley, Swinton.

House Committee.

J. FRANCIS GIBB, Chairman.

J. T. BROWNE.	MRS. A. ORR.
MRS. ALEC. DUNN.	ALAN D. ROBERTSON.
PETER EADIE.	J. SILLAVAN.
P. LINDLEY.	

THE PRESIDENT, CHAIRMAN OF THE BOARD, PAST CHAIRMEN, HONORARY SECRETARY, AND HONORARY TREASURERS, *ex-officio.*

Finance Committee.

GEORGE COMBER, Chairman.

ALFRED K. ARMITAGE.	J. F. GIBB.
ALFRED L. ARNOLD.	A. A. GILLIES.
H. BRADBURN.	G. A. T. JESSON.
JOHN DENDY.	SIR G. CHAS. MANDLEBERG.
PETER EADIE.	FRANK H. ROBY.

THE HON. H. CON. SMITH.

Dispensary Committee.

H. BRADBURN, Chairman.

ALFRED L. ARNOLD.	C. C. HEYWOOD, M.B.
H. T. ASHBY, M.D.	C. PAGET LAPAGE, M.D.
J. T. BROWNE.	

THE PRESIDENT, CHAIRMAN OF THE BOARD, PAST CHAIRMEN, HONORARY SECRETARY, AND HONORARY TREASURERS, *ex-officio.*

MEDICAL STAFF, 1924.

Hon. Consulting Surgeons—J. HOWSON RAY, Ch.M., F.R.C.S.; C. ROBERTS, M.B., B.S., F.R.C.S.; H. H. RAYNER, M.B., F.R.C.S.

Hon. Consulting Aural Surgeon—FREDC. H. WESTMACOTT, F.R.C.S.

Visiting Physicians—C. CHRISTOPHER HEYWOOD, M.A., M.B. (Cantab.), M.R.C.P. (Lond.); C. PAGET LAPAGE, M.D., (Vict.), F.R.C.P. (Lond). HUGH T. ASHBY, B.A., M.D., M.R.C.P. (Lond.)

Assistant Visiting Physician—JOHN F. WARD, M.D., M.R.C.P.

Visiting Surgeons—G. B. WARBURTON, M.B., Ch. M., F.R.C.S.; J. GOW, M.B., F.R.C.S.

Assistant Visiting Surgeon—A. H. SOUTHAM, M.D., M.Ch., F.R.C.S.

Orthopaedic Surgeon—R. OLLERENSHAW, M.D.,F.R.C.S.

Surgeon for Throat, Nose, and Ear Diseases—
J. ARNOLD JONES, O.B.E., M.B. (Vict.), F.R.C.S. (Ed.)

Hon. Ophthalmic Surgeon—T. MILNES BRIDE, M.D.

Hon. Dental Surgeon—P. I. WIGODER, L.R.C.P., L.R.C.S., L.D.S.

Anæsthetists—EDWARD MOIR, L.S.A.; J. F. O'GRADY, L.A.H.; K. B. PINSON, M.B.

Radiologist—W. J. S. BYTHELL, M.D.

Pathologist—ARTHUR SELLERS, M.D., C.M., D.P.H.

Resident Medical Officers—A. ROSENSTONE, M.B.; G. L. MEACHIM, M.B.

Lady Superintendent—MISS M. NEVILLE.

OUT-PATIENTS' DEPARTMENT.

Medical Officer—T. N. FISHER, M.B.

Assistant Medical Officer—MISS W. M. EDGHILL, M.B.

Out-Patient Sister—MISS M. L. McMURTREY.

Pharmacist and Head Dispenser—A. TEESDALE, M.P.S.

Bankers.

THE DISTRICT BANK, LTD., KING STREET BRANCH.

Honorary Solicitors.

MESSRS. LINGARDS, SUTTON, ELLIOTT & CO.,
24, Fountain Street, Manchester.

Honorary Auditors.

MESSRS. HALLIDAY, PEARSON & CO., Chartered Accountants.

Secretary.

W. M. HUMPHRY.

The Hospital, Pendlebury (Telephone Nos. 319 and 335 Pendleton), and Gartside Street, Manchester (Telephone No. 584 City).

Board of Governors and Medical Staff 1924, showing the great growth in services over 45 years.

Table 4: Most Frequent Causes of Admission to the Children's Hospital, Manchester.

	1862	1872	1882	1892	1898
No. of Cases discharged during the year	229	328	979	1191	1347
DIAGNOSIS					
Abscesses & ulcers	29	17	5	22	26
Catarrh & inflammation of respiratory organs	26	1[a]	nc[c]	nc[c]	nc[c]
Typhoid fever	20	32[b]	25	27	4
Diphtheria	15	1	9	22	2
Diseases of bones & joints	14	29	196[d]	253[d]	373[d]
Injuries & accidents	14	13	14	13	25
Scarlatina	13	18	153	130	nc
Measles	10	6	18	nc	nc
Consumption & mesenteric disease	9	nc	5[g]	9[g]	44[g]
Pneumonia	nc	19	100[e]	77[e]	40[e]
Chorea	5	17	44	43	67
Bronchitis	nc	13	22	64	24
Morbus coxae (Hip disease)	nc	13	51[f]	78[f]	106[f]
Disease of the eye & ear	6	11	3	22	34
Phthisis	nc	nc	38	48	43
Malformations	0	2	33	88	125
Knee joint	nc	nc	38[f]	27[f]	31[f]
Caries & necrosis of bones	nc	nc	29[f]	33[f]	31[f]
Spinal curvature	nc	nc	25[f]	33[f]	2[f]
Spinal caries	nc	nc	7[f]	17[f]	64[f]
Tonsils & adenoids	nc	nc	nc	2	77

nc No classification
[a] Catarrh now classified separately to inflammation of respiratory organs, which is replaced by bronchitis.
[b] Including cases of typhus.
[c] Catarrh now classified with bronchitis.
[d] Diseases of bones and joints now subdivided into various categories.
[e] Now subdivided into croupous pneumonia and catarrhal pneumonia.
[f] Also included in 'disease of bones & joints'.
[g] Now disease of mesenteric glands only.

Sources: Relevant Annual Reports.

A table of recorded admissions from 1862 to 1898 in the 1901 Annual Report of the Hospital.

Table 6: Chief Medical Disorders Entailing Admission to Pendlebury, Manchester, 1874–1900.

	1874	1882	1886	1888	1893	1897	1900
ZYMOTIC DISEASE							
Typhoid	36	25	42	16	18	4	1
Scarlatina	72	153	196	89	130	101	nc
Measles	46	18	1	nc	nc	nc	nc
CONSTITUTIONAL DISEASES							
Rickets	2	14	nc	5	17	7	13
Syphilis	7	12	1	4	10	4	1
Acute general tuberculosis	8	17	33	16	20	23	nc[f]
Acute rheumatism	15	8	4	17	25	4	7
Malnutrition	nc	5	5	nc	nc	15	31
RESPIRATORY SYSTEM							
Laryngitis	14	10	4	6	11	4	1
Bronchitis & catarrh	37	22	29	81	54	26	22
Empyema[a]	nc	5	22	20	19	28	27
Croupous pneumonia	40[b]	50	23	39	45	16	5
Catarrhal pneumonia	nc	50	48	57	38	20	31
Phthisis	11	38	75	58	50	43	64
Pleurisy	9	14	9	5	14	8	14
CIRCULATORY SYSTEM							
Valvular heart disease	13[c]	12	29	21	20	24	14
ALIMENTARY SYSTEM							
Diarrhoea	1	16	38	26	23	nc	1
Gastro-intestinal catarrh	nc	5	11	17	37	11	11
Abdominal tuberculosis	2	5	10	4	15	12	24
NERVOUS SYSTEM							
Chorea	28	44	40	58	63	57	60
Epilepsy	11	11	9	13	7	6	4
Infantile paralysis	nc[d]	7	18	12	2	6	7
Tubercular meningitis	3	6	15	10	4	7	17
Spastic paralysis	nc[d]	2	3	nc	nc	12	nc
SKIN							
Eczema & lichen	nc[e]	18	15	25	18	12	9
Lupus	nc[e]	3	1	7	3	6	16

nc Not charted
[a] Usually considered medical, although often requiring surgical intervention.
[b] Actually 40 cases classified as 'pneumonia'.
[c] 13 cases under the general heading of 'diseases of the heart'.
[d] Six cases under one general heading of 'paralyses, etc.'.
[e] 17 cases classified under "diseases of skin".
[f] Ten cases are classified, oddly enough, under a revived heading of 'scofula'.

A table of recorded medical disorders from 1874 to 1900 in the 1904 Annual Report of the Hospital.

PRESIDENTS OF THE HOSPITAL SINCE 1857:

1857–1864	Robert N. Philips
1865–1892	Oliver Heywood
1893–1910	Sir William Agnew, bart.
1911–1920	Sir George W. Agnew, bart.
1921–1946	The Rt. Hon. Lord Colwyn

CHAIRMEN OF THE BOARD SINCE 1865:

1865–1866	G. F. Hinshelwood
1867–1870	H. M. Steinthal
1871–1878	J. H. Agnew
1879–1880	Edward Cross
1881–1883	H. M. Steinthal
1884–1889	J. B. Close Brooks
1890–1892	Stewart Garnett
1893–1896	E. Tootal Broadhurst
1897–1898	J. F. Richardson
1899–1902	George Comber
1903–1907	Gerald Peel
1908–1909	George H. Leigh
1910–1912	H. A. Heywood
1913–1915	William Buckley
1916–1919	Frank H. Roby
1920–1921	Alfred K. Armitage
1922–1924	John Dendy
1924–1925	Peter Eadie
1925–1927	J. Francis Gibb
1928–1931	G. A. T. Jesson
1932–1934	A. V. Sugden
1935–1937	James Sillavan
1938–1942	Alan D. Robertson
1943–	F. S. Stancliffe

Presidents and Chairmen of the Board who served the Hospital from 1837 to 1948 and the NHS.

MANCHESTER CHILDREN'S HOSPITAL.

DIRECTIONS FOR THE MANAGEMENT OF INFANTS & YOUNG CHILDREN.

1. An infant should be kept perfectly clean, and its clothing should be thoroughly aired every day and washed frequently.

2. Its clothing should be light, warm, and loose, and should cover the limbs and body equally. No tight binder should be used.

3. It should have as much fresh air as possible without a draught, and should be taken out of doors whenever the weather is fine. Doors and windows should be opened every day to air the rooms, and the bedroom chimneys should not be blocked up.

4. No medicine should be given without a doctor's orders, and no "soothing syrup" or "teething powders" should ever be used.

5. All nourishment, whether it be breast milk, bottle, or other food, should be given at regular times, and in regular quantities. (See table **A.**)

6. Breast milk should be an infant's only food until it is seven months old. When the mother's milk is scanty, cows' milk should be given in addition to it, but not in place of it.

7. All milk used for feeding infants should be boiled as soon as it comes to the house, and should then be kept covered up in a cool, airy place. No milk that is not **quite sweet at the time of being used** should be given to any child.

8. When seven months old, an infant should have two meals a day of milk and flour food or other food, and three meals of milk. (See table **A.**)

9. Weaning should be begun at seven months and completed at one year. The sucking of "dummy teats" is harmful.

10. When a year old an infant should have daily a little plain broth, beef tea, or gravy.

11. Meat should not be given to any child under 18 months old. It should then be given pounded or finely minced.

12. Condensed milk is good; but none should be used that has any part of the fat removed. One teaspoonful of condensed milk to eight teaspoonfuls of water is about the right strength; in special cases it must be made weaker.

13. No child should be given any beer, spirits, wine, new bread, currants, or unripe fruit.

14. No tea or coffee should be given to any child under the age of four.

15. Porridge, made of oatmeal or hominy, is very nourishing. Whole meal flour and seconds is more nourishing than white flour.

Table A.—Showing how much an Infant should be given at a time, and how often.

	How often in Day.	How often in Night.	How Much.	Strength.
From Birth to Four Weeks old..	Every 2 Hours.	Every 4 Hours.	4 table-spoonfuls.	One-third Milk.
From Four to Eight Weeks old	Every 2½ Hours. Increasing	Ditto. gradually.	6 table-spoonfuls.	One-half Milk.
From Three to Six Months old...	Every 3 Hours.	Twice.	8 to 16 table-spoonfuls.	Two-thirds Milk to Pure Milk.
From Seven to Twelve Months old.................	Five meals a day—Three of 12 tablespoonfuls of Pure Milk, and Two of 12 tablespoonfuls of Milk thickened with baked flour, bread, or prepared food, and boiled.			

Diet for a Child from 12 to 18 Months old.

First Meal, 7 a.m.—Bread and milk, or oatmeal or hominy porridge, with plenty of milk.

Second Meal, 11 a.m.—Twelve tablespoonfuls of milk.

Third Meal, 1.30 p.m.—Bread Crumbs and gravy, or a lightly boiled egg and bread and butter.

Fourth Meal, 5.30 p.m.—Bread and milk.

Fifth Meal.—Milk to drink.

All milk should be sweetened with sugar (milk sugar if possible).

The bottle used should be of this description. It should be scalded each time after use, and the teat turned inside out and washed; and bottle and teat kept in clean water until wanted again.

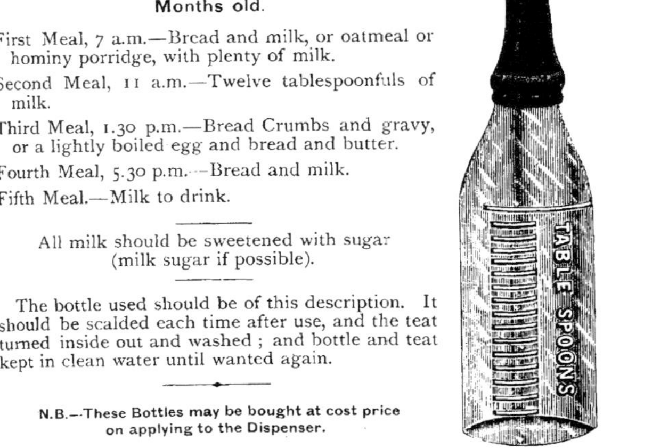

N.B.—These Bottles may be bought at cost price on applying to the Dispenser.

Management and diet sheets produced by the Hospital in 1906 to help nurses and mothers.

Rules of Governance for the Manchester Children's Hospital, Pendlebury, in the 1890s.

These rules remained little altered from 1879 to 1945. Every member of the Board was issued with a copy. The doctors and the 'head nurse' on each ward were also issued with the 'rules', which were not to be taken away from the Hospital.

RULES

FOR THE

GOVERNMENT OF THE HOSPITAL.

I.—*Title, Trustees, and Government.*

This Charity is denominated the "MANCHESTER CHILDREN'S HOSPITAL."

There shall be a President and Vice-Presidents elected by the Subscribers.

The Government of the Charity, subject to these rules, shall be vested in a Board of Governors, consisting of the President, the Visiting Physicians and Surgeons (*ex-officio*), and not less than twelve members, including Hon. Treasurers and Hon Secretary, who shall be elected at the Annual General Meeting, with power to add to their number, to continue in office until the end of the next Annual General Meeting.

The official year of the Hospital shall commence on the 1st January and end on the 31st December.

The property of the Charity shall be vested in three or more Trustees, to be elected by the Board of Governors.

All moneys belonging to the Charity which may not be required from time to time for the current expenses of the Charity shall be invested in the names of the Trustees, in accordance with directions to be given by the Board of Governors, in or upon any investments in or upon which the Trustees may for the time being be by law authorised to invest trust moneys, or in any other mode of investment which may be approved by the Board of Governors

The Board at their first meeting, to be held within fourteen days after the Annual General Meeting, shall appoint a Chairman and Vice-Chairman, and shall also appoint not less than five of their number to form a House Committee, and not less than five of their number to form a Dispensary Committee, the President, the Chairman of the Board of Governors, the past Chairmen, the Hon. Secretary and Hon. Treasurers being *ex-officio* members of these Committees. The Chairman of any meeting of the Board of Governors shall have the right to vote on every question, and if the votes are equal he shall have a second or casting vote.

II.—*General Meetings and Special Meetings.*

An Annual General Meeting of the subscribers to the Charity shall be held before the end of March in each year, on a convenient day to be fixed by the Board of Governors to receive the preceding year's reports, to elect the Board of Governors, the Honorary Treasurers, the Honorary Secretary, the Public Auditors, and to transact such other business connected with the general arrangements of the Charity as may be necessary.

The Chairman of any meeting of the Subscribers shall be appointed by the Board of Governors.

The Chairman of the Board of Governors shall call a Special General Meeting of the Subscribers within a month after receiving a requisition in writing from three Governors or from twenty Subscribers. The notice convening such meeting shall specify the object for which such meeting is called, and no other business shall be entertained at such Special General Meeting.

Subscribers of five pounds per annum, whether to the General Fund or to the Ladies' Fund, to have three votes; of one guinea, two votes: and half a guinea, one vote at the Annual General Meeting or any Special General Meeting, in the election of Governors, or other business of the Charity. A poll may be demanded upon a requisition to the Chairman of the meeting, signed by three Governors or twenty Subscribers.

The Committee of the Hospital Sunday Fund and also the Committee of the Hospital Saturday and Convalescent Homes Fund Incorporated shall each of them, so long as they contribute to the funds of the Hospital, be deemed to be a Subscriber, and any person nominated by either of them for that purpose shall be entitled to attend and vote at an Annual General or any Special General Meeting of the Subscribers.

Every meeting of the Subscribers shall be deemed to be sufficiently called if notice thereof shall be inserted in two Manchester newspapers not less than eight days before the date of the meeting, and it shall not be necessary to give notice to the Subscribers individually.

III.—*Meetings of the Board of Governors.*

The Board of Governors shall meet at least once every month (five to form a quorum) for the transaction of business, to receive the monthly general and numerical reports of the House Committee and Medical Staff, to regulate the accounts, and to take cognisance of the general state and working of the Charity.

At such meetings the Governors shall be entitled to make and alter bye-laws for the government of the Charity, provided that such bye-laws be not contrary to the rules of the Hospital.

At such meetings no resolution shall be taken on any subject outside routine business, unless notice of such subject shall have been given in convening the meeting.

No Governor shall vote upon any question personal to himself.

The minutes of the proceedings shall be regularly entered in a book to be kept for the purpose by the Secretary.

IV.—*House Committee.*

The House Committee shall meet at least once a week; minutes of the proceedings to be regularly kept and presented for confirmation to the monthly meetings of the Board of Governors. Subject

to the rules and bye-laws of the Charity and to the decisions of the Board of Governors, it shall have the entire direction of the internal management of the Hospital, and all officials, excepting such as are exclusively employed at the Dispensary, shall be under its control. It may appoint Sub-Committees and delegate to any Sub-Committee any of its powers or duties.

V.—*Dispensary Committee.*

The Dispensary Committee shall meet at least once a month, minutes of its proceedings to be regularly kept and presented for confirmation to the monthly meetings of the Board of Governors. Subject to the rules and bye-laws of the Charity, and to the decisions of the Board of Governors, it shall have the entire direction of the internal management of the Dispensary and all officials employed exclusively at the Dispensary shall be under its control. It may appoint Sub-Committees and delegate to any Sub-Committee any of its powers or duties.

VI.—*Medical Board.*

The Medical Board shall consist of the Visiting Physicians and Visiting Surgeons, the Hon. Aural Surgeon, and the Hon. Dental Surgeon.

VII.—*Meetings of the Medical Board.*

The Medical Board shall meet at least once every month, at some convenient time previous to the meeting of the Board of Governors, to draw up its monthly general and numerical reports, and to concert measures for its united action; the minutes of its proceedings shall be regularly kept and presented to the monthly meeting of the Board of Governors; and for the Annual General Meeting it shall furnish reports and yearly statistical returns, both from the Hospital and Dispensary, upon a form to be regulated from time to time by the Board of Governors. The Medical Board shall at its first meeting in each year elect a Chairman, who at its meetings shall, if the votes be equal, have a second or casting vote.

The Chairman of the Medical Board shall draft the Annual Medical Report and submit the same for adoption to the Medical Board before presenting the same to the Board of Governors.

VIII.—*Officers of the Charity.*

All officers of the Charity shall be appointed by the Board of Governors on such terms and for such time as the Board may determine.

The officers shall consist of three or more visiting physicians, three or more visiting surgeons, an aural surgeon, an honorary dental surgeon, a pathologist, one or more anæsthetists, two resident medical officers to the Hospital, an honorary ophthalmic surgeon, a medical officer to the X-ray department, and a medical officer and one or more assistant medical officers to the dispensary, who together shall form the medical staff; of a lady superintendent, an out-patient sister, dispenser, and a secretary.

The visiting and other physicians and surgeons shall be selected from candidates whose qualifications shall have been

to the rules and bye-laws of the Charity and to the decisions of the Board of Governors, it shall have the entire direction of the internal management of the Hospital, and all officials, excepting such as are exclusively employed at the Dispensary, shall be under its control. It may appoint Sub-Committees and delegate to any Sub-Committee any of its powers or duties.

V.—*Dispensary Committee.*

The Dispensary Committee shall meet at least once a month, minutes of its proceedings to be regularly kept and presented for confirmation to the monthly meetings of the Board of Governors. Subject to the rules and bye-laws of the Charity, and to the decisions of the Board of Governors, it shall have the entire direction of the internal management of the Dispensary and all officials employed exclusively at the Dispensary shall be under its control. It may appoint Sub-Committees and delegate to any Sub-Committee any of its powers or duties.

VI.—*Medical Board.*

The Medical Board shall consist of the Visiting Physicians and Visiting Surgeons, the Hon. Aural Surgeon, and the Hon. Dental Surgeon.

VII.—*Meetings of the Medical Board.*

The Medical Board shall meet at least once every month, at some convenient time previous to the meeting of the Board of Governors, to draw up its monthly general and numerical reports, and to concert measures for its united action; the minutes of its proceedings shall be regularly kept and presented to the monthly meeting of the Board of Governors; and for the Annual General Meeting it shall furnish reports and yearly statistical returns, both from the Hospital and Dispensary, upon a form to be regulated from time to time by the Board of Governors. The Medical Board shall at its first meeting in each year elect a Chairman, who at its meetings shall, if the votes be equal, have a second or casting vote.

The Chairman of the Medical Board shall draft the Annual Medical Report and submit the same for adoption to the Medical Board before presenting the same to the Board of Governors.

VIII.—*Officers of the Charity.*

All officers of the Charity shall be appointed by the Board of Governors on such terms and for such time as the Board may determine.

The officers shall consist of three or more visiting physicians, three or more visiting surgeons, an aural surgeon, an honorary dental surgeon, a pathologist, one or more anæsthetists, two resident medical officers to the Hospital, an honorary ophthalmic surgeon, a medical officer to the X-ray department, and a medical officer and one or more assistant medical officers to the dispensary, who together shall form the medical staff; of a lady superintendent, an out-patient sister, dispenser, and a secretary.

The visiting and other physicians and surgeons shall be selected from candidates whose qualifications shall have been

XII.—*Patients.*

The Medical Officers shall be entitled to admit patients to the benefits of the Charity without recommendation, and every sick child, under 14 years of age, is admissible to the Charity as an out-patient or a home-patient, or, at the discretion of the Medical Officers, as an in-patient of the Charity. The circumstances of patients shall be investigated by the Secretary.

XIII.—*Visitors.*

Parents or friends of patients are permitted to visit them on such day or days, at such hours, and upon such conditions as the House Committee may from time to time determine; provided that the House Committee may at any time, if they consider such a course advisable for the prevention of infection, suspend all visiting, and that visitors are subject to the control of the Resident Medical Officers.

XIV.—*The Clergy.*

Ministers of any denomination may visit patients, at the request of their parents, and subject to the approval of the Resident Medical Officers in respect of the health of the patient.

XV.—*Alteration of Rules.*

The above Rules, or any of them, may be altered at any Ordinary Annual or Special Meeting of Subscribers. Eight days' notice of the intention to make an alteration shall be advertised in at least two Manchester papers.

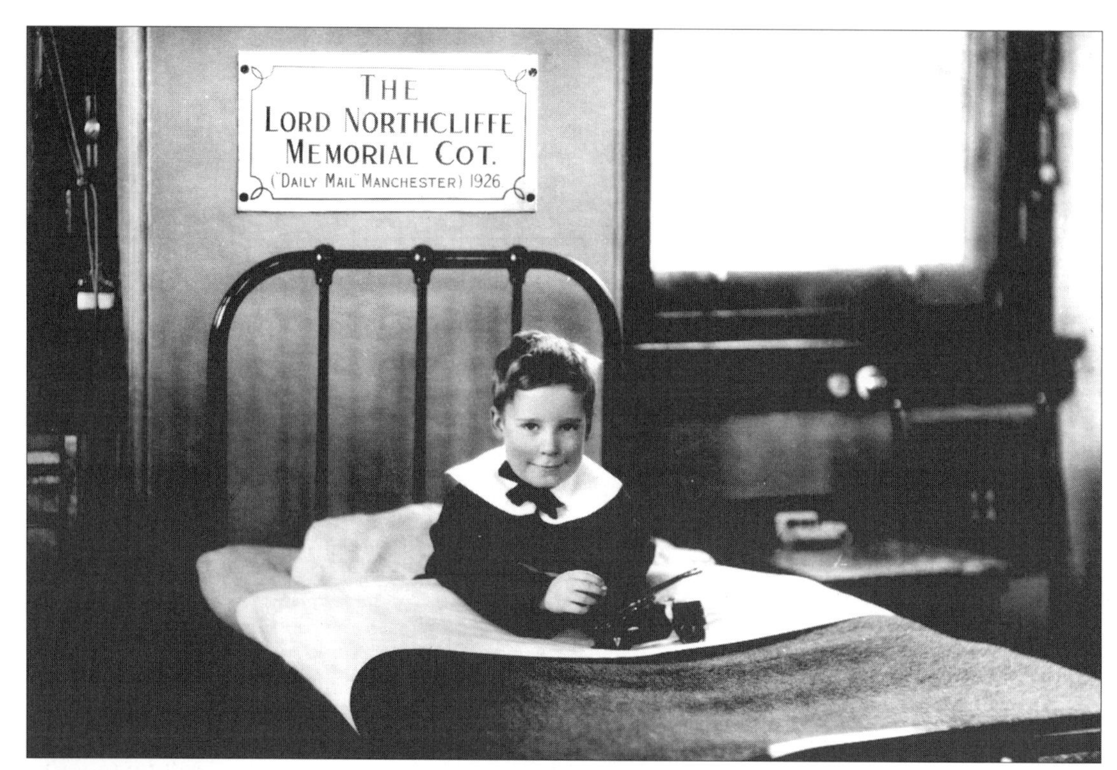

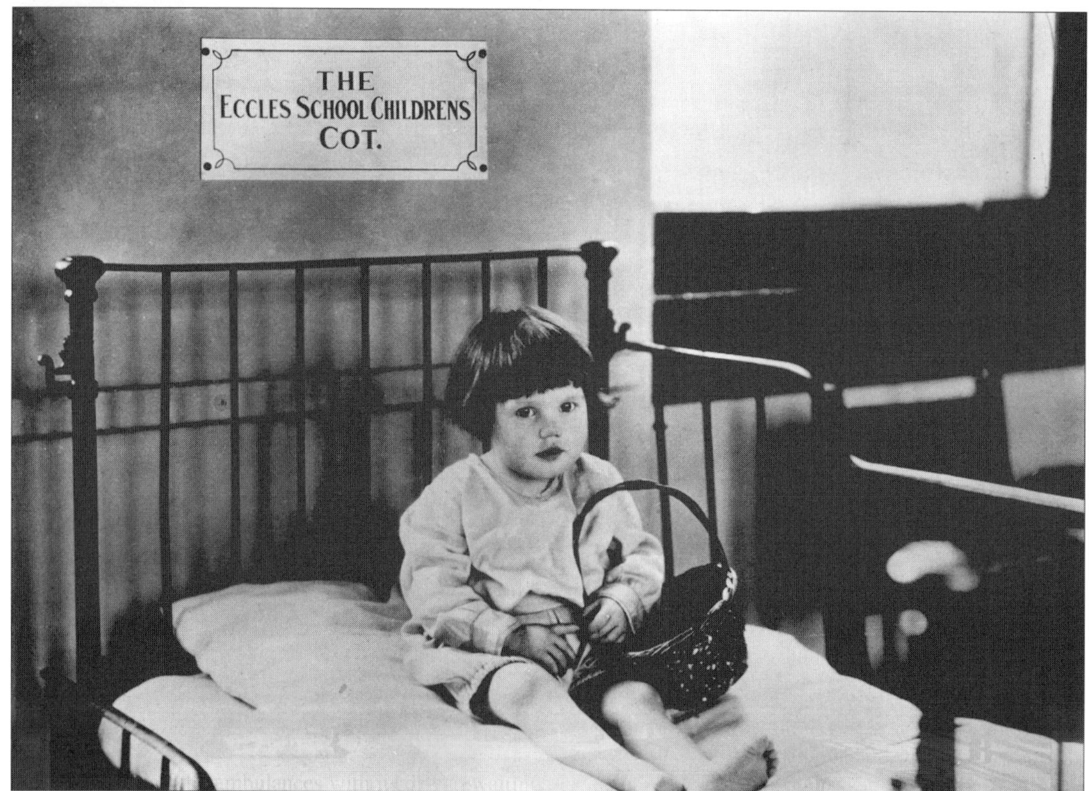

Endowed cots were an important source of funds.

CHAPTER 3

VICTORIAN PHILANTHROPY & FUNDRAISING

In Victorian Britain child welfare was generally considered to be the concern of the parent and any outside intervention was felt to undermine parental obligations.

The Factory Act of 1833 legislated for children between the ages of 9 and 13 to work shorter hours and to prevent children under this age working. The Act of 1844 allowed for the half time system. The legislation was simply a restriction against overwork, but employers and parents alike connived to escape detection in the employment of underage children.

Neither was the system of compulsory education for factory children as beneficial as first envisaged, the conditions under which the children were 'schooled' being almost worse than the factory and certainly colder. Children's health was not improving, but these moves were certainly steps in the right direction. Vaccination, too, was considered to be necessary for the 'factory children' and after the epidemic of 1837-41, vaccinations were provided free by Boards of Guardians, although they were not popular at first and the uptake was poor. Towns were beginning to make efforts to improve conditions through municipal improvement acts, first a good water supply, as set up in Manchester, and then by the middle of the century public baths and wash houses to improve the conditions and health of the community.

Against this background the cause of children began to engender philanthropic effort. *"Thus humanitarian concern, expressed in the foundation of voluntary institutions, dispensaries, hospitals and other societies afforded help to the weakly and debilitated."* (M. Cruickshank, *Children and Industry*, Man. Univ. Press 1981)

It was not until 1868 that a medical officer of health for the City of Manchester was appointed, although a health board had been in existence since the 1790s.

As the wealth of the few in Manchester and Salford increased, so too did philanthropy along with cultural development. 1806 saw the building and opening of the Portico Library, with membership through subscription, which provided an important venue for leading citizens wishing to initiate social progress.

An urban aristocracy was arising in Manchester and Salford. Local trading warehouses were as large as palaces and Manchester and Salford became a centre of trading with banks such as Heywoods (later to become William Deacons) and the Manchester & Salford Bank leading the way. The insurance industry was also developing, centred on the city, and new systems of transport and communication contributed to the economic success of businesses.

Alongside this new affluence a new social ideology was developing, with, already by the 1830s, two distinct factions within the city - the Tories and Anglicans and the Liberals and non-conformists. Leading Tory families tended to marry into the local gentry but the liberal and non-conformist families married amongst themselves and remained within the city. They included such families as Phillips, Heywoods, Percivals, Hibberts, Potters and Gregs.

The governance of Manchester was changing, with the last meeting of the 'Court' in 1845 and the granting of the Charter to Manchester Corporation ushering in a liberal era of politics within the city. In 1824 there had been an attempt at setting up an adult education movement and leading citizens and their families were being drawn towards health issues. The motives of those who looked towards this 'good work' were mixed. Some had compassion and religious zeal which was particularly inclined to favour children in need. Many gave without thought for reward; for others it was a route to status. Public and prominent citizens were expected to be patrons of the 'worthy' poor and helpless; it was considered part of their civic duties. The names of all subscribers to charitable causes were published and on the whole, the main giving was limited to one charity of choice. The subscribers had the opportunity to display not only public spirit but also their authority and power.

During the late 1840s and 50s a group of influential and well educated emigrés, who possessed many entrepeneurial skills, moved into Manchester. This group came mainly from Germany after the revolution there of 1848. Many well known Manchester families moved in at this time including the Schwabe and Behrens families. They were joined by others, including Charles Hallé, Frederick Engels and of course Louis Borchardt. Charles Hallé founded the Hallé Orchestra, the oldest existing orchestra in England. His family were subscribers to the Children's Hospital.

Manchester was becoming a cosmopolitan city with interests in the arts, music, literature and philanthropy. Mrs Elizabeth Gaskell, the famous author, who was married to the Rev William Gaskell, the Minister at Cross St. Chapel for 52 years from 1832, was part of a group of influential writers including Charles Dickens, who were interested in social reform.

The Art Treasures Exhibition in Manchester in 1857, which Queen Victoria attended, set Manchester and Salford's feet firmly on the ladder, allowing the worthy citizens to display their cultural interests. Alongside this need to demonstrate culture, there were also genuine philanthropic ideas and fundraising activities to benefit the needy.

During the 1860s to 1890s there was a large increase in charities which coincided with the increase in the number of people eligible to vote for Parliament (doubled in 1867) and the number of Members of Parliament. Those who achieved recognition were reinvesting in their community by philanthropic deeds.

The Manchester & Salford Ladies' Sanitary Reform Association was set up in 1862, eventually becoming a health visiting and social work service. The first paid health visitor in Manchester was appointed in 1890. The association trained working class women to teach hygiene to poor women in their homes. The Manchester Ladies' Association for the Protection & Reformation of Girls & Women, was a further development and was set up in 1882.

During the 1860s medical charities became popular. But the big development of charities for children came with the two immigrants to Manchester - Dr Louis Borchardt from Berlin and Prof. Merie from Budapest. Both men already had an interest in children's diseases in their own country and both were well connected with immigrant merchant families locally.

Manchester, with its high death rate on one side, and its cosmopolitan and wealthy middle class on the other, was the right environment for voluntary charities to succeed. A paternalistic mood enabled poor children and their mothers to be identified as worthy of their interest. The Heywood family, Unitarian bankers, great philanthropists, and members of the Cross St Chapel congregation, were some of the Childrens Hospital's greatest supporters at this time. By the mid 1850s fundraising for women and children became prominent amongst many new philanthropic objectives. A special Ladies' Committee was organised in 1849 to raise funds for the Lying in Charity, St Mary's Hospital. A similar Ladies' Committee was initiated for the Children's Dispensary & Hospital and was very involved in the Grand Bazaar of 1875. The 3 day event in April was a tremendous philanthropic project. A set of rules were set up in aid of the Sick Children's Dispensary & New Hospital:

1. All visitors to enter the Hall with their pockets filled with gold, silver, notes, cheques, post office orders, bank stock (railway script etc).
2. No visitors to leave the Hall with more money about them than is sufficient to pay their expenses home, and to remunerate a strong porter for carrying their purchases.

£21,359 was handed to the building committee towards the new hospital, after expenses had been paid.

This Victorian fundraising continued to be central to the progress of Pendlebury and Gartside Street alongside the subscription system, and in truth fundraising has remained thus ever since. Even after the advent of the NHS it was clear that it would continue to be an important component in the hospital's success and without it the high level of patient care could not be maintained. Th dedication of voluntary organisations, that continue to this day to provide much needed funds, comes from a long and distinguished history of 'giving'.

Saturday Funds and Sunday Clubs

This was another source of funding. The Sunday Club was primarily an association of voluntary workers whose sole aim was to raise money in aid of the hospitals and medical charities of Manchester and Salford. The method of collection was that on one Sunday in the year at various places of worship in the district a collection was taken. At the turn of the century this became highly organised and they incorporated other organisations into their movement to become the Medical Charities Fund.

The Saturday Fund was set up to systemise weekly contributions of the people of Manchester, Salford and Districts. It conferred the free use of hospital treatment and the work people's convalescent homes for those who contributed. Saturday Funds continue to this day.

Children treated at Pendlebury benefited from these clubs when their parents were contributors. By the 1930s their were over 2000 firms in Manchester, Salford and districts whose employees subscribed to the Saturdays Funds with a membership of over 100,000.

LADIES' COMMITTEES/LADIES' COUNCILS

For the Victorian middle class woman, charitable work provided one of the few outlets into public service. It was implicitly understood that the appropriate sphere for a middle class woman was that of the 'home'. Charity work, however, was acceptable; i.e. fundraising, visiting the workhouse and sanitary campaigning. All other areas of public life were on the whole barred to this group of women. In the last years of the century this work came to be understood as social work, and the Manchester and Salford middle class women played a very significant role in the development of this aspect of philanthropy in their cities.

The Ladies' Committee for the General Dispensary for Sick Children was set up in 1859. This was at the time when Robert N. Philips Esq. was the President of the Governing Body. Ladies' Committees already existed in various hospitals in the area - at Manchester Lying In Hospital St Mary's, such a committee was set up in 1807 and their duties included supervising the domestic management of the hospital, supplying linen and baby linen to new mothers and visiting patients in their own homes. So a model was already well established.

The Ladies' Committee for the General Dispensary for Sick Children coincided with the move of the Dispensary to Bridge St. The ladies at first began by donating clothing for the outpatients and were then asked to distribute the clothing and to visit the patients in their homes after discharge from the Dispensary. The Ladies' Committee made monthly reports to the Board. The first members of the Ladies' Committee were:

Mrs S.T. Armitage
Miss Brendon
Mrs Furniss
Mrs D. Lee *
Mrs Parker *
Mrs J. A. Petty
Mrs Philips *
Mrs C. Souchay *
Mrs Skinner *
Mrs Thompson
Miss Walker

*Wife of Governor

Their rules of governance allowed for them to add to their number when required.

Looking at the Board of Governors of the time, at least five of the Ladies' Committee were the wives of governors. When they opened the beds for children at the Dispensary in 1866, the Ladies' Committee helped with fund raising, furnishing the wards, supervising the domestic management of the hospital and looking after the welfare and amusement of the children in hospital. The children were given books and pictures, donated and distributed by the ladies, in order to "amuse" them.

At Christmas time Mrs A. Schwarbe gave each in-patient a set of clothes. The Matron mentions the receipt of some seasonable presents at the 1867 Annual General Meeting. *"The Board very gladly acknowledges:- from Mrs Steinthal four parcels of clothes; Mr Steinthal a bag of rice; Mrs Stoehr toys and clothes; Mrs Madden, books; Miss Barnes, £1 for toys and pictorial papers sent monthly; Mrs Adolph Schwabe, her usual Christmas gift of clothing and toys to every child in hospital; and a similar gift from Mrs Halliday, of Alderley Edge."* This practice of donating gifts was to continue until the introduction of the NHS and indeed in some form to this present day.

The Ladies' Committees were on the whole drawn from the subscribers of a voluntary hospital, and Pendlebury was no exception. The way in which money was raised gave an interesting glimpse into the social life of Victorian Manchester and Salford. Money was raised by soirees, coversazioni, lectures, exhibitions, fancy dress parties and many other ways in which Manchester and Salford 'society' entertained itself.

The rules of governance for the Ladies' Committee/Council seem to be implicit within the Hospital Rules of Governance. They worked very closely with the House Committee and their activities were always incorporated in the annual report. By far the largest task was to initiate fundraising for the hospital. They also appointed 'Lady Visitors', whose duty it was to visit the hospital, examine the efficiency of arrangements and report back to the Board of Management on a monthly basis. Lady Visitors also contributed to the home visiting program. *"Any child recommended by a subscriber and residing within Manchester and Salford was entitled to home visits."* (*Small and Special; the Development of Hospitals for Children in Victorian Britain*, EMR Lomax, Welcome Inst. 1996) They would check on patients previously discharged and offer ongoing advice. Home visiting was taken over by nurses in the 1900s.

Annual subscribers to the hospital were allowed to recommend patients according to their contribution - known as Governor's tickets or recommendations. It is difficult to get a full breakdown of how this worked for the Children's Dispensary, as the annual general reports were much more interested in the amounts donated than the criteria for recommendation. In the Rules for the Government of the Hospital it was laid down in 1903 that subscribers of £5 p.a. could have 3 votes, 1 guinea 2 votes and half a guinea (10s. 6d.) 1 vote. This differed from the method used at both Belfast and Glasgow children's hospitals. Subscriptions affected the number of patients that could be 'recommended' to the hospital. The annual general reports carried Bequest Forms. After 1891 The Mortmain & Charitable Uses Act enabled bequests to be given duty free to the hospital. By 1900 there were approximately 700 subscribers to the hospital, compared with 30 in the very early days.

During the 1880s little can be found in the Annual Reports regarding the Ladies' Committee. It must be assumed that in the move to the new hospital and the new dispensary in Gartside Street, and their development and maitenance, that the Ladies' Council would be a very important part of the new service. Subscribers' lists and gifts donated were still recorded in the Annual Reports. With the transformation in hospital management countrywide in the

1890s, the Ladies Council reappears and seems to be a newly constituted body.

By 1896 the Ladies' Council was again flourishing. They had an office at 46 Brown Street, Manchester and approximately 70 members on the council. The President of the Ladies' Council was a Mrs Moorhouse, the Vice Presidents were the Lady Mayoress of Manchester and the Mayoress of Salford, the joint secretaries were a Mrs Bradley Moore and a Mr A.A. Gillies. The hospital relied heavily on the funds collected by the Ladies' Committee/Council which in the year 1896 was £1,041.14s 0d.

The Ladies' Committee held their 1896 meeting for the first time at Pendlebury, and were offered an opportunity to see the hospital at work. All gifts to the hospital were carefully listed in the Annual General Report including such items as scrapbooks, magazines, dolls, toys, and they were acknowledged by name of donor. A Mr Samuel Armitage of Pendlebury gave 10 brace of pheasants, and also for Christmas dinner, four turkeys and two geese. One member of the Steinthal family, who lived in Marple, gave 50 eggs. There was £5 from Mr M.F. Hardcastle, High Sheriff of Lancashire - this being used for a tea party and a Punch & Judy Show for the children at Christmas time. Gifts ranged from rocking horses and toys to those of purely utilitarian nature - fruit, semolina, calico and cod liver oil. Gifts came not only from subscribers but also from parents, former patients, Sunday Schools and Schools.

The numbers of patients treated continued to increase, drawn from an ever widening geographical area. This coincided with the introduction of small satellite Ladies' Committees. Children came to the Hospital and Dispensary from Manchester, Salford and Suburbs, but many others travelled from as far afield as Blackpool, Buxton, Chester, Colne, Crewe, Darwen, Disley, Garstang, Hale, Hayfield, Holmes Chapel, Lancaster, Newton le Willows, Southport, Warrington and Wilmslow to name but a few, and Ladies' Committees were to be found in the majority of these districts.

The Ladies' Council remained at 46 Brown Street until World War Two, but when Manchester suffered severe bombing, it moved from the city centre in 1941 to an office at Pendlebury. The President of the Council was The Lady Mayoress of Manchester and the Vice President, The Mayoress of Salford. Many districts continued to have Ladies' Auxiliary Funds to raise money for the hospital. Each district branch had a small committee with a President and each branch endeavoured to raise £50 or more. In 1941 the branches contributed approximately £2,350 to the hospital fund.

When the Convalescent Home was set up in 1897 in Lytham St Anne's at the sole expense of Sir William Agnew, a Ladies' Committee was formed to support this accommodation for 26 children. Their role was to provide entertainments for the patients and raise funds. The Ladies' Committee was known as 'The Ladies' Fund' and the president was Mrs Robert S. Boddington of the brewery empire.

In conclusion Ladies' Committees/Councils played a very important role in the life of the Hospital. Until the National Health Service the finances of the Hospital always depended solely on volunteers - and so also did the social and welfare work of the hospital. The members of the Ladies' Committees in the early days, were mainly drawn from amongst the hospital's subscribers and relatives and played a vital part in the life of the hospital. Their 'work' took them not only onto the wards, but also into the homes of patients. They helped families to understand the importance of carrying out the advice of the physicians and surgeons. In summing up in one annual report it was said *"We owe a great debt of gratitude to our Ladies' Committee."* Importantly the Ladies' Committees also raised the social profile of the Institution.

ENDOWED BEDS & COTS

Another Victorian practice was that of raising money to endow cots. Donors could endow a cot in order to commemorate a loved one's name e.g. Souchay Cot January 10th 1873, paying a sum for a permanent inscription. What this sum was for each cot endowed is not clear, but as there were only 26 named between 1873 and 1900, it would seem that the amount required was substantial.

In the annual general report of 1942 there is an advertisement encouraging the endowment of cots or beds: £1,000 endows a bed and £500 endows a cot. This practice continued until the hospital was incorporated into the National Health Service.

BEQUESTS

Bequests were actively sought for the Hospital from private estates. Many citizens bequeathed both small and large amounts, and the Hospital is still the grateful recipient of continued funding from such sources.

It needs to be remembered that the entire life of the hospital at Pendlebury before incorporation into the National Health Service was that of a charity. Annual reports were very important in order for those who had contributed in anyway to receive recognition. Without such generosity there would simply have been no 'Pendlebury'.

THE FOLLOWING COTS HAVE BEEN ENDOWED IN PERPETUITY.

Perpetual Endowment ... ... £1000.
Annual Endowment ... ... £50.

Subject to the regulations of the Hospital, persons endowing Beds or Cots enjoy the privilege of naming them and nominating patients to occupy them.

Year		Cot	*Bed No.*	*Ward.*
1866	The	Steinthal Cot	13	Liebert
1866	,,	Schwabe Cot	19	Liebert
1873	,,	Hinshelwood Cot	7	Liebert
1873	,,	Hertz Cot	11	Holden
1873	,,	Souchay Cot	15	Holden
1874	,,	Lambe Cot	9	Liebert
1875	,,	Atkinson Cot	1	Holden
1879	,,	Armitage Cot	9	Heywood
1879	,,	Hope Cot	18	Liebert
1879	,,	Thomasson Cot	1	Liebert
1880	,,	Claremont Cot	8	Liebert
1880	,,	Aunt Laura Cot	14	Holden
1883	,,	Mothersill Cot	2	Holden
1883	,,	Thomas Agnew Cot	17	Holden
1888	,,	Sir Joseph Whitworth Cot	16	Holden
1889	,,	Carrie Ogilvie Cot	24	Liebert
1890	,,	Daniel Proctor Cot	12	Holden
1891	,,	Walter Haworth Cot	3	Liebert
1891	,,	Florence Bolton Cot	3	Holden
1892	,,	John Henry Agnew Cot	13	Heywood
1892	,,	Mary Agnew Cot	10	Heywood
1892	,,	Edith Mary Cot	23	Liebert
1896	,,	Florence Lee Cot	13	Holden
1898	,,	Steinthal Cot (To commemorate the services of the Rev. S. A, STEINTHAL as Hon. Secretary.)	4	Holden
1900	,,	Yates Cot	14	Heywood
1901	,,	Hannah Dawson Cot	16	Heywood
1901	,,	Gladys Pilkington Cot	16	Liebert
1902	,,	Edward Hampson and Lettice Brooks Cot	19	Heywood
1905	,,	Cornelius Tattersall Cot (In Memoriam from his Sons, Bowdon)	17	Heywood
1905	,,	Lily Peacock Cot	6	Holden
1905	,,	Eliz. Ann Milner Cot	15	Liebert
1905	,,	Louisa Whitehead Cot (Bury)	8	Holden
1905	,,	Manasseh Gledhill Cot	5	Holden
1905	The	King Edward VII. and Queen Alexandra Cot (To commemorate their visit to Salford on July 13th, 1905.) The gift of Elizabeth Fox Wood	7	Holden
1906	,,	Mary Middleton Cot	9	Holden
1908	,,	Bhainee Cot	15	Heywood
1910	,,	Frank Gemmell Crowther Cot (In memory, from his widow Mrs. Helen Crowther)	10	Holden
1911	,,	Gerald Peel Cot	2	Liebert
1912	,,	Helen Swindells Cots (In Memoriam)	5 & 6	Liebert
1915	,,	J. Grimble Groves Cot	25	Liebert
1916	,,	E. Wadsworth Cot	22	Liebert
1917	,,	Aline Cot	21	Liebert
1917	,,	Mary Ann and Jane Higgin Cot	26	Liebert
1917	,,	Agnes Riddick Cot	4	Heywood
1917	,,	Charles Stanley Haslam Cot	5	Heywood
1919	,,	Atherton Cot (Endowed by Mrs. Philip Fletcher.)	20	Heywood
1920	,,	Elizabeth Denyer Cot (In Memory of the late Mrs. Elizabeth Denyer.)	20	Liebert
1920	,,	Peel & Co., Ltd., Cot	11	Heywood
1922	,,	Law Binns Cot	24	Heywood
1922	,,	Emma A. Harwood Cot	26	Heywood
1922	,,	R. N. Hudson Cot	1	Heywood
1923	,,	Richard Hudson Cot	2	Heywood
1923	,,	Heath House Cot	25	Heywood
1924	,,	John James and Jennette Mellor Cot	22	Heywood
1924	,,	William and Alice Briggs Cot	23	Heywood
1924	,,	Anne Pownall Cot (In Memoriam)	6	Heywood
1924	,,	Mary Neville Cot	3	Heywood
1925	,,	William Henry Armitage Cot	8	Heywood
1925	,,	Manchester War Memorial Cot	7	Heywood
1925	,,	John George and Elizabeth Litton Cot	12	Heywood
1925	,,	Colonel John Chadwick Barlow Cot	18	Heywood
1925	,,	Eliza Entwistle Cot	21	Heywood
1926	,,	Margaret Mouat Cot	4	Liebert
1927	,,	Robert Guest Cot	10	Liebert
1927	,,	Goodhehere Cot	11	Liebert
1927	,,	Ancient Order of Frothblowers Cot	19	Wrigley
1927	,,	Milner-Cowburn Cot	17	Liebert
1928	,,	John George and Elizabeth Litton Cot	14	Liebert
1928	,,	The Rev. J. W. and Mrs. Kiddle Cot	12	Liebert
1929	,,	Christopher & Lavinia Higginbottom Cot	18	Holden
1929	,,	Joseph Hugh Monk Cot	19	Holden
1929	,,	Margaret Stanway Wood Cot	26	Holden
1930	,,	Bredbury & Romiley Cot		Holden
1930	,,	Mary Burrows Cots	20 & 21	Holden
1931	,,	John Wolstencroft	22	Holden

Cots endowed in perpetuity 1932 Annual Report
(many others were endowed on an annual basis, £50 a year in 1932).

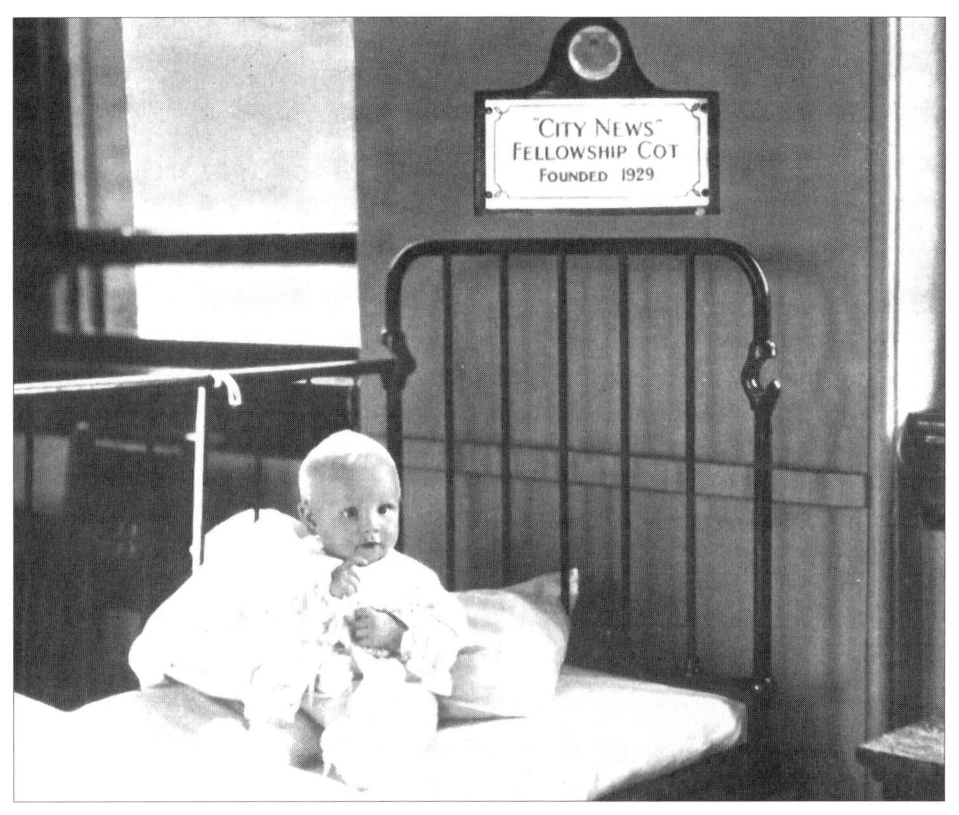

Wall plaques above endowed cots. The practice of endowed cots disappeared in the reorganisation of the National Health Service.

This marble bust of Dr Louis Borchardt is in an alcove outside Borchardt Ward at Pendlebury. Dr Borchardt was the Physician to the Hospital 1854-1879.

Dr Henry Ashby succeeded Dr Borchardt as the Hon. Physician to Pendlebury (1879-1908). He trained at Guys Hospital, London.

CHAPTER 4

PART I - PIONEERS IN PAEDIATRICS (1829-1900)

The history of paediatrics in Manchester reflects the history in Great Britain of child health care. As previously stated, children's hospitals and children's medicine were to come late to Britain. France had already experienced a loss of life through continual wars and had established the view that healthy children were a national asset. The initiative of 1802 in establishing the Enfants Malades hospital showed this and in 1815 it was a large institution with its six to eight hundred patients.

The lack of progress in Britain was in many ways due to the concept that state or charitable intervention in family life was not acceptable. The Parishes were considered to be the place for the growing numbers of deserted children who were ending up in workhouses. There was an enormous increase in the population at this time and no shortage of workforce. Healthy children were not high on local community agendas. However, the high levels of infant mortality in the slum districts particularly of the urbanised Midlands and North, began to persuade some members of the local communities of the need to serve children better.

Thomas Coram, a retired sea captain, had as early as 1729 established the Foundling Hospital in London with the support of leading members of the aristocracy. It was to be another 100 years before the small General Dispensary for Sick Children was initiated in Manchester. The main London Dispensary was brought back into high profile again by the physician Charles West in 1839, which led to the establishment of the Hospital for Sick Children, Great Ormond Street in 1852.

At the turn of the 18th century, Manchester was referred to as the "*largest village in England*". (*Manchester, This Good Old Town*, Brooks & Haworth 1997). The population was growing rapidly, but this was not totally due to the birth rate. There was a huge increase in immigrants drawn to Manchester and its surrounds by industry. This steady influx of newcomers was to have a lasting influence on the development and growth of the area. Immigrants were drawn particularly from Scotland but also from abroad. There was an ever increasing Greek and Jewish population with a large community of Germans, who settled in the area known as Greenheys. The community of Manchester and Salford with its growing population was taking on a very cosmopolitan flavour.

This growing population gave rise to problems of housing, health and basic public provision including water. The Manchester conduit was the main source of domestic water, but 1836 still saw water being brought in by stone pipes from private reservoirs, just outside the town. Not until 1850 was water supplied from the new reservoirs at Denton and Hyde.

Manchester had become the prosperous trading centre for the Lancashire industrial belt. The plight of the 'labouring' poor however was soon to become a focus of concern. More and more of the physicians and other leaders in the community became worried about these ill fed, scantily clothed and badly housed families living in the overcrowded town. In 1792, at a cost of £30,000, the Poor House opposite the Cathedral (Collegiate Church) was built, supporting a considerable programme of provision for the poor in Manchester.

The conditions were a hotbed for infection. Many of the successful inhabitants of the town now began to support charities that offered help to the poor, including the development of the voluntary hospital movement and this became seen as an acceptable and worthy practice. By 1828 a small group had recognised the significance of children's health needs, and after an initial meeting in November 1828, the General Meeting of a committee was held on 14th January 1829, to inaugurate the General Dispensary for Children.

The two doctors who helped to found the General Dispensary for Children were Walter Barton Stott, a surgeon, then only 28 years of age, and Dr John Alexander, a physician in Manchester.

Walter Barton Stott 1800-1878 MRCS 1827 LSA 1826

During the meeting, in the Manchester Exchange Committee Room on 27th November 1828, the idea for a 'Children's Dispensary' was agreed. Amongst those giving generous support were Daniel Grant and members of the Byron and Atherton families, who were private patients of Stott.

Walter Barton Stott was the fifth son of Thomas and Lucy Stott, fustian manufacturers of Deansgate, Manchester. His elder brothers were educated at Manchester Grammar School, but he was educated in Bradford and afterwards became a pupil of the well known surgeon Joseph Jordan, of Bridge Street, Manchester. His grandfathers, Thomas Stott and George Barton, had both been former Borough Reeves of Manchester. They would also certainly have been members of the John Shaw Club, as was Stott himself. Sunday afternoons were the usual gathering time for members of this club, where drinking port, a bottle apiece being the recognised quota for the day. A close friend of W.B. Stott's was James Hancock, also a member of the club, who became a surgeon at the Children's Dispensary, and later Pendlebury.

When he became a full member of the club, Stott was described as a widower. In 1830 he had married, at the Cathedral, Rosamond Ollier, daughter of the surgeon, Thomas Ollier, and much older than her husband. On her death, he married Amelia Stanhope from Eccleshill Hall in Yorkshire who was 18 years younger than himself. They lived at 28 St John Street, Manchester. By 1864 they had removed to Unwin Terrace, Disley, a village on the edge of the Peak District regarded as a healthy place to live because of the abundance of springs and serviced by the new railway line from Manchester to Buxton. Stott continued his practice in Manchester until his death in 1878. Amelia Stott died in 1864. They are both buried in St. Mary the Virgin's Churchyard in Disley with a significant headstone of pink marble.

Disley Church where William Barton Stott and his wife are buried.

During his career Stott had been surgeon to the Poor Law Guardians, and the New Bailey Prison, in which capacity he would have been required to attend executions, as well as sick prisoners. However, Stott is undoubtedly best remembered for his long contribution to the Children's Dispensary and the Hospital. His tombstone reads:

William Barton Stott MRCS LSA
Late of St John's St. Manchester
For many years surgeon to the New Bailey Prison
and to the Children's Hospital
Died at Disley April 8th 1878
aged 78 years
"He visited the sick and needy"

Dr John Alexander

The other co-founder of the Sick Children's Dispensary was Dr John Alexander, a Physician. Little is known about him. It is probable that he was the Dr John Alexander living in 4 Princess Street in 1833, who moved away in the next few years as no Dr John Alexander appears in entries for the 1841 census in Manchester. Dr John Alexander continued as Physician to the Children's Dispensary until 1853, when he seems to have left the district altogether. The annual reports throw no light on his reasons for leaving. Dr Louis Borchardt succeeded him to the position of Physician in 1854.

Although the Children's Dispensary had continued to treat sick children since 1829, there was no real progression or development in this service until the advent of the two immigrant physicians, the Hungarian, Professor Schoepf Merei, and the German, Dr Louis Borchardt. Both found it relatively easy to fit into Manchester society because of their connections with the immigrant merchants already established in business here. Both also had already specialised in children's diseases before leaving their own countries and were able to easily identify the gap in services within the city confines, and thus look to use their specific expertise in work with children.

Professor August Schoepf Merei

Professor August Schoepf Merei was born in Pesth, Hungary and had a particular interest in childhood disease. He settled in Manchester as a result of the 1848 uprisings in his own country with financial support from Salis Schwabe. His working colleague was James Whitehead, a surgeon from the St Mary's Lying In Hospital. Both were interested in the relationship between growth and disease. Their study in early physical development *On the Disorders of Infantile Development and Rickets*, aimed to show that infants who showed growth deficiency at a given age were more liable to subsequent illness such as rickets.

His work was carried out at a small children's dispensary and hospital in Stevenson Square set up at the time of the Lying In Hospital, he was never directly involved in the General Dispensary for Sick Children. The work that he carried out on childhood disease, however, must have had some influence on the work of Dr Borchardt and it would be supposed that they moved in the same social circles.

Professor Merei gave lectures on diseases in childhood at Chetham Street School of Medicine and helped to raise the awareness of paediatrics amongst the profession. With the death of Professor Merei in 1858, the beds and dispensary which had opened in Stevenson Square, moved with the hospital to Cheetham Hill, later to become the Northern Hospital for Women and Children. The children's services relocated to Booth Hall in the 1940s.

Dr Louis Borchardt

Dr Louis Borchardt was born in Landsberg an der Warthe (Brandenburg) in 1813. He qualified as a doctor in Berlin in 1838 and practised medicine in Breslau. During the typhus epidemic in Silesieu in 1845 he had distinguished himself through his ability to organise medical relief. His political activities were brought to the attention of the authorities by being named first of all in the Karl Marx - Engels correspondence and then as a political agitator. Borchardt was imprisoned in the Fortress Glatz for a short time and when the reactionaries triumphed, he was released from prison.

He then came to Bradford, where he met Mr H. M. Steinthal in about 1848. The Steinthals moved to Manchester in 1852 and Dr Borchardt followed and began to build up an excellent medical practice in Manchester. Here he joined the Liberal Party and eventually became President of the Withington Branch.

1854 saw the appointment of Dr Borchardt to the General Dispensary for Children as the honorary physician. Dr Borchardt quickly recognised that many children from the working classes were dying because of inadequate nursing at home and he began agitating for a ward of six beds to be attached to the Dispensary. He also wanted a "fever ward" for sick children. When the hospital moved from North Parade to Bridge Street there were more beds made available for in-patients. It was very much due to his encouragement and his renowned powers of organisation that the Board of Governors was persuaded to build a new hospital and that Pendlebury was chosen. Dr Borchardt was known for his devotion that was *"higher than could be looked for towards his patients"*. In Berlin he had given special attention to diseases of childhood and through his work in Manchester he was able to develop this interest and his expertise. His knowledge of foreign hospitals and administration was most beneficial when it came to the construction of the new hospital at Pendlebury for which he was on the Building Committee.

In 1879 the Board of Governors resolved *"to mark in some permanent way the sense which the Board of Governors have for the value of Dr Borchardt's services rendered as honorary physician to the General Hospital and the General Dispensary for Sick Children for five and twenty years. One pavilion, therefore, has been named the Borchardt Ward"*. Dr Borchardt was also awarded £1,000. Percival Ball was commissioned to make two busts of Dr Borchardt, one to stand outside the ward and one presented to Mrs Borchardt.

In March 1876 Dr Borchardt made an application to the governors to be relieved of his duties as physician and he was appointed honorary physician until his untimely death in 1883. He occupied at the time of his death the position of President of the Lancashire & Cheshire Branch of the Council of the British Medical Association. At a meeting of the Association in Bath in 1878 he demonstrated that he was a convinced advocate of admitting medical women on an equal footing with men.

His active and energetic approach together with his interests in childhood disease and the Children's Hospital helps to identify Dr Borchardt as very much a founder of this service. His marble bust still remains in the alcove outside the entrance to Borchardt Ward, a reminder of his great influence on the hospital. He was to be followed by another physician of great note in the care of children.

Henry Ashby (1846-1908)

Dr Henry Ashby was appointed to the medical board of the General Sick Children's Hospital in 1879. He had trained in London at Guy's Hospital and been awarded the Gold Medal for his studies in 1878. Dr Ashby came to Pendlebury (the Children's General Hospital) from Liverpool when Dr Borchardt left. He had been Assistant Physician for children at the Liverpool Infirmary and a lecturer in physiology and anatomy at the Liverpool School of Medicine. When he came to Pendlebury Miss Grace Campbell was Lady Superintendent (Matron) and a pioneer in nurse education. Dr Ashby also recognised the value of nurse education and gave a very instructive and supportive lecture in 1879 to nurses, soon after his arrival, which became a regular feature in the hospital, and raised the status of nurse education.

With his colleague George Arthur Wright, who was attached to the surgical staff at both the Children's Hospital and the Royal Infirmary, they wrote a work on Diseases of Children, which enjoyed world wide circulation as well as running through several editions and was still in demand in 1930. Ashby became a lecturer of diseases in childhood at the Owens College, Manchester, and subsequently the University of Manchester Medical School.

He was only involved in the treatment of children and went on to promote "health in the Nursery", a topic in which he extended his fame. He became a very well known authority on

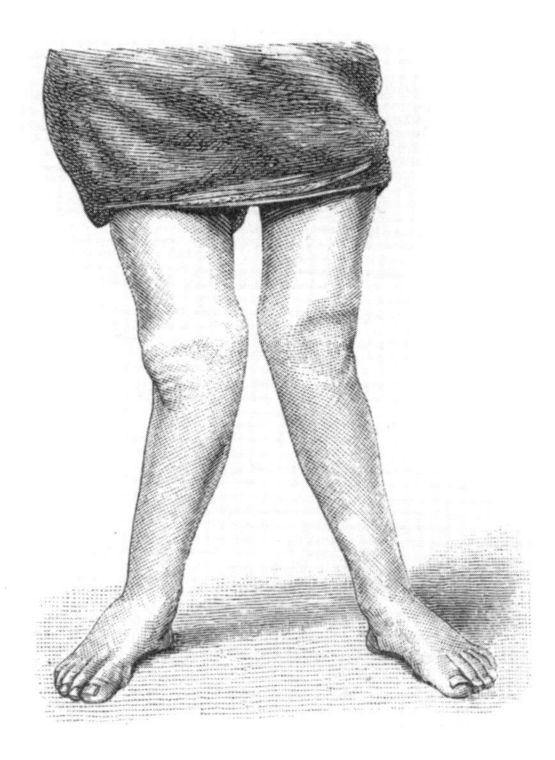

Ashby and Wright's *Diseases of Children*, and two of the drawings from it, showing the effect of rickets on a child's spine and legs.

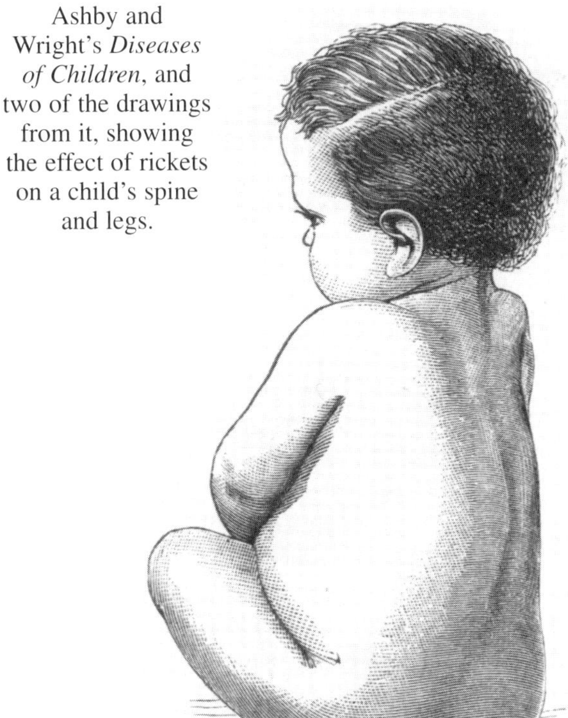

children within the medical world, not only in the North West, but worldwide. He often went to the Hospital on Sunday mornings, taking his family with him to visit his patients, or to take other medical men. Amongst his O.P. treatments he regarded "rhubarb and soda" as a panacea for many ailments of children. He wrote various articles regarding children and one especially for the Medical Times Gazette in 1882, as an authority on children's diseases. When he died in 1908 his son Hugh had just become a junior doctor at Gartside Street Dispensary.

The two surgeons who contributed to the early pioneering work in paediatrics in Manchester were Mr W. Barton Stott and George Arthur Wright (1851-1920) who was co-author with Henry Ashby of *Diseases of Children*. George Arthur Wright was considered a man of sound judgement and his advice was much sought after.

By 1900, services for children as a discrete entity were firmly established in Manchester and Salford. Paediatrics was not yet a recognised speciality but knowledge of the diseases of children was now essential for all doctors in general practice. Much had been accomplished by these pioneers at the Children's Hospital, establishing Manchester and Salford as a training and research centre in the diseases of childhood.

PART II - 1900 ONWARDS - THE WORLD STAGE

At the turn of the century, Pendlebury was still very much a charitable institution. As such, senior hospital medical officers, visiting physicians and surgeons, volunteered their services very much on a part-time basis. Most derived income from private practice which was rarely confined to children. Paediatrics was not on the whole remunerative (and still remains so), and physicians and surgeons avoided specialisation in paediatrics.

On the Continent hospital attendants were salaried and in the States there was a more positive attitude to private practice in paediatrics. Because of this part-time status less time was spent on research than was spent by their French and German counterparts. University teaching was also slow and it was thus relatively late on that departments of paediatrics were established in this Country's universities. This accounted for the slow development of the science of paediatrics. The considerable development in Manchester and at Pendlebury in the field of paediatrics is therefore all the more remarkable. It remains just as important an issue as we come to the end of the century and paediatricians fight again for discrete services in child health.

Louis Appleby in *A Medical Tour Through the Whole Island of Great. Britain,* 1994, says that Britain has a very rich medical history. *"Illnesses do not rise spontaneously - they stem from the way in which people live and work. Medical treatments emerge, not merely from science, but also from folklore, social fashion and political upheaval."* This surely sets the scene for Manchester and Salford.

As the Cities moved into the twentieth century, the diseases being treated in the Dispensary and Children's Hospital continued to be the group of "killer" infections known then as zymotic diseases. The term meant fermentation of some disease-carrying entity; the theory of miasma. This theory was undergoing radical change by the end of the nineteenth century with the discovery of microbial pathogens. However, in the discharge tables of 1899 and 1900 diseases continue to be listed under the headings of Zymotic Disease (Typhoid, Diphtheria, Influenza); Constitutional Diseases (Rickets, Syphilis, General Tuberculosis, Malnutrition, Purpura and others); Respiratory System (Laryngitis, Pneumonia, Phthisis, Pleurisy, Tonsils and Adenoids); Circulatory System (Congenital Heart Disease, Valvular Heart Disease and Pericarditis); Alimentary System (Carious Teeth, Ulceration Navel, Stomatitis, Diarrhoea,

Hernia, Constipation and others); Liver (Interstitial Hepatitis); Spleen and Glands (Hodgkins Disease, Abscess, Splenic Anaemia and others); Genito-Urinary System (Nephritis, Albuminura Tuberculosis of Kidney and others).

The total number of children being treated in 1900 was approximately 1,450; there were 130 beds on five wards available with bed occupancy approximately 118.6 daily. The mortality rate was 7.3 per cent. Wards were emptied during the spring for purposes of cleaning and on occasions when there was an outbreak of 'zymotic disease'. By this time children who contracted scarlet fever were sent to Monsall Hospital.

Patients admitted to Pendlebury came from an enormously widespread area. There was a very large proportion of children from Manchester City and Suburbs, and Salford. But it is interesting to note that as many as 39 came from Bury, 37 from Sale, 28 from Stockport and 39 from Stalybridge during the year. Children were admitted from Preston, Blackpool, Lancaster, Leek, Northwich and Warrington, to name but a few places.

Many outside factors that would have a bearing on the services for children were emerging at the turn of the century. The isolation of the 'tubercle bacillus', and the introduction of tuberculin as a 'cure', and the development of vaccines to prevent diseases such as tetanus and diphtheria in 1890, began to set the scene for medicine for the 20th century. Medical breakthroughs in the early part of the 1900s included drug treatment, the beginning of chemotherapy, the development of the gastroscope and the recognition of vitamins. Alongside these developments was the discovery that sunlight killed bacteria. The contagion theory of spread of disease had replaced the fermentation theory. All the wards at Pendlebury were to begin to add verandas for 'sunlight' treatment and fresh air.

The National Insurance Act, brought in by Lloyd George in 1911, was a further significant advance. Most working men were registered with Friendly Societies and other insurance companies and had their payments supplemented through taxes, and obtain unemployment benefit and medical aid from doctors who were registered with local panels. This change was especially beneficial in the long treatment of tuberculosis. Importantly, however, this 'national insurance' did not cover their families.

The real discussion regarding the nation's health in the Edwardian Era, i.e. the time from 1900 through to the First World War, continued to be that of poor housing, and a still very high infant and child mortality - and this was not producing a healthy population for the Country, in fact the reverse. The situation was highlighted when, in the Manchester area, of "*11,000 who volunteered for service in the Boer War [1899] only 3,000 passed as fit to fight and only 1,000 fit for line regiments*" (*Medicine and Industrial Society*, J. V. Pickstone 1985). The leaders of the district now had a very clear view of the problems they were facing in children's health.

The services for children now began to develop quite rapidly. The new Memorial Dispensary built in Gartside Street in 1907 was a great step forward. Any child who visited the Dispensary needing admission to the hospital was taken to Pendlebury in an omnibus belonging to the hospital. Much was made of "*removing these little sufferers*" to Pendlebury to enable them to have constant attention of *"skilled nurses"*, frequent visits of the best "*medical men*" and to "*enjoy the fresh warm air and sunny light*" that the hospital offered. Comments within hospital documents of 1906 describe the doctors wearing top hats and frock coats, the nurses wearing dresses with very high collars, long sleeves and cuffs. Promotion to Sister took about ten to fifteen years and they were very proud of their red and white beds, and blue and white cots. Some sisters were considered very formidable. Horse-drawn omnibuses were the transport to the Heights and many had bikes. Professor Marsden, when he worked at

Pendlebury in the early days of the NHS, after the Second World War, continued with this mode of transport, coming from Withington daily by bicycle in the early 1950s.

There was no General Office at the Hospital and the Hospital Secretary came up to the Hospital once a week. The Resident Medical Officer had to do all the buying of dressings and other medical equipment. He had a huge box of thermometers, and should a nurse break one she had to pay 6d for a replacement. The Medical Officer was also in charge of stores, rubber tubing and meeting the demands from the sisters for replacement materials for their wards, which were handed out on Wednesday evenings. All requests for leave, equipment and other issues were written up in either the Lady Superintendent's Request Book or the Sister's Requisition Book. - On December 11th 1911 *"May I be absent from duty three days in January, 6, 8 and 9 - Yes. F. Roby"*, and again *"January 16, 1911 - N Hamilton went off duty last Thursday with a bad throat"*. From the Lady Superintendent's Request Book is the entry *"April 8, 1903. New cots are very badly required in 3 of the wards - Liebert, Heywood and Holden. The price for the 24 would be 31/3 each. Agreed F.S."*

The Convalescent Home built in 1897 by Sir William Agnew at Lytham St Annes continued to offer a valuable service. The building included two large playrooms, an open air verandah with a south aspect and a croquet lawn. A 'garden house' was added around 1910 for shelter when outside.

Dr C Paget Lapage became physician to Pendlebury on the death of Dr Henry Ashby in 1908. Dr Hugh Ashby, Dr Henry's son, was appointed the Medical Officer at Gartside Street Dispensary, in Dr Lapage's place. Dr Lapage's association with Pendlebury was to last the first half of the 20th century, during which time the Department of Diseases of Children was instituted in 1913, at the Medical School. The department from its inception was under the direction of Dr Lapage but was very limited in its scope and direction until the 1940s.

Dr Lapage was a well-liked doctor of the 'old' school, considered by many a real eccentric. He maintained a very old car, to which he would retire for long periods to read; he would only drink distilled water, which had to be available to him on his ward rounds; he did not complete any of his very long sentences, and walked so fast the members of his 'round' had the greatest difficulty in keeping up with him.

In 1912 Dr Lapage, or 'Lappie' as he was affectionately known, was joined by **Dr Hugh T. Ashby** at Pendlebury when he became a visiting physician, which position he would retain the whole of his working life. **Miss Renaut,** Lady Superintendent, joined the hospital from Edinburgh. A new isolation unit was built and opened on 12th June by the President, Sir George Agnew. The year saw fewer deaths, 169 as opposed to 181 in the previous year, despite an increase in admissions, but there was still a very high mortality rate. The London-based King's Fund had laid down criteria for outpatient department lectures on the management of T.B. (tuberculosis) cases in connection with Public Health. The hospital staff commenced a series of postgraduate lectures upon diseases of children as a result of this directive.

At this time there were beds at Gartside Street. **Mr Westmacott** had six beds for ENT work. The X-ray equipment here was also being used more extensively.

All Medical Officers of the Charity - that is the doctors - were appointed by the Board of Governors. The Medical Officers were all unmarried and had to devote their whole time to the hospital. They were required to visit all the patients every morning and to call in the Consultant Physician or Surgeon when in any difficulty with a case.

With the outbreak of World War I in 1914 there would be enormous changes that would have far-reaching effects, not only on Pendlebury but on all aspects of medicine and the delivery of medical service world-wide.

CONVALESCENT HOME, LYTHAM ST ANNES

By 1896 it had become the practice of the medical staff at Pendlebury, (by means of a Convalescent Fund), to send children, who might benefit from it, away for convalescence. During that year over 200 children benefited in this way, staying for a period of three weeks each. The children were received into the Children's Sanitarium at Southport, the Abraham Ormerod Children's Convalescent Home at St Annes and the Barnes Convalescent Home in Cheadle - although not by the sea, the air was considered 'healthy'. '

Open air' treatment was becoming recognised as an important aspect of paediatric treatment and this coincided with a shortage of convalescent home beds. It initiated the extraordinary generosity of the President of the Board of Governors, Sir William Agnew, in building at his sole expense a convalescent home entirely for the use of children from Pendlebury, at Lytham St. Annes. A building committee chaired by Mr George W. Agnew was set up with an architect, and the building began. The report in 1897 says that the autumn of 1896 had been a particularly wet one and the building had become somewhat delayed. By the summer of 1897 accommodation for 30 children in four wards, with two large play-rooms, was to be available. The building had an open air verandah with a southerly aspect, an out of doors shelter, croquet lawns and sandhills, and was to be run by 8 staff.

With this new home of their own, they could increase the severity of case that was able to benefit. Children who were still wearing splints or had unhealed wounds were now able to be admitted for convalescence.

The Board appointed Miss Stevens, who for eleven years had been Sister on Wrigley Ward, as the first Matron of the Convalescent Home. The Board was confident that under her care "*the welfare and happiness of the inmates*" would be assured.

Convalescent Home, Lytham St Annes, built at the sole expense of Sir William Agnew in 1897.

Sir William Agnew Bart. President of the Hospital from 1893 to 1910.

The Rules of Governance were set out explicitly in the Annual Report in 1897. The Home was to be called the "Manchester Children's Hospital Convalescent Home." The governance of the Home became vested into the Board of Governors of the Manchester Children's Hospital and all property belonged to the trustees of the Children's Hospital. A House Committee was set up to administer the Home; the committee was to meet monthly and present a report on a regular basis to the Board of Governors. The nurses were under the direction of the Matron. The patients had to be under fourteen years of age and not suffering from infectious diseases. Parents and relatives could visit their children at the discretion of the Matron. This was allowed between 2pm-4pm daily, through application to the matron.

In 1898 there was a committee of nine to run the Home. In the first report of this committee, 258 children were admitted, 244 remained for 3 weeks, 13 remained for 6 weeks and 1 remained for 9 weeks.

The building was considered both substantial and comfortable. It was agreed that a further covered verandah was needed for the surgical convalescent patients. The honorary medical staff were Drs Ruxton, Booth and Elliot.

The Ladies' Committee, whose President was Mrs Boddington, provided many entertainments for the children and £150 of financial help during 1898. By 1902, the Ladies' Committee were very active and continued to support the Home through fundraising and visiting. The Home was costing about £704 per year to run and there were about 300 children benefiting.

Little is documented further regarding the home except that it continued to benefit children needing convalescence well into the 1970s. The rules of government continued to be printed in the annual reports, but little of the activities within the home were recorded. By 1932 we know that Mr G.A.T. Jesson was Chairman of the 'Home' Committee, that Dr H.T. Ashby and Dr C.P. Lapage were members of the committee, the Matron was Mrs E. Wynne and the honorary medical officer was Dr E.R. Ormerod.

The convalescent home at St Annes continued to be used up until 1972. A group of children at this time were taken out and another brought back each Wednesday in the Hospital's own ambulance. Many young girls wishing to train as nurses would spend a period of time working there until they were old enough to commence their training.

When the home closed in 1972 it was deemed that it had served its purpose. The convalescent opportunities provided by this accommodation at St Annes must have benefited many thousands of children. With advances in treatment and modern medicine it had become financially unviable and inappropriate to treat children at such a great distance from their families. The Home had for over seventy five years been a key component of recovery for very sickly children and given opportunities to help sick children unavailable in any other way.

GARTSIDE STREET DISPENSARY - EARLY DAYS

When the Dispensary with the in-patient beds outgrew its premises in Bridge Street, it was relocated to the green fields of Pendlebury. However, a conscious decision was also made at this meeting in 1867 that a convenient dispensary should be erected in the city, capable of treating the growing number of patients requiring medical relief but not in-patient care. A plot of land near the old Dispensary was purchased and a plain but substantial building erected in 1868. It cost £3,000 to build the new dispensary in Gartside Street. Around 7,000 patients were being seen at the Dispensary in 1867, at the time the decision was taken. There was a continued increase in out-patient attendances and towards the end of the century a rebuilding was recommended to give more space.

At the turn of the century an increase in chronic ear disease and deafness was recognised and a measles epidemic was responsible for a large increase in home visits. Dr Lapage, the medical officer in the Out Patients department, paid 4662 visits to patient's homes and a second medical officer was engaged to assist him. Much discussion took place about establishing an Infant Milk Depot, as in Paris and London. Liverpool developed a municipal milk depot in 1905/6, but by the time of the opening of the new Dispensary out-patients department, there was no sign of the milk depot in Manchester. Such a depot allowed mothers to give young children non-contaminated milk in order to reduce disease associated with milk. The depot was finally established shortly after the opening of the new building in 1907.

The increase in work in the dispensary outpatients' department gave an impetus to the appeal for the funds for the new building. The appeal was issued to the public in 1904 to

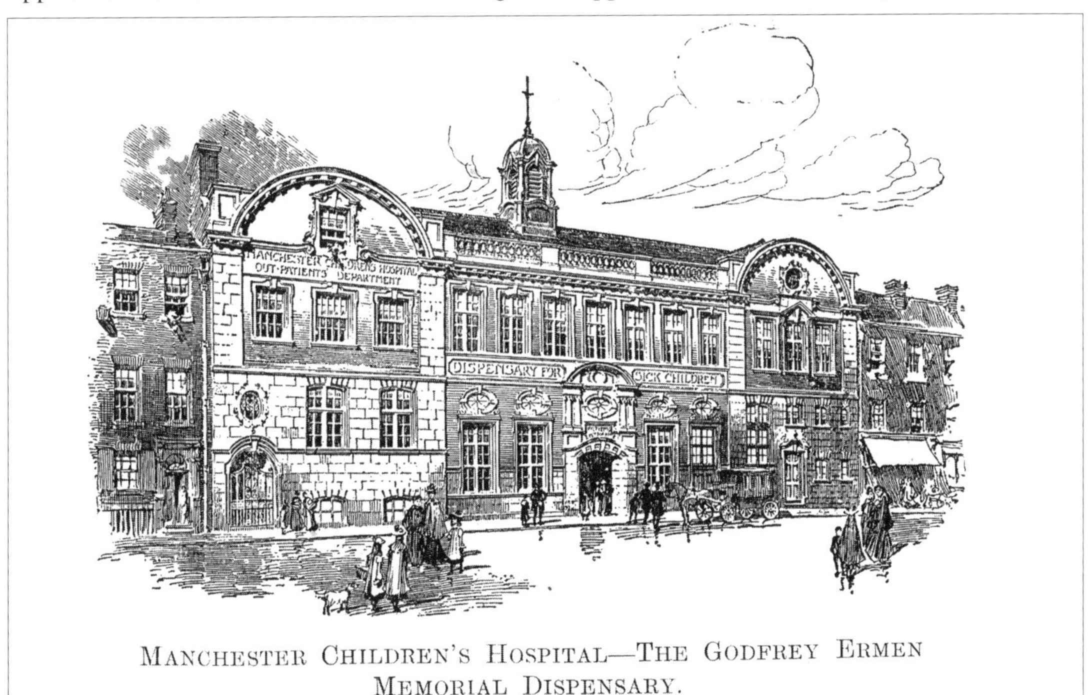

MANCHESTER CHILDREN'S HOSPITAL—THE GODFREY ERMEN MEMORIAL DISPENSARY.

provide a new and modern "Out Patients Department". By 1905, £11,500 of the £20,000 required had been raised. The Residuary Legatees of the late Mr Godfrey Ermen then offered to subscribe £12,000 to purchase land, and to build and equip the new Out Patients Department. A building committee was formed, which recommended that the new building be built on the old site and extended to double its size. The City of Manchester Corporation generously gave a piece of land adjoining and so the new building speedily went ahead.

On the 7th March 1907 the new building called The Godfrey Ermen Memorial Dispensary was opened by Mrs E. Tootal Broadhurst in the presence of the High Sheriff, Mr E Tootal Broadhurst. Sir William Banks from Liverpool at the opening declared that, *"the really great work of every Children's Hospital is done in the Out Patients Department."* Dr Henry Ashby, Chairman of the Medical Board responded, *"Your country has need of all her children and humanity demands your best efforts on their behalf."* Arthur G. Roby, a trustee of the Godfrey Ermen Trust, followed by saying, *"England's greatest asset, her children might be made stronger and have better health and be better able to fight the battle of life and fulfil, when they grow up, their duty to their fellow citizens and God by the opening of this building".*

At the main entrance of the building a level pavement was made for 'spinal carriages'. The Waiting Hall was 60ft by 40ft and could accommodate 380 waiting out-patients. Each consulting room had its own 'cosy fireplace' with beautiful wall tiles in the waiting area. The caretaker of the building was provided with a flat. The building sub-committee had also decided on radiators and hot water piping for the building generally. At the meeting of the Dispensary Sub-Committee of Governors in September 1907, the work carried out in the new dispensary for one month was recorded.

New patients	594	Operations done	91
Old patients visiting	648	Visits of M.O. to homes	529

The new building had an operating theatre. Children at this time were still queuing for the 'Tonsils Day' operation, if required. They returned straight home, the method of anaesthesia being a chloroform mask. The post of Sister for the Out Patients was advertised. It was also reported that 79 applications has been received for the post of Sister in the Out Patients Department at a wage of £120 p.a. In 1910 a Porter was engaged for duties at a wage of 25 shillings per week. The new X ray apparatus was also installed at this time, a gift of Mr Peter Eadie.

By 1915 the governors were advertising for a Masseuse (the first physiotherapist) and Miss Maudsley was appointed and would serve the Dispensary for 19 years.

By 1910 the reputation of the Children's Hospital was worldwide, and the Dispensary in Gartside Street where all the outpatients were seen played a major role in these developments. The severe cases seen at Gartside Street were sent off to the hospital at Pendlebury, taken there by an *"omnibus belonging to the Hospital."* Between the 5 years 1905-1910, 148,748 patients were treated involving 474,037 attendances. The Outpatients department was extending its role into health education giving information to the very poorest members of the population regarding feeding and treatment of children. Early statistical information was able to be given to the authorities on zymotic diseases eg cholera, typhus, etc, which would benefit the calculation of, and the response to, the still appalling infant mortality rate. The average expense of a patient in the dispensary was 1s. 5d., which seemed very economical to those running the service.

By 1926 the attendance of patients in the Godfrey Ermen Memorial Dispensary increased to 89,128. 1,898 were admitted to hospital, 2,309 operations were carried out at Gartside Street and the X Ray Department examined 781 cases. The Out-patients Dispensary was a very important aspect of the Children's Service and would continue to play a vital role until its closure in 1991, when the out-patient service was transferred to Pendlebury, to the Nurses' Home, Colwyn House, which was no longer used as nurse accommodation.

The Godfrey Ermen Dispensary at Gartside Street built in 1907.

The old switchboard at Gartside Street, photographed in 1991 just before the move to Pendlebury.

The Godfey Ermen Out-patients department in Gartside Street.

NO SMOKING

Opposite page:
'Waiting' at Gartside Street Out Patients, 1950, Godfrey Ermen Memorial Dispensary.

Right: X-ray Dept, 1950s at Gartside Street.

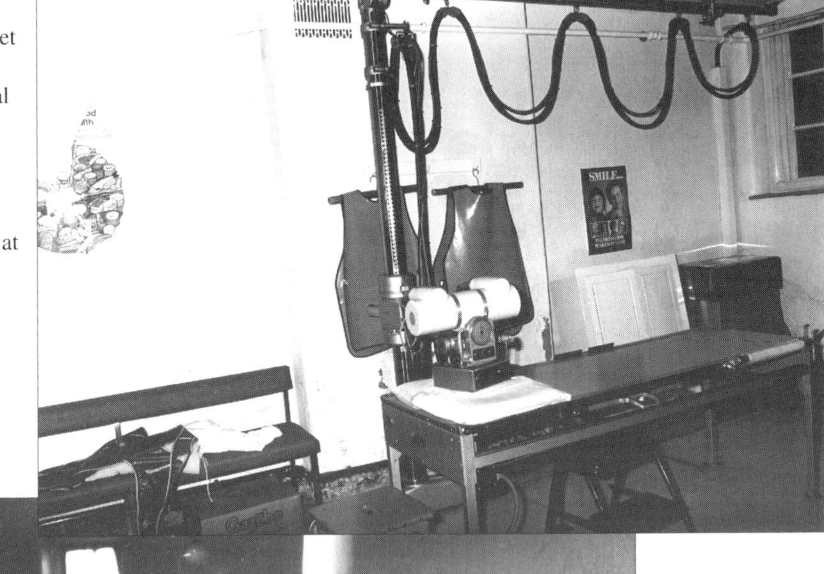

The waiting room and wendy house just before the Out-patients was closed and moved to Pendlebury in 1991.

Inside the office of the Godfrey Ermen Dispensary shortly before closure and moving to Pendlebury.

PUBLIC HEALTH IN MANCHESTER AND SALFORD

The establishment of a public health service within the Cities of Manchester and Salford had great relevance to child health services. Manchester's first Medical Health Officer was appointed in 1868. In 1889 this medical officer was permitted an assistant.

	Living under five years of age.		Deaths under five years of age.		Per centage of Annual Mortality under five years of age.	
	Manchester.	Salford.	Manchester.	Salford.	Manchester.	Salford.
1841	24,917	9648	2788	1031	11·189	10·68
Seven yrs., of which 1841 was the centre.			3218	1115	12·908[a]	11·324[a]
1851.	28,652	11,514	3098	1058	10·58	9·18
1860	30,050[b]	13,798[b]	3408[c]	1259[c]	11·34	9·05

Monsall Fever Hospital was opened to deal with the infectious diseases within the city and by the mid 1920s there were 600 beds. The Children's Hospital now sent cases of infectious disease to Monsall where the death rate was running at around 13 per 1,000 - a great improvement on the turn of the century statistic of 33 per 1,000. Infant mortality was running at 187 per 1,000 towards the end of the nineteenth century. By 1927 it had decreased to 91 per 1,000.

The main ailments presenting at the fever hospital were, at the turn of the century, typhus, typhoid and scarlet fever, diphtheria and epidemic diarrhoea. By the mid 1920s these diseases had decreased in number, but cases of encephalitis lethargica and puerperal fever were on the increase. There was now a considerable Maternity & Child Welfare programme in both Manchester and Salford, enhanced by the 30 beds at the Babies Hospital - the Duchess of York Hospital for Babies. A vast programme of treatment for infants suffering from rickets and other diseases of malnutrition had been introduced, which included research into the incidence of rickets within the city.

Manchester was the first city to voluntarily adopt the policy of the notification of tuberculosis as early as 1899. There were several Sanatorium Institutions set up to treat adults. Some of the children were sent to Abergele in North Wales, where there were ten beds. A Youth Training programme was available in Frimley, Surrey. By 1928, 540 beds were available at Abergele for children with pulmonary and non pulmonary tuberculosis.

By the 1920s Public Health Departments had become increasingly aware that the fogs caused by industrial pollution were responsible for adversely affecting all diseases of the respiratory system. A District Regional Smoke Abatement Committee was set up, but it was to be many years before the dense smogs of the industrial cities of the North and Midlands, like Manchester, would begin to abate.

By 1925 cancer was recognised as a rising disease and a Manchester Committee on Cancer was set up to campaign against the disease and to monitor the situation.

The supervision of the City's milk supply was also regulated and farmers were visited by veterinary officers, a service that was introduced in the early 1900s. This was the start of the gradual progression towards a tubercle-free milk supply and also a decrease in the incidence of gastroenteritis in children.

The Public Health Department was also responsible for general sanitation and housing and the maintenance of Corporation Hospitals, together with a Schools Medical Service. Salford was very much to the fore in the development of services within their authority for children of school age. They set up open air schools and other special schools, including one for blind children in 1921. School Medical Officers arranged for the operative treatment of tonsils and adenoids at general hospitals in the city. In the 1920s nearly all the ENT surgery for the Children's Hospital was carried out in Gartside Street. Children were referred by subscriber recommendations, usually through the family doctor.

It is interesting to note the various changes within the Greater Manchester and Salford areas as the story of paediatrics has unfolded. From a time when children were not considered worthy of treating, through to the present day where there is no more emotive subject, the changes have been enormous.

The breakthroughs in medicine, technology and science over the last fifty years save so many more lives than would have ever been thought possible a hundred and fifty years ago.

Changes were slower prior to the advent of the National Health Service. The story of a children's service in the twin cities of Manchester and Salford is unique to the area, but also follows patterns in other health care institutions for children in other parts of the country.

However it must not be overlooked that some of the most significant improvements in child health have come through improvements in public health, immunisation, housing and sanitation.

PUBLIC HEALTH

CITY OF MANCHESTER—DAYS OF FOG

Year	Jan.	Feb.	March	April	May	June	July	Aug.	Sept.	Oct.	Nov.	Dec.	No. of Days
1892	4	6	5	3	—	—	—	—	—	7	9	10	44
1893	6	4	6	3	—	—	—	—	1	3	5	6	34
1894	6	6	12	2	—	—	—	—	3	10	4	7	50
1895	8	10	8	1	—	—	—	—	4	10	4	9	54
1896	12	12	5	3	—	—	—	—	2	9	10	5	58
1897	7	3	2	2	—	—	—	—	7	5	3	5	34
1898	7	4	7	—	—	—	—	—	—	3	3	2	26
1899	4	7	6	1	—	—	—	—	—	8	3	10	39
1900	1	3	3	2	—	—	—	—	4	—	1	2	16
1901	3	9	2	—	—	—	—	—	—	3	12	5	34
1902	2	10	2	—	—	—	—	—	4	2	1	1	22
1903	—	—	—	—	—	—	—	—	1	—	7	5	13
1904	9	4	4	1	—	—	—	—	3	1	9	12	43
1905	2	2	2	—	—	—	—	—	1	8	4	4	23
1906	1	6	—	1	—	—	—	—	2	1	7	7	25
1907	2	6	5	—	—	—	—	1	2	3	4	3	27
1908	10	1	1	2	1	—	—	—	2	2	8	6	33
1909	6	5	3	3	—	—	—	—	—	1	8	3	29
1910	3	1	1	—	—	—	—	—	3	1	6	—	15
1911	5	5	—	—	—	—	—	—	—	4	1	2	16
1912	5	1	—	—	—	—	—	—	—	5	5	1	17
1913	2	4	—	—	—	—	—	—	—	2	2	1	17
1914	1	—	—	—	—	—	—	3	—	2	3	3	12
1915	1	1	—	—	—	—	—	—	—	1	10	1	14
1916	—	—	—	—	—	—	—	—	—	—	2	10	12
1917	—	6	—	—	—	—	—	—	—	1	3	7	17
1918	—	—	—	—	—	—	—	—	—	1	6	1	9
1919	—	2	1	—	—	—	—	—	—	4	—	—	7
1920	—	1	—	—	—	—	—	—	—	1	2	6	10
1921	—	1	—	—	—	—	—	—	—	—	3	1	5
1922	2	—	—	—	—	—	—	—	—	—	3	3	8
1923	2	—	—	—	—	—	—	—	—	—	9	5	16
1924	2	2	2	—	—	—	—	—	—	—	5	1	12
1925	1	4	2	—	—	—	—	—	1	3	11	3	25
1926	—	—	—	—	—	—	—	—	—	3	6	3	12
1927	—	4	—	—	—	—	—	—	—	—	1	—	5

Days of Fog in Manchester p.192 Public Health Chart. *The Book of Manchester & Salford.*

Nurses with Lady Superintendent, Miss Cameron, and young Dr Hugh T. Ashby (whitecoat, on right) about 1910.

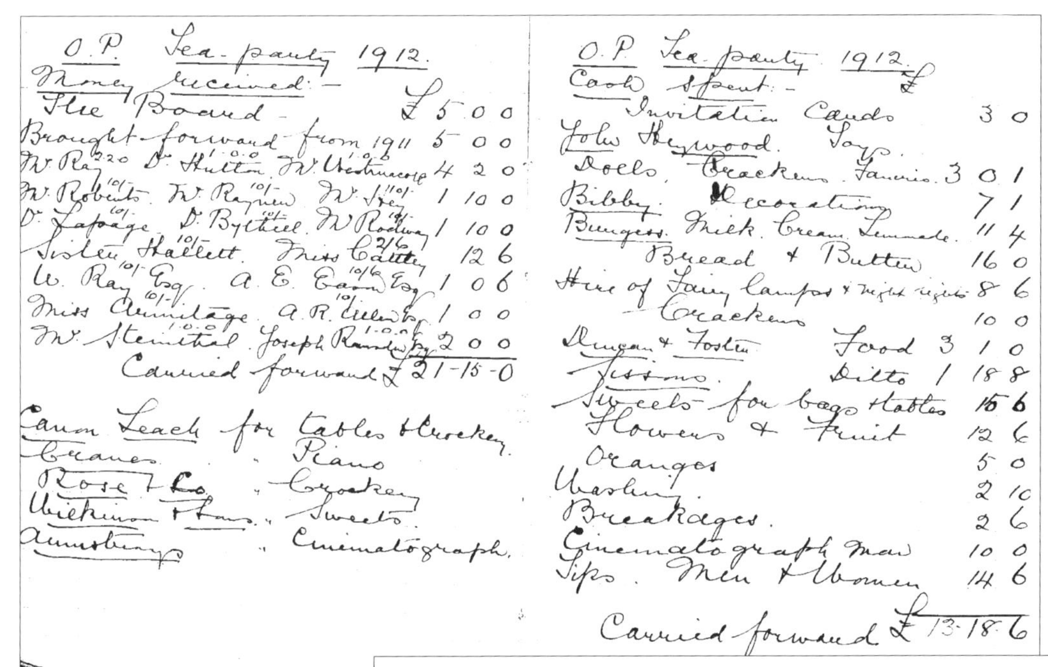

O.P. Tea-party 1912.

Money received:—

	£	s	d
The Board —	5	0	0
Brought forward from 1911	5	0	0
Mr Ray 2.2.0 Dr Hutton 1.0.0 Mr Westmacott	4	2	0
Mr Roberts 10/- Mr Rayner 10/- Mr Frey 10/-	1	10	0
Dr Lafage 10/- Dr Bythell 10/- Mr Rodway 10/-	1	10	0
Sister Hallett 10/- Miss Cattey 2/6		12	6
W. Ray Esq 10/- A. E. Eason Esq 10/6	1	0	6
Miss Armitage 10/- A. R. Allen Esq 10/-	1	0	0
Mr Steinthal 1.0.0 Joseph Rawlinson Esq 1.0.0	2	0	0
Carried forward	£21-15-0		

Canon Leach for tables & crockery
Cranes " Piano
Rose & Co " Crockery
Wilkinson & Sons " Sweets
Armstrong " Cinematograph.

O.P. Tea-party 1912.

Cash spent:—

	£	s	d
Invitation Cards		3	0
John Heywood. Toys.			
Dolls, Crackers, Fancies.	3	0	1
Bibby. Decorations		7	1
Burgess. Milk. Cream. Lemonade.		11	4
Bread & Butter		16	0
Hire of fairy lamps & night lights		8	6
Crackers		10	0
Duncan & Foster Food	3	1	0
Sissons Ditto	1	18	8
Sweets for bags & tables		15	6
Flowers & Fruit		12	6
Oranges		5	0
Washing		2	10
Breakages		2	6
Cinematograph man		10	0
Tips. Men & Women		14	6
Carried forward	£13-18-6		

1912 Expenditure on a tea party for the in-patients, and names of those who contributed.

MANCHESTER CHILDREN'S HOSPITAL.

DIET TABLE AND INSTRUCTIONS FOR RICKETY CHILDREN.—2 to 6 YEARS.

First Meal, 7 a.m.:

Bread and Milk, or oatmeal or hominy porridge with plenty of milk; bread and butter or bread and dripping with a lightly boiled egg or a little fat bacon.

Second Meal, 11 a.m.:

Cup of milk with rusks, plain biscuits, or bread and butter.

Third Meal, 1.30 p.m.:

Bread crumbs and gravy or potatoes and gravy; fresh fish or finely minced meat with bread crumbs; milk pudding, stewed prunes, or baked apples.

Fourth Meal, 5 p.m.:

Milk, or cocoa and milk, with bread and butter or bread and dripping.

Fifth Meal, half-hour before bed:

Bread and milk.

The child should be taken out whenever the weather is fine, but should not be allowed to stand or walk until the doctor gives permission.

It should have the juice of an orange or fresh green vegetables at least three times a week.

If splints are ordered they should be taken off and re-applied night and morning. Great care must be taken to avoid causing sores.

No child should be given tea or coffee.

No food must be given between meals.

Diet sheet for children with rickets.

Patients and nurse 1920s.

CHAPTER 5

NURSING

Nursing children in the early 19th century was fraught with many difficulties, not least the fear of contracting diseases from the children (indeed still a problem until after the Second World War) and the absence of a nursing profession. Great emphasis was placed on the health of prospective nurse probationers. During his medical report in 1870 Dr Borchardt refers to the careful discharge of the duties by the Matron/Lady Superintendent Miss Thompson and those under her superintendence, and the sad death of Nurse Jane Hunt from fever, *"taken in exercise of her duties."* Several nurses had died in the previous year. Dr Borchardt emphasised that with the new building, better sanitary arrangements would be in place and this *"regrettable experience"* would not happen again.

It is not clear as to where Miss Thompson received her training prior to her appointment as Lady Superintendent when the Dispensary and Hospital resided in 16 Bridge Street and very little reference is made to the appointment in 1864. The appointment coincided with the provision of beds for in-patients that Dr Borchardt had long advocated. Miss Thompson had a panel of 'lady visitors', from the ladies' auxiliary fund, who gave guidance on matters within the dispensary. They were responsible for providing almost all the amenities for the patients. She remained on the staff of the General Dispensary and Hospital for Sick Children and moved for a short time to the new site at Pendlebury. She continued to carry out her duties as Lady Superintendent until early in 1875. A Miss Peckham was then appointed in 1876 - she resigned within the year.

The appointment of Miss Grace Campbell (later to become Grace Neill) was a milestone in the history of the Children's Hospital, particularly for nursing. She has always been considered as the first Lady Superintendent at Pendlebury, General Hospital for Sick Children. Although only in residence for just over a period of two years, Pendlebury was to make great developments during this period.

Grace Neill (1846-1926) was born Elizabeth Grace Campbell, a member of a wealthy Scottish family. Her father was a retired Colonel from the Argyll & Sutherland Highlanders - a deeply religious man, but a very liberal thinker. Grace Campbell was well educated and had wanted to go to Cambridge, and wished to pursue medicine, but was not allowed to do so by her father. He did not believe in over-educated women!

The family moved to Rugby in order to educate the sons in 1870 and Grace Campbell supported her father in giving political aid to the National Union of Agricultural Workers throughout the depression of 1870. Grace Campbell then met Florence Nightingale, who advised her to join the nursing sisterhood of St. John's House in London. Her father, against his will, did eventually pay her fees and she stayed there for about five years.

At this time establishments like St John's were enlisting *"ladies of superior education and background"* to undertake the nursing of the sick. Previously nurses were recruited from *"working class"* families - they could not read or write and it was a means of livelihood. The nursing training undertaken by Grace Campbell was as part of a Sisterhood - *"nursing was a high vocation - pursued selflessly in the alleviation of human suffering."* (*The Story of a Noble Woman*). These would be the aims on which the new profession of nursing was established in later years.

By the time Grace Campbell entered nursing, the direction of nursing was well established, in particular at hospitals such as Charing Cross and Kings College in London. There were 3 grades of nurses - probationers, nurses, and sisters. Florence Nightingale had her very successful and famous school of nursing at St Thomas's Hospital.

Grace Campbell was 30 years of age when she was appointed by the Governors to Pendlebury in 1877. She met and married Channing Neill, a young doctor, in 1879 and, as Lady Superintendents were not allowed to stay in post if married, she moved with her husband to the Isle of Wight, then to Queensland Australia, and finally to New Zealand. Her father also had disapproved of her marriage as he considered doctors little more than barbers.

Sir Oliver Heywood said of her, on her retirement from Pendlebury *"Miss Grace Campbell (now Mrs Channing Neill) was for two years the efficient and greatly valued Lady Superintendent of the Hospital for Sick Children at Pendlebury - 140 beds. Her successful administration gave proof of judgment, gentleness and intelligence. She had the confidence of all members of the Board and there was general regret when she resigned her appointment."*

As a mark of recognition for the great work carried out by Grace Neill, the New Zealand Registered Nurses Association presented to Salford Hospitals Committee the Grace Neill Trophy in the 1950s. It is for an inter-hospital competition between hospitals under its administration. Grace Neill is renowned for her pioneering work in nursing in New Zealand and is considered to be instrumental in the foundation of maternity services there.

Grace Campbell must have been responsible for setting up the first nurse training at Pendlebury, as in 1879 there were 13 probationers. During this year Dr H. Ashby was appointed, Mr W. Barton Stott died and Dr Louis Borchardt finally left the hospital after 25 years of service. During her short period at Pendlebury Grace Campbell saw many major events and witnessed the completion of the six wards at the hospital. On 31st May 1879 Florence Nightingale wrote to the hospital secretary congratulating the governors on their Annual Report and the plan of the new hospital which she highly commended.

The Nursing of Sick Children has always posed its particular problems and requires a very specialised approach. Adults can usually appreciate the need for hospital treatment and are readily prepared to suffer such discomforts that treatment may incur: Children, on the other hand, simply cannot understand what is happening to them. They do not understand the nature of sickness itself - all they know is that it hurts or makes them feel unhappy - and they suffer a very real sense of loss through being removed from their homes and families. In addition to her purely technical skills, the Sick Children's Nurse must above all have a genuine feeling for children and be able to comfort them with kindness and understand their emotional needs. This is a particular tradition of nursing which has been fostered over the years at Royal Manchester Children's Hospital: the nurses are devoted to their work and the children in their care. It is a tradition of which we are particularly proud.

Florence Nightingale is, perhaps without question, the most famous nurse in history. This highly dedicated woman had tremendous influence; she knew Lord Palmerston and all the members of the cabinet, and when she took a team of nurses to Scutari during the Crimean War she changed nursing forever. Through her methods of nursing and administration she saved many lives and became known as 'the lady with the lamp'. In 1859 she wrote a small book, *Notes on Nursing*, (published by Duckworth and reissued in 1970 by Harrison & Son). She claimed that *"Bad dormitory, bad architectural and bad administrative arrangements often make it impossible to nurse."*

She followed the Miasma theory, that of gasses from putrefaction (rubbish, rotting vegetables, etc) causing illness. Hence her very warm support and commendation for the new

The Grace Neill plaque which was presented to the Hospital by the New Zealand Nursing Association. Grace Neill left Pendlebury in 1879 and emigrated to New Zealand with her husband. She was responsible for developing maternity services there.

GREAT BRITAIN.

AGES.

NURSES.	All Ages.	Under 5 Years.	5—	10—	15—	20—	25—	30—	35—	40—	45—	50—	55—	60—	65—	70—	75—	80—	85 and Upwards
Nurse (not Domestic Servant)	25,466	...	...	...	...	624	817	1,118	1,359	2,223	2,748	3,982	3,456	3,825	2,542	1,568	746	311	147
Nurse (Domestic Servant) ...	39,139	...	508	7,259	10,355	6,537	4,174	2,495	1,681	1,468	1,206	1,196	833	712	369	204	101	25	16

TABLE B.

AGED 20 YEARS OF AGE, AND UPWARDS.

	Great Britain and Islands in the British Seas.	England and Wales.	Scotland.	Islands in the British Seas.	1st Division. London.	2nd Division. South Eastern.	3rd Division. South Midland.	4th Division. Eastern Counties.	5th Division. South Western Counties.	6th Division. West Midland Counties.	7th Division. North Midland Counties.	8th Division. North Western Counties.	9th Division. Yorkshire.	10th Division. Northern Counties.	11th Division. Monmouth. and Wales.
Nurse (not Domestic Servant	25,466	23,751	1,543	172	7,807	2,878	2,286	2,408	3,055	1,225	1,003	970	1,074	402	313
Nurse (Domestic Servant) ..	21,017	18,945	1,922	150	5,061	2,514	1,252	939	1,737	2,263	957	2,135	1,023	410	614

Table of nurses employed at the time of Florence Nightingale - from her book *Notes on Nursing*.

June 17. 1903.

Dr. Ashby wishes to have a large ice chest in Borchardt Ward like the present Victoria one. The cost as far as I know will be about £5.

Dr. Lapage has asked if he may have a new wicker chair for his room. The leather chair he has is very uncomfortable. The cost of a new one will be about 30/-

S.L.L.

Nurses' Request Book 1903.

July 13th. 1915.

Miss Harrison, the new Staff Nurse was not happy here, and has left to nurse wounded soldiers. The Matron of Pendlebury has lent us a nurse meanwhile, as I cannot get a suitable one at present.

With your permission we should like to commence the holiday July 31st, 9 weeks altogether, as the Pendlebury nurse has not had her holiday yet.

July 11. 1916.

Nurse McMurtrey & myself should like to take our holidays from the end of this month, but I am unable to get a locum this year; the nurse I had engaged (late Staff nurse at Pendlebury) has withdrawn, as she does not feel strong enough to do the work; all the old locums we have had before are otherwise engaged; & Matron cannot let me have any extra help at all from the Hospital.

Sister's Requisition Book 1915.

Verandah to Holden Ward. Verandahs were added to the wards from 1906 onwards when open air treatment and sunlight became popular.

hospital for children in Salford and Manchester. It was important in her eyes, like others who followed this theory, to have continuous flow of air throughout the wards. She recommended five points for good conditions in houses and buildings:

- Pure Air
- Pure Water
- Efficient drainage
- Cleanliness
- Light

Florence Nightingale said that *"Children - much more susceptible than grown people to all noxious influences. They are affected by the same things but much more quickly and seriously."* She also felt strongly that hospitals should do no harm to their patients.

Grace Campbell would have come under the influence of Florence Nightingale during her nurse training, particularly as she had sought her advice. The Governors, the architects and the builders must also have been influenced by these theories, as they used the new European model for their hospital; a model that had already appeared on the Continent, and was known as the "pavilion style." This style was to become synonymous with the name of Florence Nightingale. In fact wards in this style were commonly called "Nightingale" wards from then on. They were designed for ventilation and surveillance. One continues to be conscious on entering any of the six pavilion wards even today, of the spaciousness, lightness and impressive architecture of these wards. Now they are 150 years old, and they still enable a positive nursing environment.

As with other industrial cities the health of children in connurbations such as Manchester and Salford continued to be very poor throughout the 19th century. The need to improve conditions for these children both physically and socially was well recognised. Alongside the advances being made in medicine this allowed the promotion of the skilled nurse training required for nurses to carry out their vocation.

Dr H. Ashby on his arrival at Pendlebury in 1879 gave a very remarkable lecture to nurses, which was to set the standard for the future in nurse training here. He was very keen to see nurses with a good level of knowledge, in order to nurse their child patients to their fullest potential.

Hospitals began to establish their own training schools for nurses. Elizabeth Fry had set up the first Institute for Nursing in London in 1840 and Florence Nightingale followed with her School of Nursing at St Thomas's in 1860.

Within the history of Pendlebury is reflected, in many ways, the history of nursing. Grace Campbell brought with her from London a dedication to nurse training. Dr Ashby, who had come from Guy's Hospital, was also aware of the high level of training needed for nurses. Nursing was fast moving forward from the view that, *"It seems a commonly received idea among men, and even among women themselves that it requires nothing but a disappointment in love, the want of an object, a general disgust, or incapacity for other things, to turn a woman into a good nurse."* (F. Nightingale, *Notes on Nursing,* 1859)

By the 1890s Pendlebury had its own well established nurse training scheme. The Rules of Governance at Pendlebury in 1896 clearly set out the Regulations for Ladies' desirous of being trained as Nurses. These probationers were received for one year's training on payment of £50 in advance and had to be over the age of 21. If they were unable to pay this amount in advance, they must remain for two years in the hospital, *"giving their services for the second year in recompense for their first years training."* They would receive during this training, courses of lectures on *"Elementary Anatomy, Physiology, Medical & Surgical Nursing and on the Diseases of Children."* They were also instructed in management. A certificate as a Trained Nurse would be awarded *"if deserved"*. They were allowed 3 weeks holiday. Caps and materials to make their uniforms were provided. They were to rise at 6.30am and *"lights out"* were at 10pm.

There was at the same time a group of Special Probationers who were *"ladies desirous of work in the wards"* - for the purpose of acquiring practical knowledge in the nursing of sick children. Again payment was £50, but in two instalments. This group of probationers were to be not less than 21 or more than 35 years of age. They were to be lodged and boarded at the hospital, they were not required to go into the fever ward as were the other probationers. They too received all lectures except for management and provided their own caps, aprons, collars and cuffs. They received a certificate as a Trained Nurse (for one year) only *"if deserved"*.

1901 saw significant changes for the nurses at Pendlebury regarding their accommodation. A new wing was provided, with suitable provision of nursing staff bedrooms. A new dining room was built - and furnished - entirely by an anonymous friend.

Nurses had previously been accommodated on a ward which now came into use as the Victoria ward. The new accommodation block was built off the main corridor between Victoria & Holden wards.

Nurses were also able to be placed outside the hospital to nurse children in their homes, and this had already become a well established practice by 1896. It was also considered as a special privilege and increased their rate of pay.

Another advance that impacted on nursing skills was the new operating theatre constructed in 1906 on the *"most approved sanitary principles and best materials available"*. This allowed a large increase of surgical patients to be treated at Pendlebury and more nurses were required with wider skills. Minor surgical operations were still being carried out at the Dispensary, which included circumcisions, removal of tonsils and adenoids and various other similar.

The most featured 'treatment' in the hospital at this time was sunlight and fresh air with all wards having a verandah attached for 'Open Air Treatment' as it was called. The nursing staff of the hospital still consisted of sisters, nurses and probationers, to be appointed by the Lady Superintendent. There does seem, however, to be a continuing arrangement for 'Special Probationers', "ladies desirous of work on the wards" who paid to come and train, lived in the hospital and provided their own uniforms, and received training for one year.

The nursing of children included advice on diet. Firm instructions were laid down for staff to follow on the feeding of children and infants. Weaning was not to take place until a child was seven months of age and completed by the child's first birthday. The sucking of *"dummy teats"* was considered harmful, as was the giving of meat to a child under 18 months of age. Instructions included a meal timetable for 5 *"meals"* per day, the fifth meal being supper of bread and milk before bedtime. Children were to be taken out if the weather was fine, have juice of an orange or fresh grown vegetables at least 3 times per week, splints taken off and re-applied night and morning, no tea or coffee to be given or food between meals.

The way in which nurses were employed, trained and carried out their duties continued almost along the same lines until the advent of the First World War. Miss Renaut, who had been appointed Lady Superintendent in 1911, together with 3 sisters and 1 nurse, were called up for military duty. So too were several of the doctors. A war bonus was given to all nurses in 1915, in recognition of their dedication to duty in a time of national crisis. Members of His Majesty's forces were not asked to contribute to the maintenance of their children whilst in hospital. The

Lady Superintendent Walker and Staff 1934.

Two photos of nurses and children at the Hospital in 1936 and a Benger's Food poster showing Pendlebury. Manchester Children's Hospital was supported by Benger's Food in 1922 through this advertisement which requested financial donations to the Hospital.

Patients and nurses making Christmas decorations in the 1940s.

War had an enormous influence on nursing practice and the future training of nurses. Because of the terrible loss of life at the front, more and more women were being employed in the workforce. This was also true of hospitals. Women House Officers were appointed in medicine and this was so at Pendlebury. Nurses were establishing their own discipline and management structure.

In 1919 a Federation for Nursing was set up nationally and Pendlebury joined this "Federation of Provincial General Hospitals for Children" in order to protect their nurses.

It was only in 1919, with the founding of the General Nursing Council (GNC), that registration for nurses was established. This was for general nurses and there was a supplementary register for those who specialised in children's nursing. Even in the 1930s there were many that believed, quite wrongly of course, that those specialising in children's nursing were inferior. It was not until after the publication of the Report of the Committee on the Welfare of Children in Hospital in 1959, the Platt Report, that paediatric nursing was really brought into the limelight. This report stated that *"children should be cared for on wards dedicated to the care of children by nurses with a specific qualification in nursing children."*

Nurse training with recognition from the General Nursing Council commenced at Pendlebury in 1922 - previous to that nurse training had been carried out under the auspices of the Board of Governors, the Lady Superintendent and the Medical staff. This would be known as ward teaching. All wards were run by a Ward Sister and the nurses were allocated a number of patients. As medical knowledge expanded and the skills of nurses increased it was seen to be necessary to increase the length of training for nurses. By 1955 there were combined SRN/RSCN training courses taking 4 years. Looking back through the archives, one is struck by remarks from various nurses and comments on their training at Pendlebury: *"It was tough being a nurse in the forties. The discipline was oppressive both on and off duty. Only nine out of the original 21 in my set completed their training" (*Nurse Mackay, *Hospital Archives).*

By the forties, in children's nursing the training was three years at Pendlebury; entry age was 18, with school certificate and by interview. They were not allowed to sit the RSCN exams until 21 years of age. They bought all their own uniforms, all food, board and laundry was provided. They received £18 in their first year, £20 in their second year and £22 in their third year. They were only allowed to sleep away from the hospital for one night per month. There were no porters or ward clerks and each ward had its own "maids." The nursing staff did all the cleaning, nursing, bathing, making beds, talking to parents and caring for the children. Visiting was restricted to 2 hours on Sunday afternoons. Christmas was a very special highlight when wards were beautifully decorated and the children received many toys.

In 1945 nursing by case assignment was introduced onto Holden Ward and extended onto other wards. It was also the custom during the forties for "*Night Staff to prepare the breakfast, making the porridge and cooking the bacon for the children with diabetes." "The Junior Night Nurse on Heywood Ward boiled the potatoes and cabbage for the Night Staff meal and made the coffee for Night Sister at 11pm,"* The night sister did a ward round with the resident medical officer and resident surgical officer at midnight. *"If a doctor was required to see a patient during the night, the Junior Night Sister went up to his room to waken him up."*

At the convalescent home in St Anne's the night nurse had the responsibility of the boiler, which was in the boiler room in the cellar, and woe betide any nurse who allowed this "monster" to go out.

At Pendlebury, tiled fireplaces were a feature of each ward and the nurses kept the fires going for a large part of the time. Steam sterilisers were at the entrance of most wards; syringes were carefully wrapped for sterilising and needles were sent off for re-sharpening. All baby feeds were made up on the ward. The night sister wrote up a report on every ward and it was read to the Matron every morning. At 6am the night sister would call all the ward maids and nurses, as all were resident. She was also responsible for serving breakfasts and taking prayers in the Chapel before the nurses went onto their own wards.

Staff were, almost without exception, resident, so many recreational activities were organised; a sports club with tennis, hockey, etc and inter-hospital tournaments. Other activities such as musical evenings, a monthly dance and jumble sales took place.

Following the comprehensive scheme of training offered at this time, selected students could take the SRN and RSCN training, which was a four year course. The first two years were spent at Pendlebury, a third year at a General Hospital (Hope) and the fourth year back at Pendlebury. During the nurse training at Pendlebury arrangements were made for training to be gained in the Eye Hospital, St Mary's Premature Baby Unit and Monsall Fever Hospital. A system of cadet nursing was also practiced, when 15 year olds started working at Pendlebury until they could commence nurse training at eighteen.

Between 1956 and 1970 the School of Nursing was based at Jesson House, where the Principal Tutor was Miss Katherine Hodkiss; the two courses offered were the three year RSCN and the experimental four year course. Male students began to be attracted to children's nursing - and it is now considered highly beneficial for the children to have both female and male nurses to offer care when sick.. Nurse training at Pendlebury began at 18 years of age, educational requirements in the 1950s were stated as being *"3 or 4 subjects at GCE O level would be an advantage"*. Student nurses were under the authority of the Matron and all entrants completed a 12 week preliminary training. They were required to live for at least the first year in the Nurses' Home; after which their own accommodation could be arranged with Matron and written consent from their parents. They were required to attend prayers daily before duty and were also allowed to attend services at a local church of their own denomination.

Nurse training has changed greatly since this regime. Now nurses study under the Project 2000 scheme and the training programmes are incorporated into colleges of health within a university. Paediatric nursing is studied in the last modules of Project 2000.

Nursing children as a profession has developed into a highly specialised skill, and Pendlebury has been in the forefront of this development in the North West, alongside Booth Hall Children's Hospital. Nursing children will always be a highly skilled, demanding yet rewarding experience, and an enormous challenge for all who enter the profession.

In any hospital, through the period of this history, a major role is undoubtedly played by the senior nurse. Many initiatives are inaugurated through their vision, and the reputation of a hospital depends as much on its nursing expertise as its medical competence. It would seem therefore appropriate to give a brief resumé of some of these "heads of nursing" over the years.

Miss Thompson, was appointed when the hospital resided at 16 Bridge Street and moved with the institution to Pendlebury. It was however due to the exceptional qualities of the Lady Superintendent appointed in 1877, Miss Grace Campbell that there began the recognition of an expertise associated with Pendlebury in the field of nursing children. From 1879 Miss Edith Elizabeth Cobb was then in post as Lady Superintendent until another nurse from Scotland, Miss Hannah Maria Turner, then aged 31 was appointed in 1891 and stayed in post until 1902. A very short appointment for a Miss Longton from St Thomas's followed prior to Miss Cameron from a hospital in Bradford being appointed in 1904.

A Miss Nicholson who trained at Pendlebury was appointed Lady Superintendent in 1910 but left to be married the following year.

Miss Neville, who was Lady Superintendent from 1914-24, was in post when the hospital received its Royal Charter in 1923.

1924 saw the appointment of Miss M.R. Walker R.R.C. who was at Pendlebury for 17 years. Apparently this lady very much made her own decisions and in 1937, a special meeting of governors was called to discuss her "*errant*" behaviour. The notes of the meeting were not to be disclosed for ten years. On reading these minutes it is difficult to unravel the problem! It would seem that it was a "*personality*" difficulty arising from the Lady Superintendent allowing cosmetics to be sold to nurses. The whole issue was resolved and Miss Walker was requested to continue to carry on with her duties. The complaint brought against her was *"executive in nature and did not reflect adversely on the professional abilities of the Matron."*

The appointment of Miss Ena D. Stevens has always been considered a great triumph for the hospital. She was brought into the post in the early years of the Second World War. It was a time of great difficulty and the unknown. She safely steered the hospital through this period, and into the National Health Service in 1948. A tall, impressive and erect figure she was considered to have brought in much enlightened practice in the care of sick children and nurse training. She left towards the end of 1952 after marrying a Czech refugee scientist and they went to live in the States.

The office was then taken on by Miss Golay in 1953, who was keen on her nurses having lots of social activity. Included in these were the hospital dances and it was at one of these that she met and later married Wing Commander Bill Deverell.

Nurse training throughout maintained its national and international reputation at Pendlebury. As far back as the census in 1881 nurses have joined the staff at Pendlebury from as far away as New Zealand, Canada and Australia, with others from London, Glasgow, Norfolk and Ireland. As there were only 25 sisters at this time, with so many coming from such a distance, the reputation of this hospital must have been considerable.

Miss Joan Jackson became Senior Nursing Officer in 1957 and continued to support the highly prestigious nurse training. In December 1994 the School of Nursing incorporating paediatric nursing moved into Peel House to become part of the Salford School of Nursing, and then became incorporated into Salford University.

After Miss Jackson retired in 1973, completing 17 years as Senior Nursing Officer at Pendlebury, Miss Vera Lumb was appointed, leaving in 1977. Nursing at the hospital was then administrated by Miss Sybil Preece from Hope Hospital as an interim measure until Miss Elizabeth Hall was appointed Senior Nursing Officer in 1978. After 6 years Miss Hall moved to Liverpool, and again an interim nurse administrator, Acting Senior Nursing Officer Miss Glenys Porter took over for two years.

Open visiting was now the order of the day. Parents were able to visit their children at all reasonable times and encouraged to stay overnight. No longer were there the terrible queues on a Sunday afternoon that trailed down to Bolton Road; no longer distraught parents and children going through separation, and nurses trying to console these unhappy children. Although the "Platt Report" took a long time to implement, the changes have been built on a solid foundation and not implemented lightly.

In 1986 Miss Anne MacDonald was appointed as Director of Nursing Services. Miss MacDonald came from Chester and Yorkhill, Glasgow, and many of the nurse innovations that have taken place at Pendlebury were due to her vision. She was able to demonstrate that nurses working with sick children must be and were of the highest calibre at this hospital. She introduced the therapeutic play service onto the wards, demonstrating its enormous importance for sick children. She received an OBE for her services to children. In 1993 Mrs Rebecca Howard, who had been appointed Director of Nursing Services at Booth Hall, became Director of Nursing Services for both sites, Pendlebury and Booth Hall. The two children's hospitals were incorporated into a National Health Service Trust in 1995, with Mrs Howard becoming an Executive Director. During 1997 she was seconded to the Department of Health as their expert on services for children, and she returned in 1999.

The very nature of paediatric nursing has changed over the years. The treatment time for children is now much quicker. Children are in hospital for a much shorter time, but also treatment has become, in some instances, quite dramatic, especially within a children's service that is considered a tertiary referral service. Pendlebury and Booth Hall for many years have always treated children from all over the North West, as well as those children who are local to these hospitals. Many children also come from overseas for treatment. The changes in children's nursing over this period of time are reflected in this hospital - a hospital that has been in the forefront of excellence in nursing over its long history.

LIST OF LADY SUPERINTENDENTS, MATRONS, CHIEF NURSING OFFICERS

1864 - 16 Bridge Street - Miss Thompson
1873 - Hospital moved to Pendlebury
Dispensary to Gartside Street prior to this move.
1875 - Miss Thomson left Pendlebury
1876 - Miss Peckham appointed - later resigned
1877 - (Jan) Miss E. Grace Campbell 1st Lady Superintendent. Left at the end of 1879 to be married to Dr Channing Neill
1879 - Miss Luckes
1880 - Miss Edith Elizabeth Cobb from Struck in Kent
1889 - Hannah Maria Turner (aged 31) from Scotland
1897 - Jeanette Stevens Head Sick Nurse on Wrigley Ward goes to Convalescent Home in St. Anne's. Had been Sister on Wrigley Ward for 11 years
1902 - Miss Longton from St. Thomas - London
1904 - Miss Cameron from Bradford (1904-1910)
1907 - Miss E. Munroe - Sister, New Gartside Street O.P. Dept.
1910 - Miss Nicholson (formerly trained at Pendlebury went to St Bartholomew's Hospital as Lady Superintendent)
1911 - Miss E.A. Renaut - Asst. Matron Edinburgh before coming to Pendlebury (Miss Nicholson married)
1914 - Miss Neville - (Miss Renaut went to War effort)
1919 - Sister M.L. McMurtrey appointed to O.P. Dept. Gartside Street
1923 - Royal Charter - Miss Neville - (1914-1924)
1924 - Miss M.R. Walker R.R.C. (commended) (1924-1940)
1929 - Centenary Year - (Miss Walker)
1936 - Miss F. Jones - Matron St. Anne's
1937 - Special Meeting of governors to discuss Lady Superintendents actions
1939 - Assistant Matron - Mrs Harland

1940 - Miss Walker retired after 37 years nursing service, Lady Superintendent at R.M.C.H. 17 years
Assistant Matron - Miss Pollard

1941 - Miss Ena D. Stevens appointed as Matron (1941-1952)
Assistant Matron - Miss Bullen
Sister in charge of Zachery Menton Home - Miss Hendy

1952 - Matron Stevens married an American/Czech Scientist - Carl Ficher

1952 - Miss Liptrot was Assistant Matron
Miss Gill Sister at Gartside Street Out Patient Dept.
Miss Liptrot Acting Matron until 1953

1953 - Miss Golay appointed (1953-1957)
Miss Golay married Wing Commander Bill Deverell (continued as Mrs Deverell)

1957 - Miss Joan I. Jackson appointed (1957-1973)

1970 - Also assumed responsibility for Swinton Children's Hospital
Assistant Matron - Miss Parncutt

1973 - Miss Vera Lumb (1973-1977)

1977 - Miss Sybil Preece from Hope (Acting Matron)

1978 - Miss Elizabeth Hall - Senior Nursing Officer

1984 - Miss Glynis Porter (Acting Nursing Officer from Hope Hospital)

1986 - Miss C. Anne MacDonald appointed. (Director of Quality 93/96)

1993 - Mrs Rebecca Howard appointed Director of Nursing Services (RMCH & Booth Hall - 2 Sites)
Seconded to Dept of Health for 6 months in 1997.
New title; Director of Nursing, Quality & Clinical Support
Further secondment to Bristol enquiry 1999

1999 - Mrs Julie Flaherty. Acting Director of Nursing Quality and Clinical Services

(Miss Fran Floyd, formerly Ward Sister on Ashby Ward, became Principal Nursing Officer for Salford Hospitals 1972 - 1974.)

NURSE TRAINING SCHOOL

The following presented the prizes at RMCH - 1956-1966

1956	Bishop of Middleton
1957	Professor Mansfield Cooper
1958	Mayor of Swinton & Pendlebury
1959	Lord Derby
1960	Sir John Barbarolli
1961	Lord James of Rusholme
1962	The Princess Royal
1963	Lady Dorothy Macmillan
1964	Gracie Fields
1965	Bishop of Manchester
1966	Duke of Devonshire

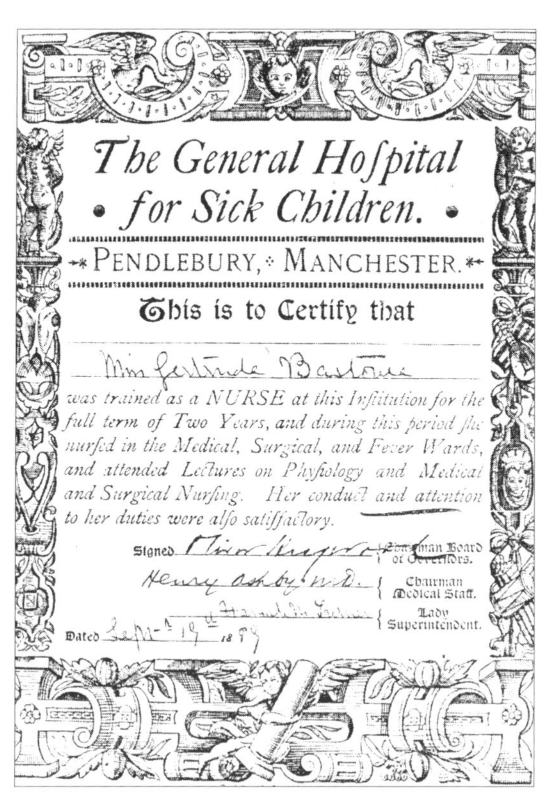

The General Hospital
for Sick Children.

PENDLEBURY, MANCHESTER.

This is to Certify that

Miss Gertrude Bastone

was trained as a NURSE at this Institution for the full term of Two Years, and during this period she nursed in the Medical, Surgical, and Fever Wards, and attended Lectures on Physiology and Medical and Surgical Nursing. Her conduct and attention to her duties were also satisfactory.

Signed .... Chairman Board of Governors.

Henry Ashby M.D. Chairman Medical Staff.

Hannah Turner Lady Superintendent.

Dated Sept 19 1889

The Nurse Training badge and Certificate presented to successful nurses on completion of training at Pendlebury. It was always something special for a nurse to be able to say she was a Manchester or Pendlebury Children's nurse. The certificate, of 1889, is signed by Dr Henry Ashby and Lady Superintendent, Hannah Turner.

Group of graduate nurses 1947 (Courtesy of P. Mackay)

1945 Group photograph of the nurses on the steps of RMCH. In the second row are the Matron, Assistant Matron, Home Sister and 5 Sisters.

1948 prizegiving with Matron Stevens.

ROYAL MANCHESTER CHILDREN'S HOSPITAL.
PENDLEBURY.

Matron:
MISS E. D. STEVENS.

TEL.
SWINTON 2021-2

EDS/EH. 13th February, 1946.

Mr. Garner,
136, Lightoaks Road,
off Lancaster Road,
Pendleton,
Salford, 6.

Dear Mr. Garner,

Your daughter was seen coming in through a window of the Recreation Room of the Nurses' Home, at 12.30 midnight, on 11th February.

As this is not the type of behaviour expected of a third year Student Nurse, or, for that matter, of any responsible intelligent girl, I think you should know of the occurence.

Yours sincerely,

E. D. Stevens

MATRON.

An irate letter from Matron Stevens to the parents of a nurse in training in 1948

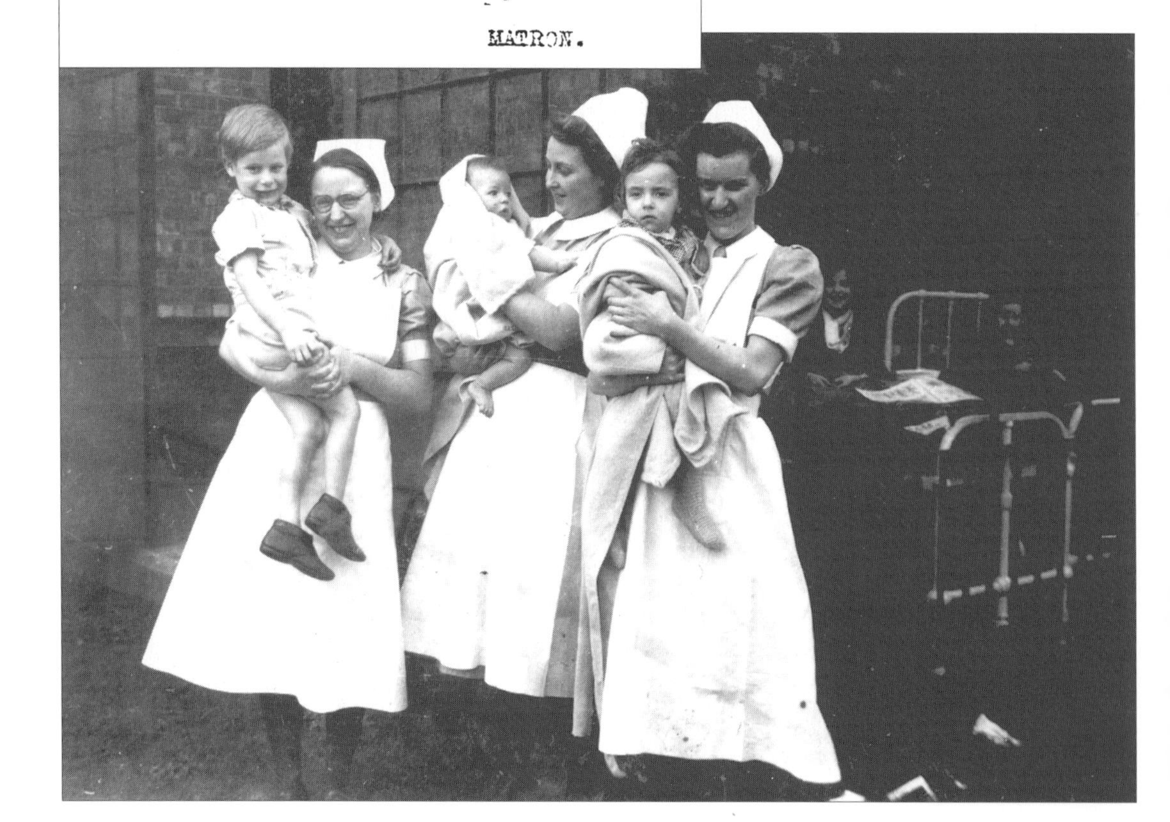

Nurse M.J. Parker and two of her colleagues and patients in 1945.

Lunchtime in 1944

A Christmas Mayoral visit to the Hospital in 1974.

Nurses dining room after refurbishment in 1924 by an anonymous donor.

Colwyn House, the Nurses Home, before the extension. This is now the Out Patients Department.

Sisters sitting room in 1936.

Sisters' sitting room 1953. Miss Golay, Matron.

Photos above and below: Nurses' accommodation in the 1940s at the Zachary Merton Home.

1956 tennis match between RMCH and Hope Hospital.

Nurse Training - keep-fit - outside the Zachery Merton Home. 1958.

Student nurses at Booth Hall, Health and Beauty Class, 1950s.

The Chapel at RMCH, which is now the Board Room. Nurses were expected to attend prayers prior to duty until well after the Second World War.

Nurses sitting their exams in 1946.

Nurse Training in 1945 - known as the Block System - which entailed keeping in the same group throughout the entire training. Trainees experienced different aspects of nursing in other local hospitals.

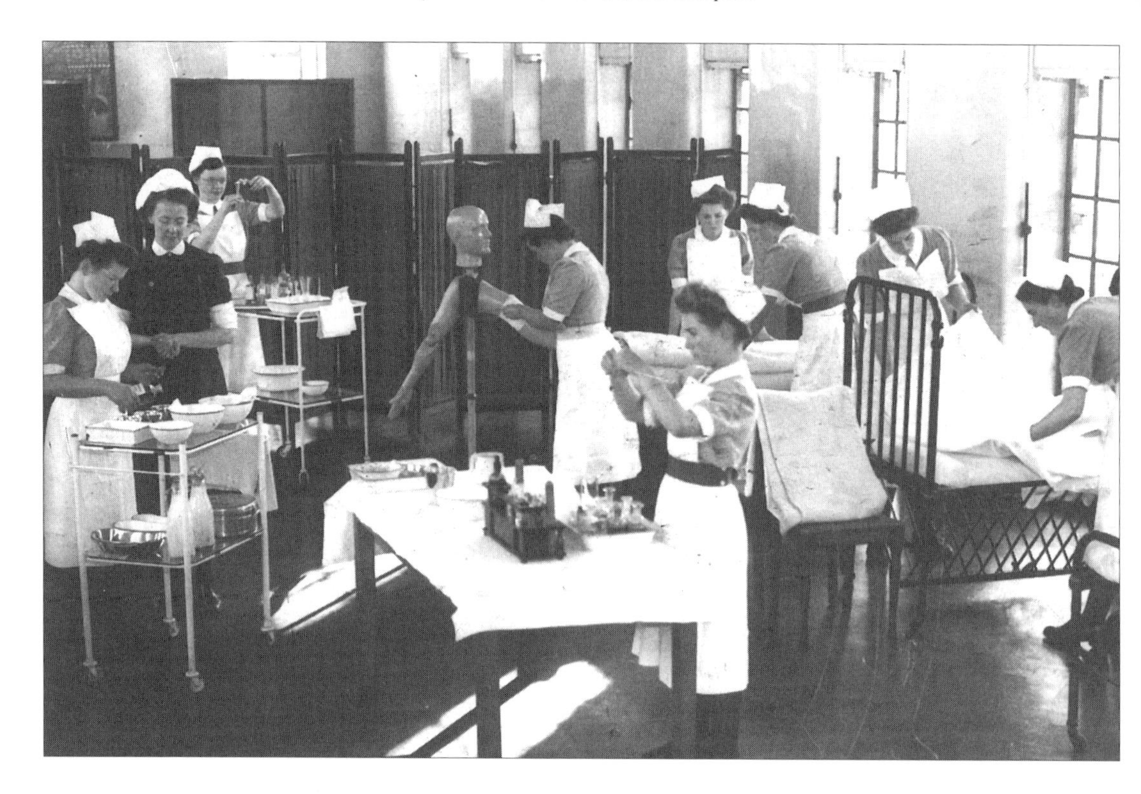

Photos above and below: Nurse Training School 1946.

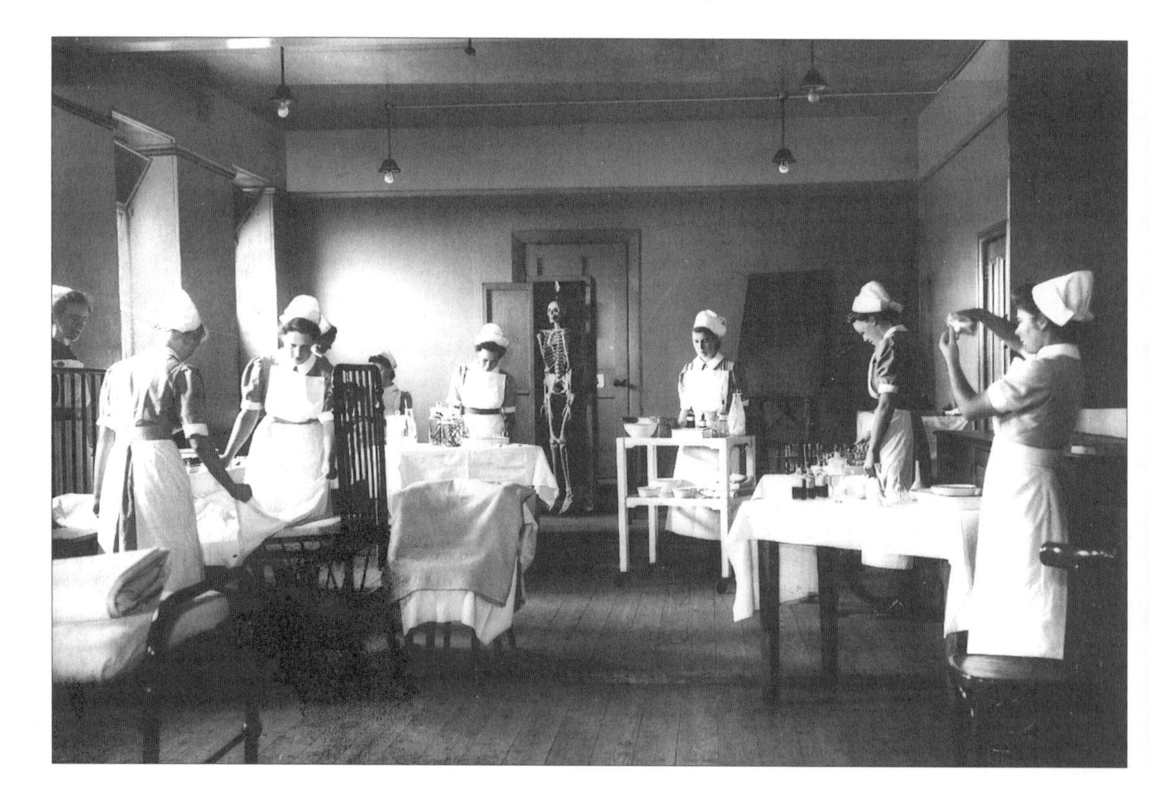

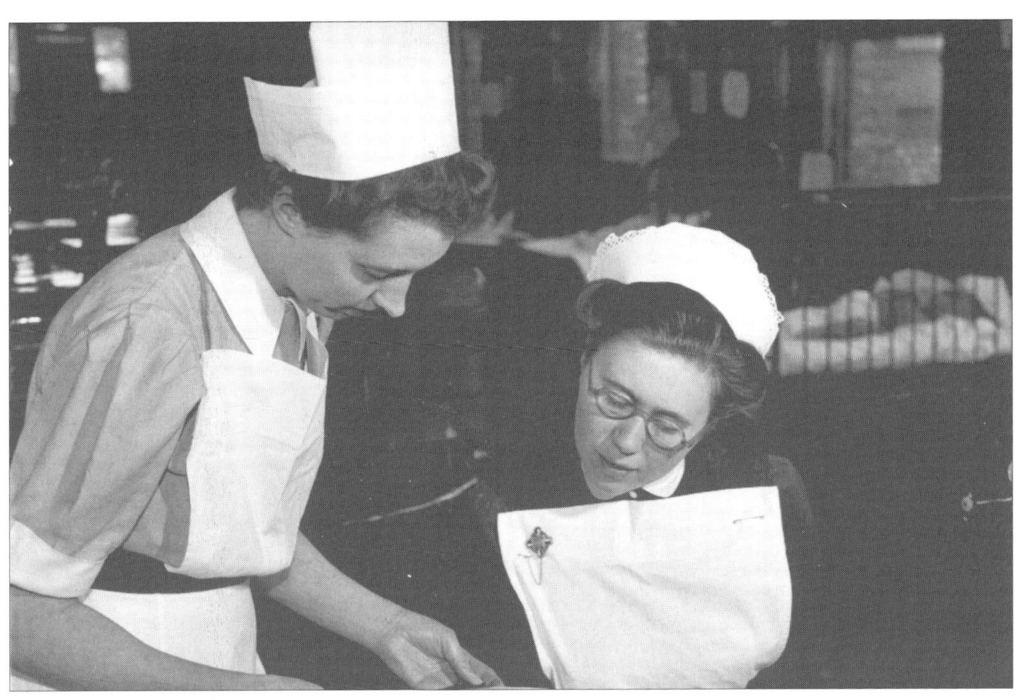

Nurses report 1944.

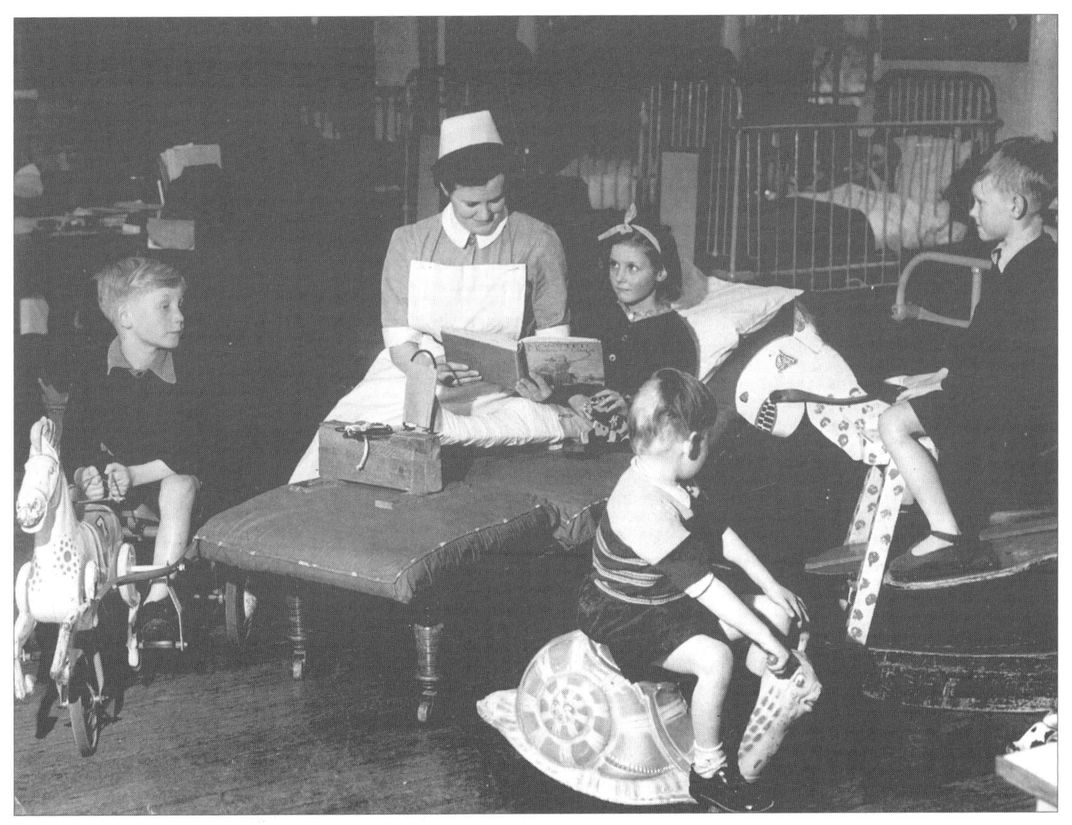

Nurse with young patients in Liebert Ward 1953.

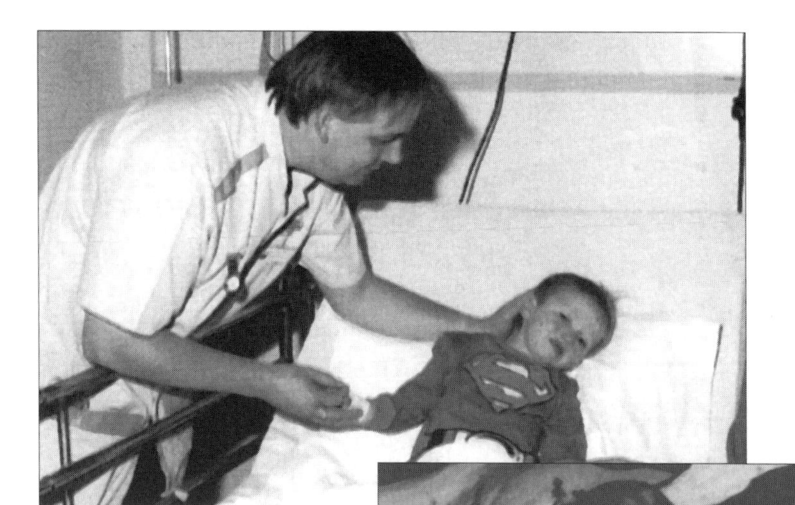

These three photos and the top photo on the next page perhaps demonstrate the progressively more technical but hopefully more patient-friendly nursing that has developed over the past 20 to 30 years.

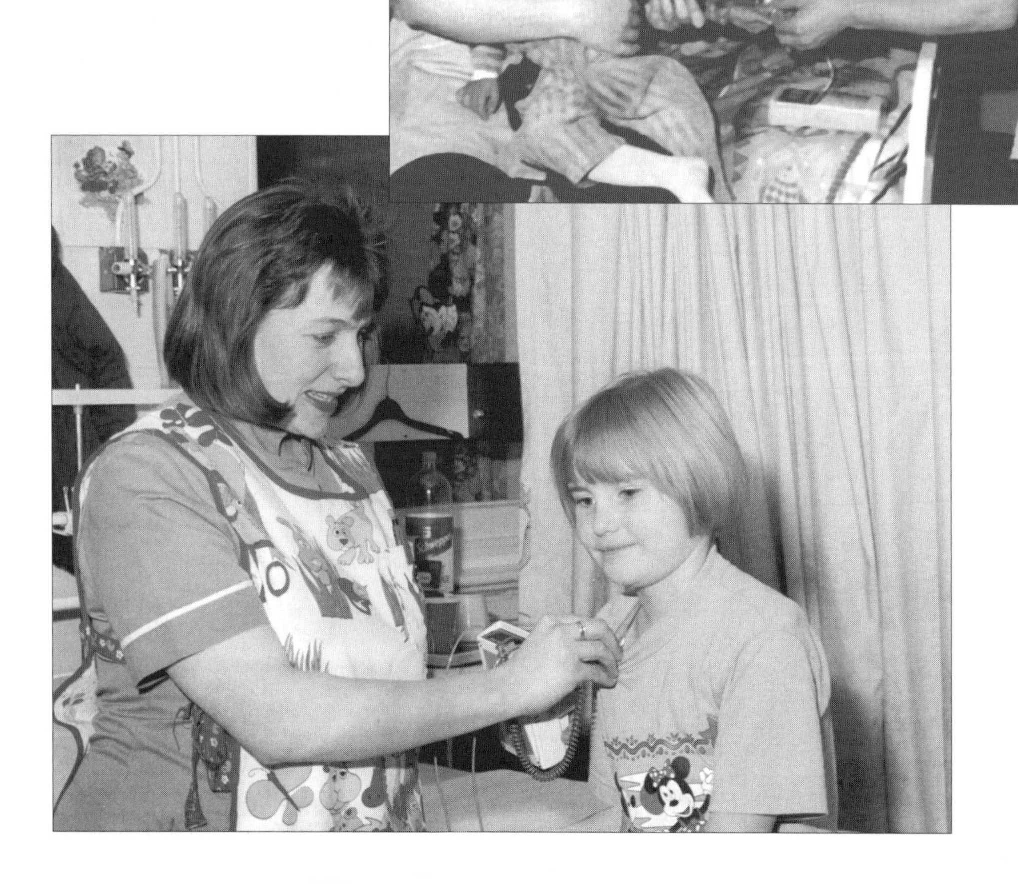

Right: The 1997 Nurses' Awards. The Children's Hospital nurses have always been at the forefront of advances in nursing.

Anne MacDonald who was appointed Director of Nursing in 1986, and was awarded an OBE for services to children in 1995.

Rebecca Howard, Director of Nursing, Quality and Clinical Support, 1993-1999, Childrens Trust.

Julie Flaherty, Acting Director of Nursing, Quality and Clinical Services 1999.

HRH the Duchess of Gloucester speaking with Nurse Whelan on Victoria Ward in 1983.

HRH the Duchess of Kent visiting the Hospital in 1995 to open the MRI machine, after £1 million was raised by charities for its purchase.

Gracie Fields presented the prizes in 1964. Mr Willink, Chairman of the Hospital Committee, is 2nd from the right on the front row.

Manchester United players showing the FA Cup of 1948 to a young patient at Booth Hall.

Three photographs of Sir Harry Secombe at Pendlebury.
Above: Harry in the Hospital's schoolroom with young patients. Opposite: with another amused patient.
Below: Unveiling the Variety Club of Great Britain plaque in the Agnew Unit to mark their support. Seen with Harry are Harry Hall, Vice-Chairman of Salford Area Health Authority, and Mrs Pamela Green, Headmistress of the Hospital School.

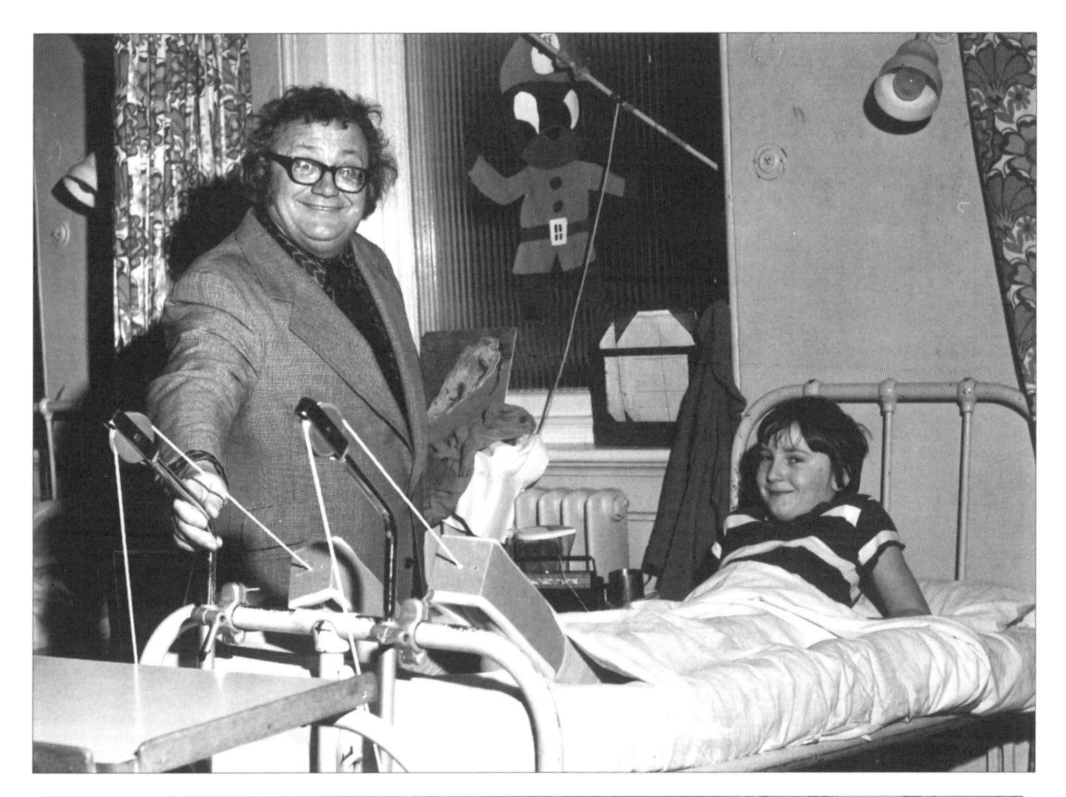

The late Sir Matt Busby with a Manchester United display in aid of Pendlebury.

Ryan Giggs, Bobby Charlton and Alex Ferguson continuing the Manchester United tradition of supporting the City's children's hospitals.

Fundraisers for the Hospital

Top: Theatre staff with a cheque from Wimpey Homes in 1989 with Kath Smith MBE a well-known fundraiser.

Middle: Captain Mike Underwood (seated) raised a large sum for a Mass Spectrometer through a charity flight to Dublin.

Bottom: Dr Ed Wraith and Pamela Barnes receiving a cheque from Bovis.

ROYAL MANCHESTER CHILDREN'S HOSPITAL, PENDLEBURY. 1931

A—Vestibule.
B—Hall.
C—Corridor.
D—Offices.
E—Engineer's House.
F—Secretary's Office.
G—Waiting Room.
H—Lavatory.
I—Water Closets.
J—Kitchen.
K—Doctors' Office.
L—Doctors' Dining Room.
M—Matron's Dining Room.
N—Matron's Sitting Room.
O—Staircase.
P—X-Ray Room.
Q—Passage.
R—Matron's Office.
S—Splint Room.
T—Dark Room.
U—Sisters' Sitting Room.
V—Housemaids' Pantry.
W—Dining Room.
X—Lecture Room.
Y—Gatekeeper's Lodge.
Z—Recreation Room.
*—Receiving Block—Doctors' Waiting and Bath Rooms.

1—Special Ward.
2—Sink.
3—Brushes.
4—Linen.
5—Lobby.
6—Ward Kitchens.
7—Box Room.
8—Porch.
9—Linen Room.
10—Dressing Room.
11—Dispensary.
12—Anæsthetising Room.
13—Sterilising Room.
14—Operating Theatre.
15—Coals.
16—Bath and Lavatory.
17—Verandah.
18—Liebert Ward for 30 beds.
19—Heywood ,, ,, ,,
20—Wrigley ,, ,, ,,
21—Holden ,, ,, ,,
22—Victoria ,, ,, ,,
23—Borchardt ,, ,, ,,
24—Artificial Sunlight Room.
25 to 44—Nurses' Bedrooms.

45—Chimney.
46—Disinfecting Room.
47—Disinfected Room.
48—Large Wash House.
49—Drying Room.
50—Small Wash House.
51—Sorting Room.
52—Ironing Room.
53—Calender Room.
54—Engineer's Office.
55—Engineer's Shop
56—Engine Room.
57—Pumps.
58—Boiler House.
59—Ashes.
60—Joiners' and Splint Makers' Shop.
61—Yard.
62—Mortuary.
63—Post-Mortem Room.
64—Garage.
65—Greenhouse.
66—Garden Tools, &c.
67—Children's Ward.
68—Nurses' Ward.
69—Nurses' Sitting Room.
70—Bedrooms.
71—Scullery.

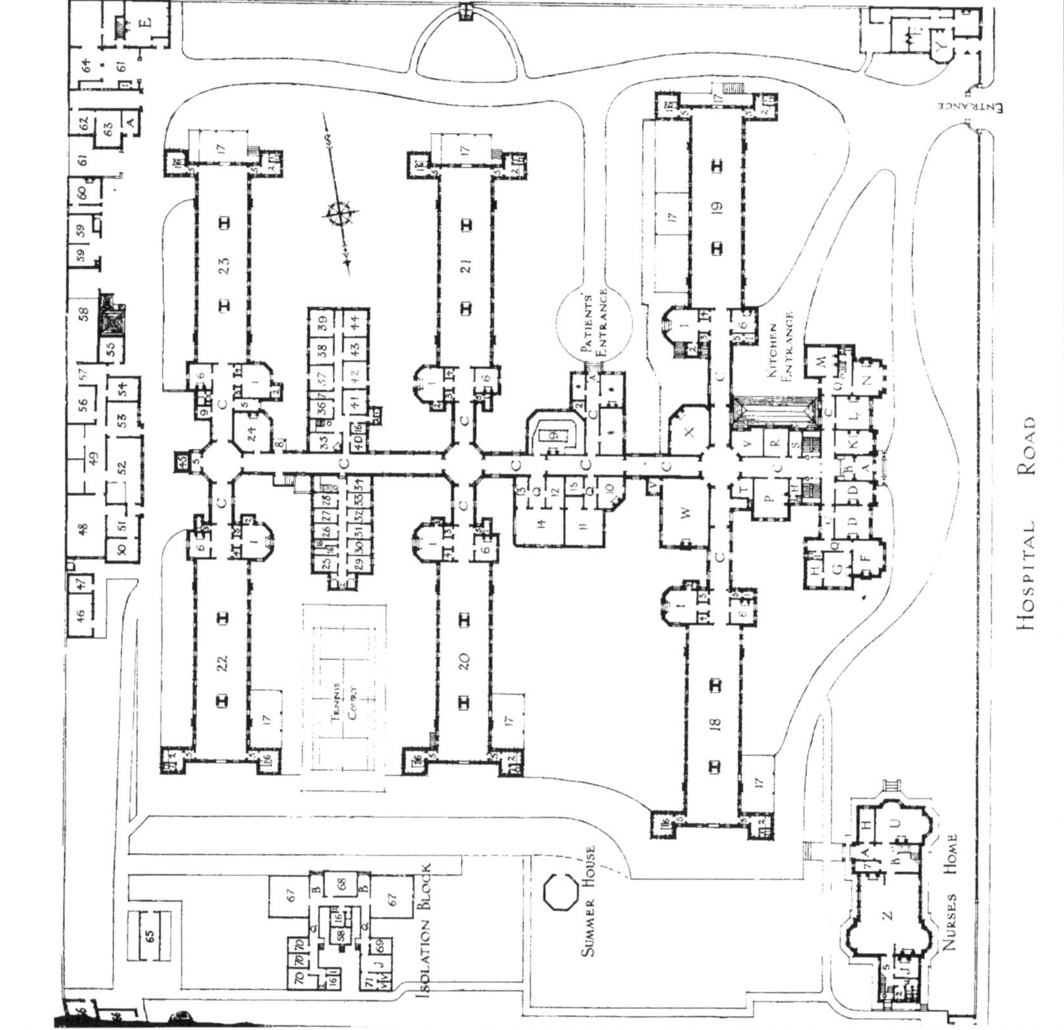

CHAPTER 7

THE IMPACT OF TWO WORLD WARS ON CHILDREN'S SERVICES IN MANCHESTER

The National Insurance Act of Lloyd-George became law in 1911, just prior to the outbreak of the First World War. This far-reaching Act covered working men through friendly societies and insurance companies, to provide unemployment benefits and medical care. The National Insurance monies enabled local corporations to offer additional hospital facilities. Tuberculosis was far and away the greatest problem, with little provision until this time, and by 1913 had become the responsibility of local authorities.

As early as 1903 Manchester Education Committee had taken over Swinton House, where they were to provide 65 beds within a residential school for children suffering from surgical tuberculosis, rickets or paralysis. Staff from the Children's Hospital supervised the bed provision. Some patients from the Hospital itself were sent here for convalescence, whilst most went to St Annes.

The outbreak of World War I was to change the health services out of all recognition. Medical science progressed at an ever increasing pace from then on.

1915 was to see the start of major developments in hospital provision across the board in Manchester and Salford. Poor Law hospitals and local government hospitals began to work together. (See J. V. Pickstone Medicine and Industrial Society p.238.) Artificial sunlight clinics and open air and sunlight treatments were established. The Children's Hospital began to have verandahs attached to the wards to give this treatment.

In 1908, Prestwich Guardians had built a new Infirmary at Booth Hall (see history of Booth Hall). The hospital was taken over as a military hospital in 1915. In 1916 it was decided to move the soldiers to Withington Hospital and Booth Hall was converted into the largest children's hospital in the North. The cases being treated at Booth Hall were mostly of a medical nature. The Children's Hospital at Pendlebury took more surgical cases and did not treat infectious diseases which were sent to Monsall Hospital.

The Great War broke out in August 1914. The medical staff and nursing staff were quite seriously depleted. Miss Renaut, the Lady Superintendent, three sisters and one nurse were called up for military duty. (Miss Renaut went on to the David Lewis Hospital in Liverpool after the War) Miss Neville was appointed Lady Superintendent. Two of the doctors who were called up lost their lives when the H.M.S. Royal Edward was sunk in 1915.

Women doctors were now appointed as resident medical officers. It would seem that Dr Nesta Perry was the first woman medical officer to be appointed at Pendlebury. Both resident medical officers were women in 1919, "Miss" Sybil Bailey M.B. and "Miss" Kathleen O'Donnell M.B. A War bonus was given to all the nurses at Pendlebury and the Governors in their annual reports commented on the huge increase in prices of groceries and the difficulties in obtaining supplies.

A quote from the Annual Report in 1917 reflected the current thinking:

> "We must all bear in mind that as the war draws out with its consequent losses, so does the value of each young life become greater and now after three and a half years of the most terrible fighting the world has ever experienced, we cannot afford to lose one single child-life, which it is possible to save by medical and surgical aid."

The Board of Governors deemed it unnecessary for members of His Majesty's Forces to contribute to the maintenance of their children whilst in hospital. A Major Haslam was killed in action and left money to endow two cots. The 1914 Star was awarded to Mr Roberts, two doctors were awarded the Military Cross and Mr Hey received the Croix de Chevalier.

The Board of Governors began to recognise the importance of child welfare, and to encourage it as a branch of hospital work. Medical staff, who were anxious to see better child care in the community, developed a special care and feeding plan., which found favour with the Board of Governors and was included in their Annual Report.

But as the War came to a close in 1918, a world wide epidemic (pandemic) of influenza was to start with far-reaching repercussions. Several wards had to be closed at Pendlebury, reducing the in-patient activity for many months to come. Staffing became very difficult, but even so the work increased as can be seen from the medical staff numbers and disciplines in 1921, compared with 1916. The increase in doctors probably reflects the advances in medicine, as it occurred despite a reduction in beds.

1916		**1921**
2	Hon. Consulting Surgeons	2
1	Hon. Consulting Aural Surgeon	1
1	Hon. Consulting Pathologist	1
3	Visiting Physicians	3 + 1
3	Visiting Surgeons	3 + 1
1	Surgeon Ear Nose and Throat	1
1	Hon. Ophthalmic Surgeon	1
1	Hon. Dental Surgeon	1
2	Anaesthetists	5
1	Medical Officer X-Ray Department	1
1	Pathologist	1
1916		**1921**
1	Resident Medical Officer	2
1	Junior Resident Medical Officer	1

The hospital's future was faced with huge financial difficulties. This increased workload could not be sustained without financial support. The bequest of Taddington Hall in Cheshire from the Bramwell family could not be utilised because of the financial situation and the estate was sold. Dry rot was discovered and needed addressing and a ward closed because of the financial situation was unable to be reopened for some time. A grant of £20,000 from the National Relief Fund allowed the immediate danger to pass.

Despite these financial difficulties, 1,316 operations were carried out and a total of 2,227 children treated during 1920. 497 cases were examined in the X-ray department at Gartside Street, and 4,325 received massage and gymnastic treatment (physiotherapy). 2,327 operations were also performed in the Outpatient Department.

Even five years on from the War, the serious accumulated dilapidations due to the War, and the financial crises, were still causing enormous concern to the governing board. A 'Propaganda Committee' was formed to address the lack of finances and a large programme of 'occasions' were designed to raise monies for the hospital.

In spite of the financial difficulties facing Pendlebury the hospital still reflected the current trends in medicine and surgery. It was a very busy period for children's orthopaedics in the 1920s, reflected in the open air balconies added to wards to nurse children after surgery. The improvement in orthopaedic surgery, aseptic practice and medical treatments, as a result of military experience in the War, helped some of the Dawson Reforms for preventative medicine to be met. There was also a greater division in labour in nursing and the development of physiotherapy and other ancillary services.

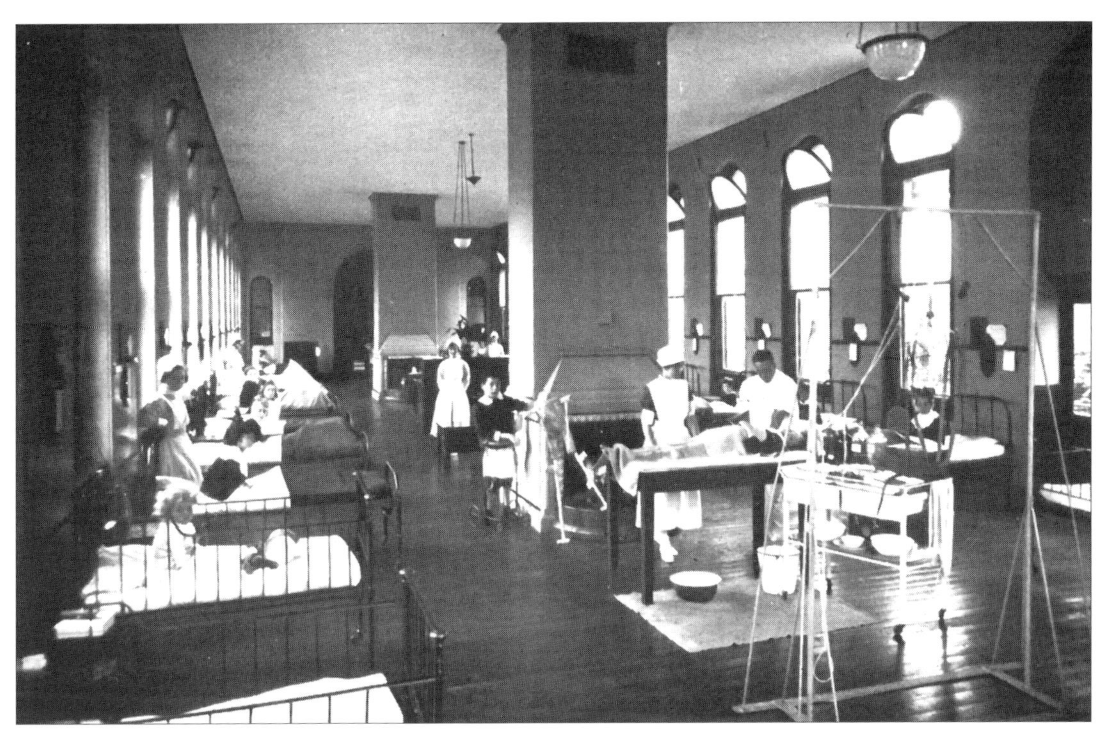

Liebert Orthopaedic Ward in the 1930s; a very busy ward. The central chimney and fireplaces are still in place, and a child is being plastered on the ward.

Borchardt Ward in the late 1930s with a roaring fire but the central chimney tower removed.

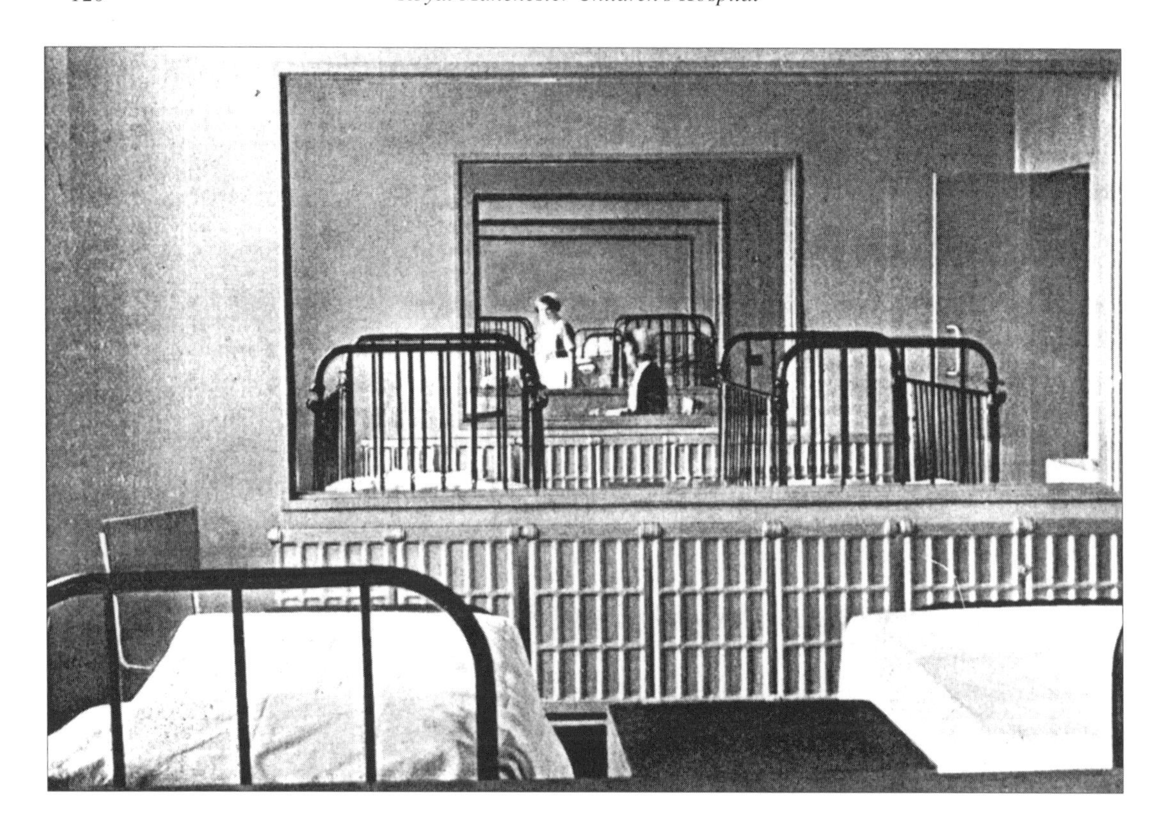

Above and below: Inside and outside the New Isolation Block built in 1937.

Lord Colwyn, 5th and final President of the Board of the RMCH.

1920 saw the resignation of Sir George Agnew, Bart, M.P. and **The Rt. Hon. Lord Colwyn,** P.C. became the new President of the Board of Governors. The governing body had already joined the new Federation for Nursing in order to safeguard their nursing staff, and were planning to build a new nurses' home as soon as the financial situation was in a happier state. This was accomplished in 1924 and Lord Derby opened the new nurses' home known as Colwyn House. (In 1991 it became the refurbished Outpatient Department at Pendlebury, as it was no longer in use as accommodation for nurses.)

During the 1920s some very colourful members of the medical world were attracted to Pendlebury. A very prestigious orthopaedic surgeon, **Mr R. Ollerenshaw** was appointed, and his family were to work tirelessly on behalf of the hospital. He edited the Centenary Gift Book that was published in 1935. Another illustrious name remembered to this day, is that of **Annie E. Sommerford** MD, DPH who was appointed pathologist in 1927. As yet there were still no women on the governing committees, except for the House Committee and, of course, the Ladies' Auxiliary Fund. But women medics were increasing in number.

Colwyn House, the 'New' Nurses' Home, in 1924.

Form. 156

Royal Manchester Children's Hospital.

Admit one visitor to ....Baby Unsworth........

in **HOLDEN** Ward

between 2 and 3 p.m. on Sunday

27 MAR 1938 ......and following Sundays.

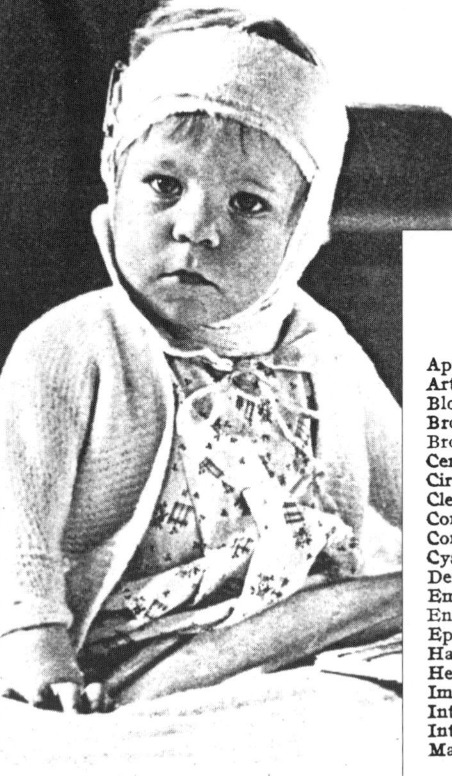

Photograph of a patient from the 1940 Annual Report alongside the list of operaions performed, and a 1938 visiting ticket admitting one visitor for an hour.

LIST OF OPERATIONS, 1939.

(Performed at the Hospital).

Operation	Number
Appendicitis	64
Arthrodesis	9
Blood Transfusions	24
Bronchial Lipiodol	4
Bronchoscopy	1
Cervical Adenitis	41
Circumcision	42
Cleft Palate	36
Congenital Dislocation of Hip	32
Congenital Pyloric Stenosis	34
Cystoscopy	11
Deflected Nasal Septum	2
Empyema	12
Encephalography	5
Epi- and Hypo- Spadias	5
Hare Lips	17
Herniæ, Hydroceles, Undescended Testicles	262
Imperforate Anus	2
Intestinal Obstruction	2
Intussusception	5
Mastoids—Simple	19
Radical	3
Maxillary Antrum	18
Meningocele	4
Miscellaneous—Ear, Nose and Throat	23
General	100
Orthopaedic	23
Myringotomy	11
Naevi	29
Nephrectomy	1
Œsophagoscopy	1
Osteomyelitis	29
Rectal Polyp and Prolapse	1
Septic Arthritis	1
Splenectomy	1
Sympathectomy	2
Talipes	40
Tendon-Elongation	36
Transplantation	3
Thyroglossal Cyst and Sinus	2
Torticollis	11
Tonsils and Adenoids	360
Tuberculous Bones and Joints	16
Tumours—Simple	5
Malignant	1
Webbed Fingers, Supernumary Thumbs, etc.	10
TOTAL	1,360

Treatments, services and the high profile of the hospital moved on apace during the 1930s. A Contributory Federated Superannuation Scheme for Nurses and Hospital Officers had been recently inaugurated and was to help achieve stability within management of the hospital, in line with other voluntary hospitals at the time. Training took on an increased status. The nurses were given a new Lecture Room and they continued to have great successes in the State Examinations.

In 1938 a Neurological Surgeon, **Mr G. F. Rowbotham**, was appointed; it was recommended that a new Pathological Department be established in the hospital; **Mr Hodgkins** was running a highly successful Speech Clinic, and **Dr W. Mary Bunbury** was appointed as Hon. Psychiatrist. The President of the Orthopaedic Section of the Royal Society of Medicine for 1938-39 was Mr R. Ollerenshaw, a very great honour for the hospital, and a fitting reward for his endeavours. The new isolation unit at the hospital was working well; Nurse Training was of a very high standard and the Board of Governors placed on record their thanks to the Honorary Medical Staff *"who are so largely responsible for Pendlebury's high reputation in the Hospital World"*.

But rumblings of War were not far away again. By the following year everyone was making ready for another world war. A sub-committee had been set up to deal with air raid precautions and the necessary training of hospital personnel. 1939 saw the country again at war. Staff were called up and there was a sub-committee for war precautions. A ward was evacuated in order to accommodate any casualties.

Putting in sandbags at the Hospital in 1939 in preparation for war.

Three nights before Christmas in 1940 there were continual air raids over Manchester, Salford and Trafford. The mass production of the Rolls Royce Merlin aero engines in Trafford Park was bringing prosperity to the area but also German bombers. Mrs Anne Feldman, then a trainee nurse, remembers clearly the blitz of December 1940. Two of the wards were damaged at Pendlebury and the whole of Trafford was ablaze from end to end. They had been preparing for Christmas. Fortunately one of the wards damaged was one of those which was emptied to receive casualties. After coming up from the air raid shelters a bewildering sight of disarray met their eyes. It was a very difficult situation for a young nurse and her patients.

Again medical and nurse staffing was depleted as many went to war. **Mr E. D. McCrea**, a staff surgeon, was killed whilst on active service.

Above: The night of the Manchester Blitz 22nd December 1940. Pendlebury suffered some small damage.

Despite the wartime conditions and the continuous obligation to reserve beds for casualty reception, the life of the hospital continued. Large scale improvements were even contemplated. The Hospital Almoner's Department was opened in 1941 and **Miss K. R. Turner** was appointed (the first 'social worker'). This was not only to benefit the children's 'after care' but to introduce an improved system of patient medical records - handicapped by the need to economise on paper as part of the war effort!

The Psychological Clinic, which was established in 1938 continued to support children with mental and emotional disturbances and increased their staffing with an Educational Psychologist and Psychiatric Social Worker in 1941. The Speech Clinic was another new service established initially to correct speech defects after cleft palate operations.

In 1941 the Hospital and Dispensary offered a wide and ever growing variety of services for children. Not only was there a comprehensive in-patient service, with 2,289 children admitted, but at Gartside Street Out-patients there was enormous activity - 62,893 patients seen. The services included an ear, nose and throat department, a dental service, an X-ray department and a pathological service, including post mortem examinations. There was physiotherapy - a Massage and Gymnastic Department - which offered massage, electrical treatment and Swedish Remedial Exercises, and treated 2,251 patients in the year. The Artificial Sunlight Department treated over 6,000 patients and the Speech Clinic 1,000. Approximately 700 patients were seen in the Psychological Clinic. 240 patients were sent to St Anne's Seaside Home for convalescence and 356 used the Zachary Merton Home. Patients were still being admitted from as far afield as Leeds, Skegness, Saddleworth, Nottingham, Stoke-on-Trent and Colwyn Bay.

As the war ended in 1945, a new era in the history of the Hospital began. Important changes took place within medicine and within the personnel of the hospital, people who would influence the next fifty years. The stage was being set for the greatest milestone within the history of medicine in Britain, the National Health Service. There were to be enormous changes in the provision of health care for children. At last the country and the public recognised that the future of their country lay in their children. The dedicated staff at the children's hospital had always believed this.

Preparing for war at Zachery Merton with the building of a bomb shelter.

1944. Removing sandbags and unblocking the windows in the Theatre Block at the end of the War.

ZACHARY MERTON CONVALESCENT HOME - PENDLEBURY

At the annual general meeting 1934, the board were able to announce some good fortune. The country had come through difficult times, including a terrible recession. There was very welcome news that improving prospects, with a return to trade, was indicative of a movement towards future prosperity. The governors had delayed the celebration of the 100 years of their hospital because of these circumstances and now, after six overdue years, they announced a new development. The trustees of the late Zachary Merton, a business man with interests in Manchester, were to build and equip an up to date convalescent home to accommodate 40 patients and the necessary staff. This was to be built on the site of 'Westwood', formerly the residence of Sir Lees Knowles, at a cost of over £20,000. The Lord Mayor of Manchester would lay the foundation stone in March 1935.

Although there was already the convalescent facility in St Anne's, the physicians and surgeons felt that there were many less straightforward cases that would benefit from convalescence under closer supervision. It would also enable the medical staff to deal more effectively with the 'Waiting Lists'. During 1935 the new Zachary Merton Home was laid out. and further money for the purpose of a Lodge and entrance gates on the Manchester Road boundary was offered. The Home was opened in March 1936 by R M Holland-Martin Esq, CB, Chairman of the Zachery Merton Trustees.

Zachary Merton, a wealthy copper smelter from the London area with interests in Manchester. The convalescent hospital was built with money bequeathed in his will. Another home was built in Leicester and another in the South of England.

The Zachary Merton Home provided a very useful resource for the hospital, proving of inestimable value. A programme of entertainment for the children was set up. Miss C.G. Hawksworth was Sister in Charge and when she accepted a senior appointment at the Leicester Royal Infirmary Miss Winifred Hardy became Sister in Charge. Mr James Sillavan was Chairman of the Zachary Merton Home Committee with Mr J. Gow FRCS, Mrs John Orr, Lady Stewart and Mr G.A.T. Tuchet-Jesson MBE. The latter was the Chairman of the Medical Board. Mr Tuchet-Jesson and Miss Walker, the Lady Superintendent had had the 'famous' disagreement.

The aim of the home was for young patients to enjoy as much sun and fresh air as possible to aid their recovery. There were day rooms and 2 dormitories with french windows leading to a verandah. A two storey building attached to the children's accommodation was built for the sisters, nurses and maids. The interior furnishings were entirely donated by Heal & Sons of London, the famous furniture store, and all the crockery was designed with small flowers and 'Z.M.' painted in blue on each piece. There was an interesting new approach to heating with radiant panels fixed in the ceilings, and a modern Telematic" system of internal telephones with 25 instruments installed throughout the home and a central switchboard.

In 1936 a 5 valve Marconi wireless set was donated to the home by a local firm to help entertain the children. They were also given access to play materials by a member of staff specially employed for these duties. A detailed scheme of play therapy and re-educational exercises were introduced. The home continued to provide care for convalescent patients throughout the Second World War and well into the days of the National Health Service

As new patterns in child care took place after the War, the nature of the Zachary Merton Home also began to alter. The dormitories became wards and were renamed the Ashby and Sillavan Wards; the Ashby ward being for medical patients, the Sillavan ward for post-operative care. The Sillavan Ward was named after the Chairman of Governors of the Zachery Merton Home, who had a long association with the Hospital as Honorary Secretary, and the Ashby ward after the famous father and son doctors of the Hospital.

The Zachary Merton Home still plays a very important role in the care and treatment of sick children but in a different way from the original objectives. It is no longer thought necessary to have children convalescing in hospital. Not only is it expensive, but it is inappropriate to retain children in hospital any longer than necessary. With good community care and the better modern housing children can now recuperate in their own homes.

For many years the first floor of the Zachary Merton Home was used to provide accommodation for nurses but the Komrower Genetic Unit is now located here. The Zachary Merton Home provides acute in-patient care for many local children and is as busy as it ever was.

A corner of the dormitory in the New Zachery Merton Home from the booklet produced in 1936.

OUTSIDE INFLUENCES ON GROWING AND LEARNING - EDUCATION, PLAY AND HEALTH

With the passing of the 1944 Education Act, Local Education Authorities were required to make special educational provision for children who fell into the category of special needs. In the North West of England, and particularly in Manchester and Salford, hospital schools were set up. These schools have played and still play a very important part in the holistic life of the patient in hospital. Considerable resources have been allocated to hospital schools at both Royal Manchester Children's Hospital and Booth Hall Children's Hospital, one funded by Salford Local Education Authority, the other by Manchester Corporation.

Today we have the Department for Education Document 1994 to give local guidance on the education of sick children. This offers guidance on the organisational provision in light of the 1993 Education Act. Education is now seen as part of the integral treatment of a sick child in hospital, alongside the importance of parents, opportunities for play, recreation, and being kept fully informed.

A history of the service for sick children in Manchester and Salford would not be complete without reference to this well used and valued service. The first attempt to combine health issues alongside education for the patient was probably the kindergarten founded in Salford in 1873 by William Mather of the engineering firm. This was organised on Froebelian lines and small children were bathed, fed, given rest times and play. Friedrich Frobel in Germany had advocated this and his philosophy is still the basis on which current practice in the very early years of education is structured.

A Ragged and Industrious School had been opened in Salford in 1854, prior to William Mather's kindergarten. But the first joint venture of a hospital with attached school was the Greengate Hospital and Open Air School, opened by Dr Theodore Grimble in 1876. It is believed to be the first of its kind in England. This was a charitable institution, containing 30 beds and mainly used alongside the treatment of rickets. The children attended school daily, lived in the hospital and returned home for weekends. The average length of stay was approximately two years. The facility was used by the Children's Hospital. This "open air" treatment was very popular at the turn of the century. Dr Henry Ashby recognised the links between health, education and school, and was a leading and well-known figure in the promotion of healthy nurseries at the time.

Another development of note was that of the David Lewis Manchester Epileptic Colony, built in 1904 near Knutsford in Cheshire. As many children were admitted to this institution, the Children's Hospital had a particular interest there. Dr Richard Newton, a paediatric neurologist at the Children's Trust in Manchester, continues the liaison work with children who are treated in this centre.

The convalescent homes began to recognise that during the long day time hours of convalescence children needed occupation. Nurses were detailed to 'entertain' the children and in St Annes Convalescent Home a member of staff was employed to occupy and play with the children. Perhaps the very first Hospital Play Specialist?

Salford Authority established special schools for children with disability as did Manchester Corporation in the early 1920s, both linking closely to the School Medical Service. The first attempt to establish a school within Pendlebury was in 1936 and with some success, but the looming pressures from Europe did not allow this development to progress.

Post-war, and with the advent of the National Health Service and the 1944 Education Act, the schooling of sick children took on a new impetus. Today there is a highly qualified teaching staff of 15 who offer a wide range of the national curriculum for in-patients and selected out-patients at Pendlebury.

The service of hospital play specialists, to help meet the social and psychological needs of sick children, has become important within the Hospital, and they are a recognised professional group within the National Health Service. They have their own specialised training and registration.

The Department of Health emphasises that education and play services should be available for all sick children; a philosophy endorsed by Action for Sick Children and with a high profile within the Children's Trust in Manchester.

Action for Sick Children (formerly Mother Care for Children in Hospital, then National Association for the Welfare of Children in Hospital) has always played an important role in the welfare of hospitalised children in the North-West. The charity was set up as a direct result of the Platt Report. This committee, chaired by Sir Harry Platt, a well known surgeon connected with Pendlebury, published their report in 1959. They recommended far-reaching changes that would revolutionise the way in which children were cared for in hospital, where parents and professionals would work closely together to achieve a high quality service for sick children.

This close relationship between the staff and parents was demonstrated with the opening of the mother and child unit in 1965, attached to Ashby Ward. Ledbrooke House parent accommodation was opened in the 1980s with monies raised by the League of Friends. Today the Trust has a continuing policy of working closely with parents to provide the best service possible for children.

Fundraising for RMCH in the 1920s at the St Annes Convalescent Home Garden Party.
The little house was later used in the grounds of the Home, for the children to play in.

THE ROYAL MANCHESTER CHILDREN'S HOSPITAL

An aerial view of the Hospital 1920s.

(Photo by Lafayette.)

Mr. G. A. T. JESSON,
Honorary Secretary.

(Photo by Yevonde.)

Mr. JAMES SILLAVAN,
Chairman of the
Board of Governors.

(Photo by Yevonde.)

The Hon. H. CON. SMITH,
Honorary Treasurer.

Some members of the Board, 1936.

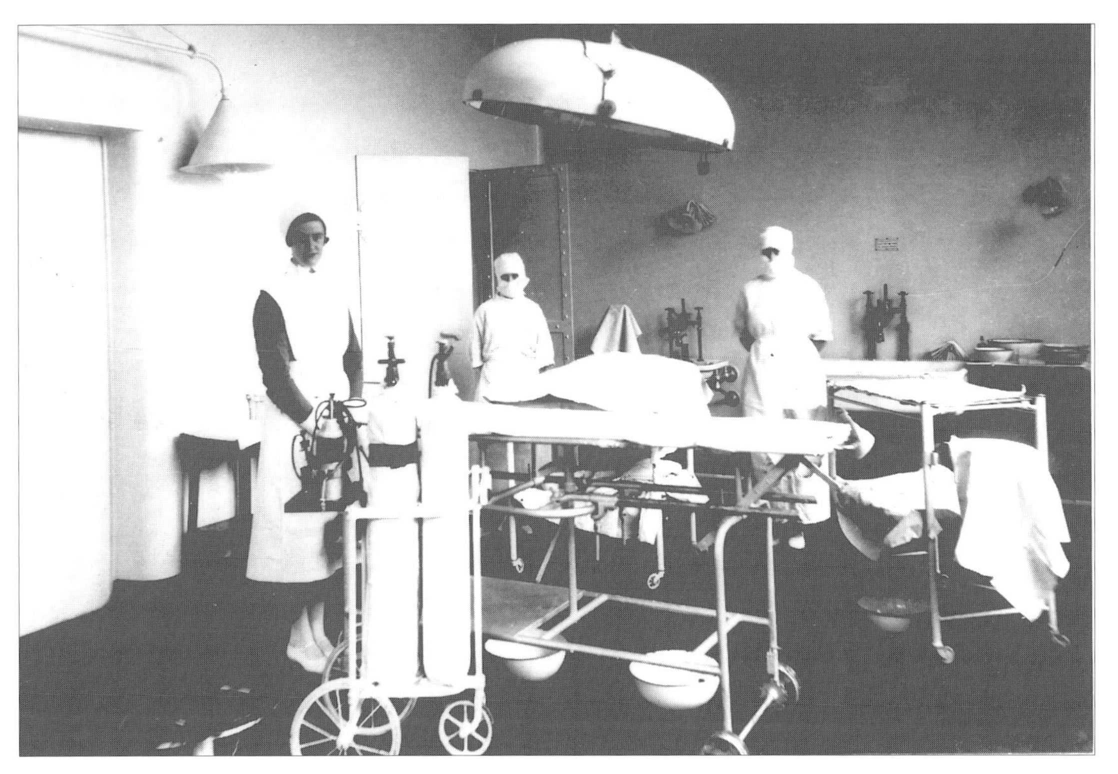

Operating theatre at Pendlebury in 1931.

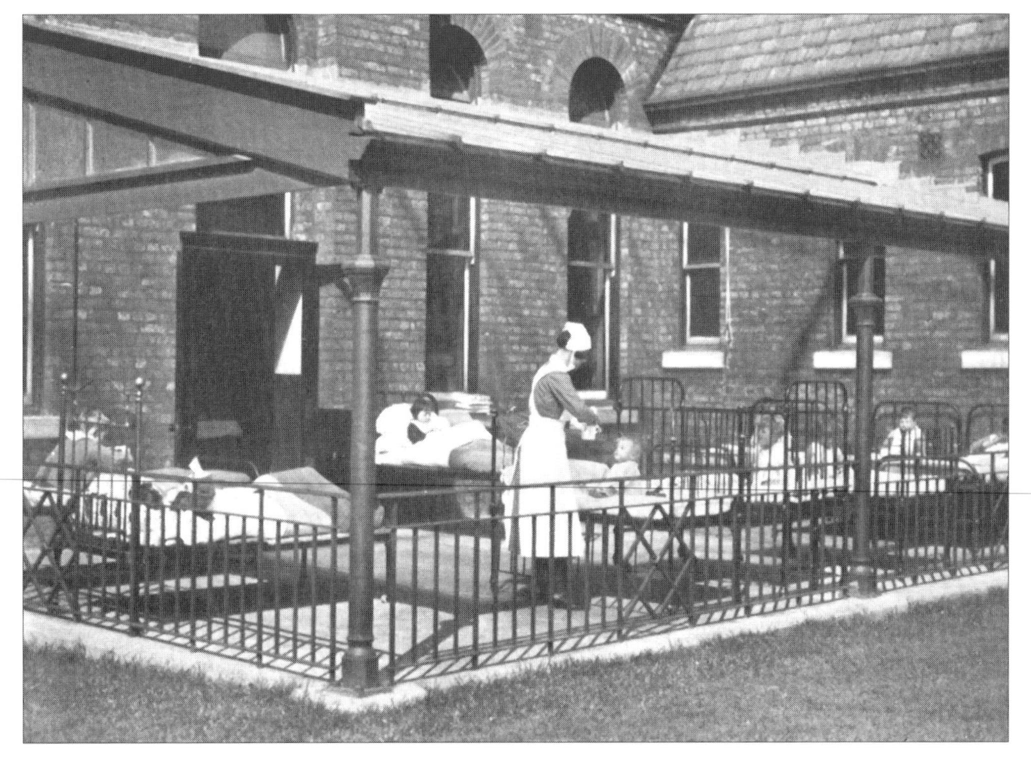

Open air treatment on a ward verandah 1931.

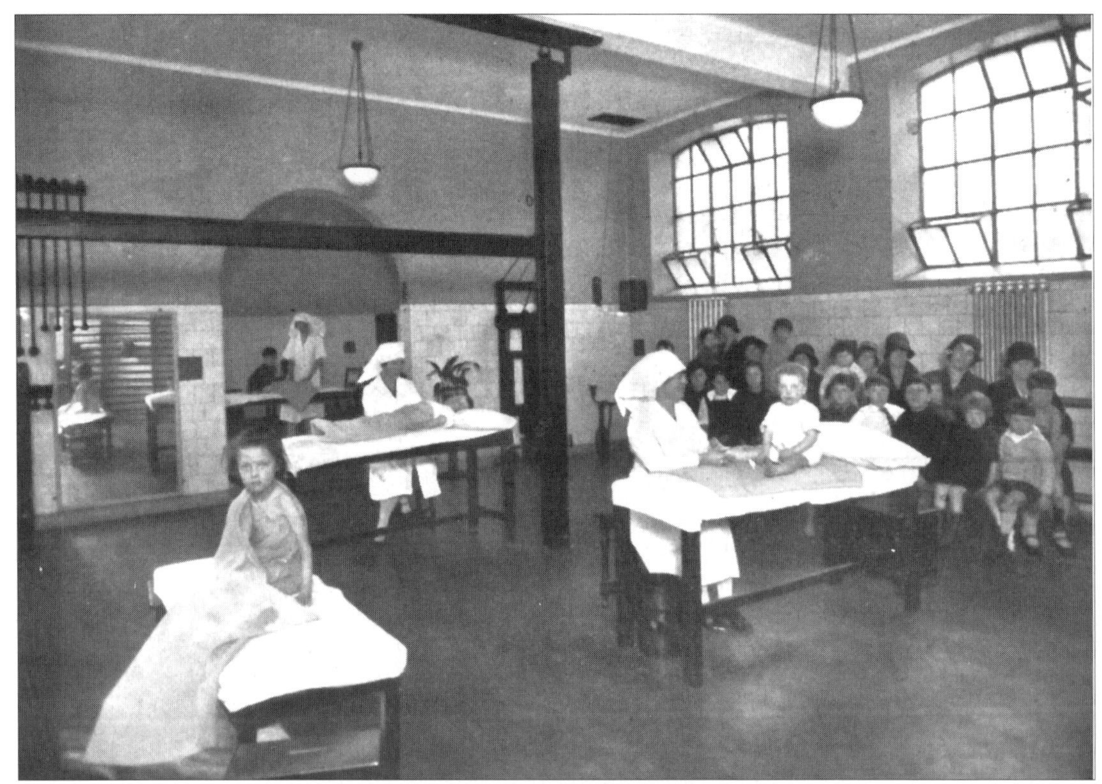

The Massage, Electrical and Artificial Sunlight Department early 1930s.

Pendlebury staff, governors and dignitaries in the late 1930s. First left on front row, Dr C Paget Lapage, first Head of Child Health Manchester University. Dr Komrower is last right back row. Col. Willink is last right second row. Other names, pencilled onto the photo, can be made out with a magnifying glass.

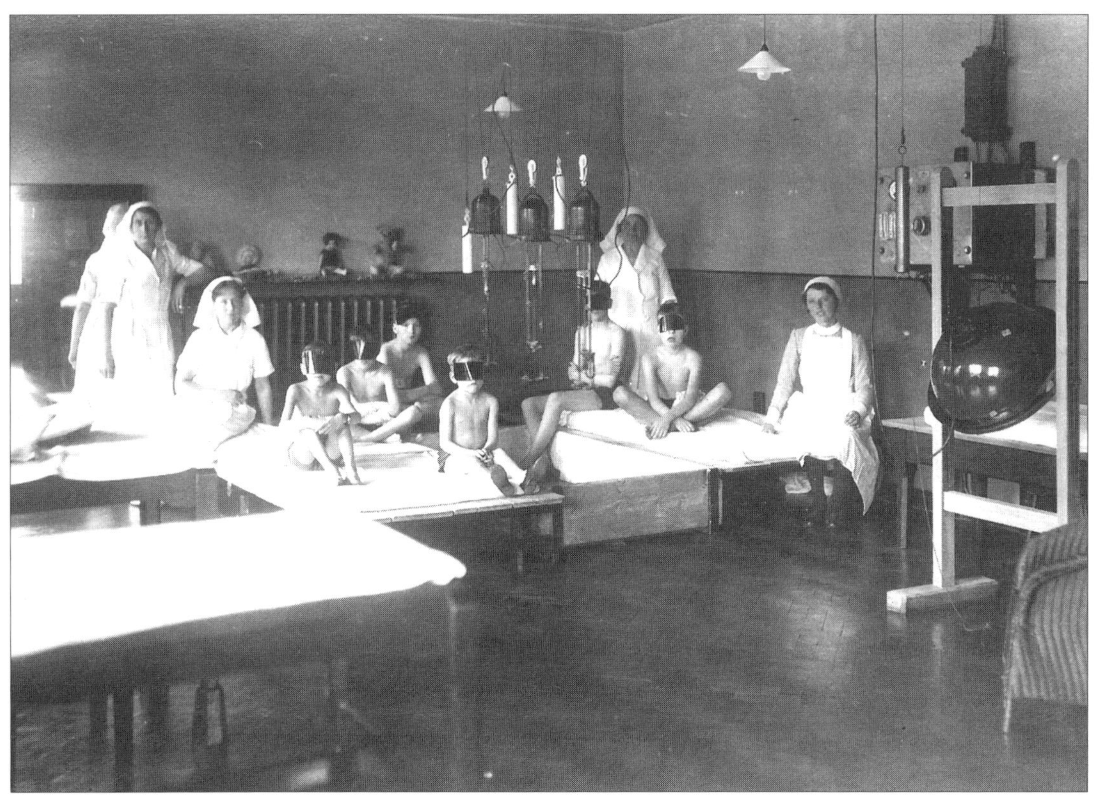

1930s Artificial Sunlight treatment, with children in protective visors for their eyes.

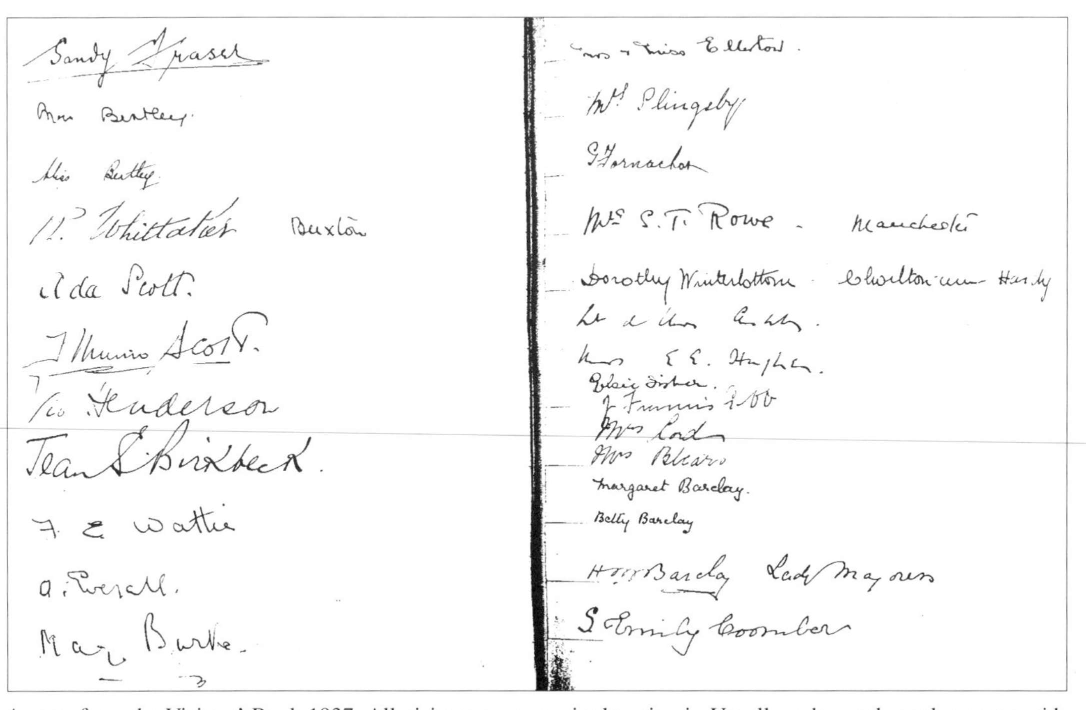

Sandy Fraser
Mrs Bentley
Miss Bentley
Whittaker Buxton
Ada Scott
Scott
Henderson
Birkbeck
F. E. Wattie
Mary Burke

Mrs & Miss Ellerton
Mrs Slingsby
Mrs S. T. Rowe Manchester
Dorothy Winterbottom Chorlton-cum-Hardy
Elsie Fisher
Margaret Barclay
Betty Barclay
Barclay Lady Mayoress
S. Emily Coomber

A page from the Visitors' Book 1937. All visitors were required to sign it. Usually a day each week was set aside as a visiting day for governors, the ladies committees and other dignitaries.

Playing with child, late 1940s.

The Rotary Club of Alberta, Canada, sent food gifts in December 1948. Here 3 year old Pauline Walsh is receiving chocolate from Mr Abbott of the Manchester Rotary Club. Children who were too ill had a bar placed in their locker so that no child missed out on this rare treat.

Many ancillary staff, like laundry staff, catering staff, maintenance and engineering staff, estates staff and porters, have worked hard over the years to make Pendebury the fine hospital it has been. Top photo: Kitchen at RMCH about 1930. Below: Laundry at RMCH about 1918.

THE EXTRACTS FROM THE ANNUAL REPORTS OF 1932 AND 1938 ON THESE TWO PAGES DEMOMSTRATE THE LEVEL AND NATURE OF ACTIVITY AT PENDLEBURY PRIOR TO THE SECOND WORLD WAR

RMCH INFORMATION FROM THE 1932 ANNUAL REPORT

R. OLLERENSHAW.	C. PAGET LAPAGE.
D. M. SUTHERLAND.	HUGH T. ASHBY.
J. ARNOLD JONES.	JOHN F. WARD.
W. J. S. BYTHELL.	T. N. FISHER.
OGILVIE M. DUTHIE.	G. B. WARBURTON.
P. I. WIGODER.	J. GOW.

Number of Available Beds :—	1930.	1931.
Hospital	190	190
Convalescent Home	30	30
Remaining in Hospital, 1st January	154	154
Admitted during the year	2,505	2,737
Total under treatment during the year	2,659	2,891
Remaining in Hospital, 31st December	154	155
Average number of beds occupied	153.7	158
Days spent in Hospital	56,099	57,646
Average number of days per patient spent in Hospital	22.39	21.06
Sent to the Convalescent Home at Lytham St. Annes	250	310
Operations at the Hospital	1,675	1,841

Out-Patients' Department Statistics.

	1930.	1931.
Total attendances, Out-patients	97,843	92,989
New Out-patients	14,546	15,632
Renewals	5,591	4,838
Admitted to Hospital	1,843	2,020
Operations ,Out-patients	2,454	2,746

Throat, Nose, and Ear Department.

(included above.)	1930.	1931.
New Patients	1,059	1,093
Total attendances	2,985	3,021
Operations	882	1,017

Dental Department.

New Patients	308	343

X-Ray Department.

The number of cases examined and treated in the two X-Ray Departments is almost the same as in the previous year.

	1930.	1931.
Cases examined at Gartside Street	1,008	1,003
Cases examined at Pendlebury	694	744
Treatment Cases at Gartside Street	333	287
	2,035	2,034

Pathological Department.

	1930.	1931.
Agglutination Tests	13	7
Blood (General Examination)	149	218
Blood (Special Test)	218	214
Cerebro Spinal Fluid	70	104
Fæces	49	60
Inoculations (Guinea Pig)	9	4
Pus	112	98
Sputum	36	40
Swab (Nose, Throat, Vagina)	978	922
Tumour	78	63
Urine	168	108
Wassermann Reaction	179	250
Vaccine	27	39
Miscellaneous	301	471
Total	2,387	2,598
Post-mortem Examinations	32	42

Massage and Gymnastic Department.

		1930.	1931.
Treatments Out-Patients	Massage	7,539	7,966
	Electrical	364	446
	Swedish Remedial Exercises	2,246	1,824
		10,149	10,236
New cases during year (Out-patients)		222	235
In-patient Massage Treatments		1,128	1,238
,, ,, New cases		107	121

Artificial Sunlight Department.

New patients at Gartside Street	492	530
,, ,, Pendlebury	188	163
Number of treatments at Gartside Street	11,674	10,751
,, ,, ,, Pendlebury	1,676	1,317

Convalescent Home.

Number of available beds	30	30
Average number of occupied beds	18.6	22
Number of patients admitted	250	310
Average number of days per patient spent in Home	27.2	25.6
Total days spent in Home	6,760	8,191

AVAILABLE BEDS.

	1937.
Hospital	192
Zachary Merton Home	40
Sea-side Home	30
	262

HOSPITAL.

	1937.
Remaining in Hospital, 1st January	141
Admitted during the year	2,860
Total under treatment during the year	3,001
Remaining in Hospital, 31st December	164
Average number of beds occupied	148
Days spent in Hospital	53,848
Average number of days per patient spent in Hospital	18.83
Sent to the Sea-side Home at Lytham St. Annes	274
Sent to the Zachary Merton Home	384
Operations at the Hospital	1,866

OUT-PATIENTS' DEPARTMENT STATISTICS.

	1937.
Total Attendances—Out-patients	98,440
New Out-patients	15,311
Renewals	5,366
Admitted to Hospital	2,110
Operations—Out-patients	2,246

THROAT, NOSE, AND EAR DEPARTMENT.

	1937.
New Patients	1,097
Total attendances	4,140
Operations	796

DENTAL DEPARTMENT.

New Patients	322

RMCH INFORMATION FROM THE 1938 ANNUAL REPORT

X-RAY DEPARTMENT.

The numbers of cases dealt with for the last two years are as follows:—

	1937.
Cases examined at Gartside Street	1,520
Cases examined at Pendlebury	884
Treatment Cases at Gartside Street	172
Treatment Cases at Pendlebury	—
	2,576

The examinations made at Gartside Street include 70 cases sent from St. Mary's Hospital.

PATHOLOGICAL DEPARTMENT.

	1937.
Agglutination Tests	83
Blood (General Examination)	271
Blood (Special Test)	116
Cerebro Spinal Fluid	70
Fæces	124
Inoculations (Guinea Pig)	12
Pus, etc.	124
Sputum	65
Swab (Nose, Throat, Vagina)	1,938
Tumour	50
Urine	570
Wassermann Reaction	102
Vaccine	21
Miscellaneous	498
Total	4,044
Post-mortem Examinations	38

MASSAGE AND GYMNASTIC DEPARTMENT.

		1937.
Treatments Out-Patients	Massage	8,563
	Electrical	273
	Swedish Remedial Exercises	3,139
		11,975

MASSAGE AND GYMNASTIC DEPARTMENT (*continued*)

	1937.
New cases during year (Out-patients)	349
In-patient Massage Treatments	1,473
,, ,, New cases	134

ARTIFICIAL SUNLIGHT DEPARTMENT.

New Out-patients at Gartside Street	465
New In-patients at Pendlebury	241
Number of treatments at Gartside Street	9,034
,, ,, ,, Pendlebury	1,473

SPEECH CLINIC.

New Out-patients	68
Attendances—Out-patients	650

SEA-SIDE HOME.

	1937.
Number of available beds	30
Average number of occupied beds	18
Number of patients admitted	274
Average number of days per patient spent in Home	23
Total days spent in Home	6,410

ZACHARY MERTON HOME.

	1937.
Number of available beds	40
Average number of occupied beds	28
Number of patients admitted	384
Average number of days per patient spent in Home	26
Total days spent in Home	10,035

C. PAGET LAPAGE.
HUGH T. ASHBY.
JOHN F. WARD.
T. N. FISHER.
M L. THOMSON.
J. GOW.
R. OLLERENSHAW.
D. S. POOLE WILSON.
N. W. BOLTON.
NEVILLE A. J. YOUNG.
H. M. MORRIS.
OGILVIE M. DUTHIE.
G. F. ROWBOTHAM.
P. I. WIGODER.
W. M. BURBURY.

THE ZACHERY MERTON HOME

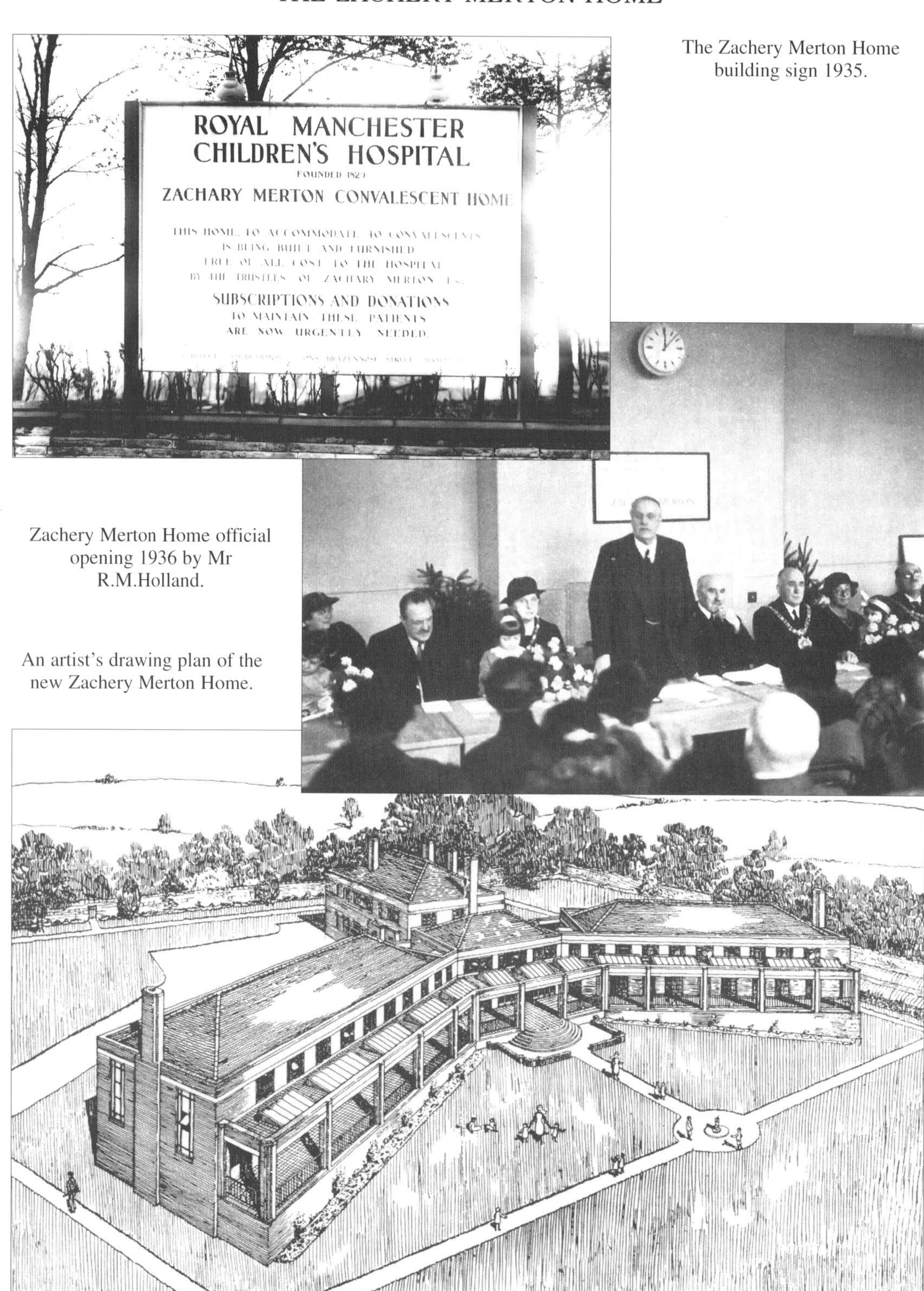

The Zachery Merton Home building sign 1935.

Zachery Merton Home official opening 1936 by Mr R.M.Holland.

An artist's drawing plan of the new Zachery Merton Home.

Members of the board, dignitaries and trustees of the Zachery Merton Trust at the opening of the Home in 1936.

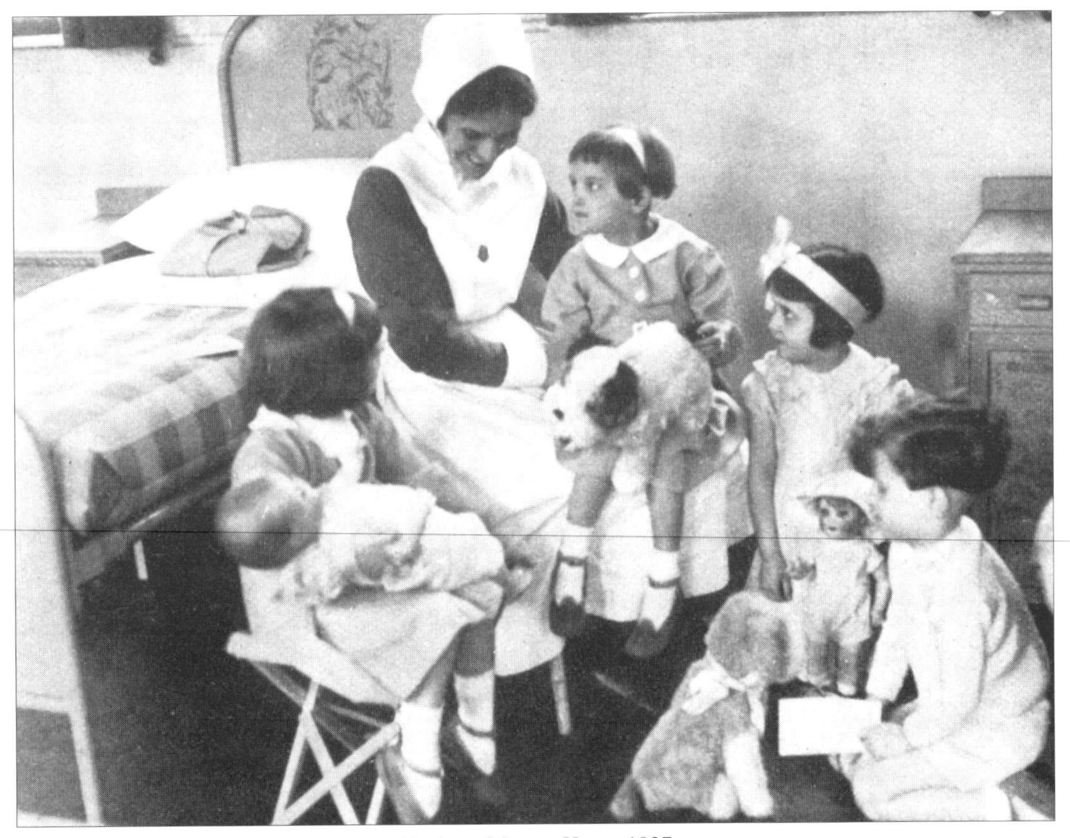

Zachery Merton Home 1937.

Zachery Merton Home
Christmas 1944.

Zachery Merton Home
- the sun verandah.

Zachary Merton Home kitchen 1936.

On the balcony of Zachery Merton Home in 1936. Now Ashby Ward.

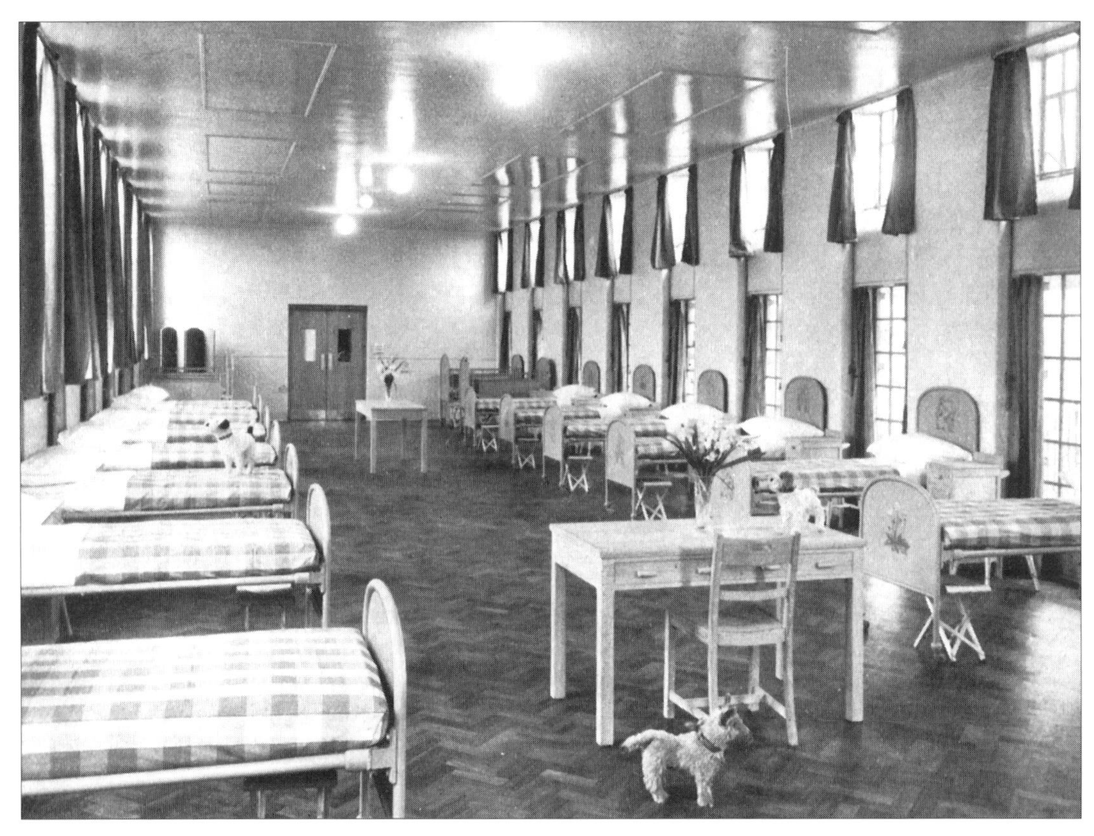

The Zachary Merton dormitory, now Sillavan Ward.

1947 Sister supervising a nurse making up baby feeds. All wards made up their own feeds.

EDUCATION AND PLAY

Greengate Hospital and open air school 1916.

Greengate Hospital and open air school 1924. Education for sick children was provided at least as long ago as 1916. Both Pendlebury and Booth Hall had, and still have, their own hospital schools.

Library books Ashby Ward 1952.

'At play' RMCH 1948.

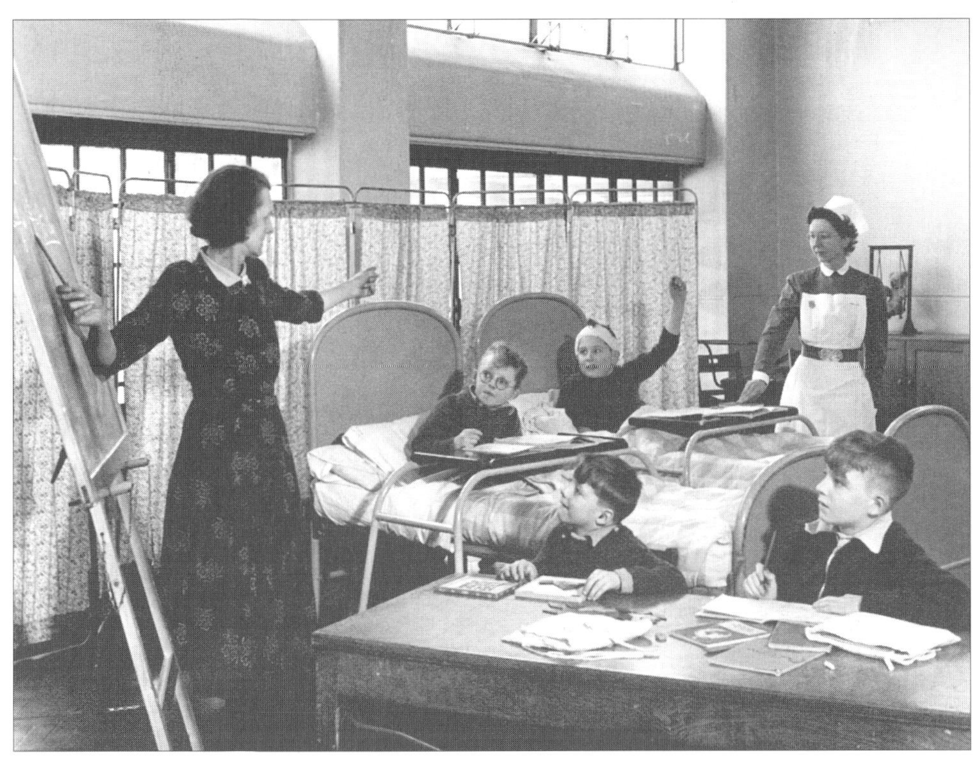

School classes on Ashby Ward (Zachery Merton) in 1952.

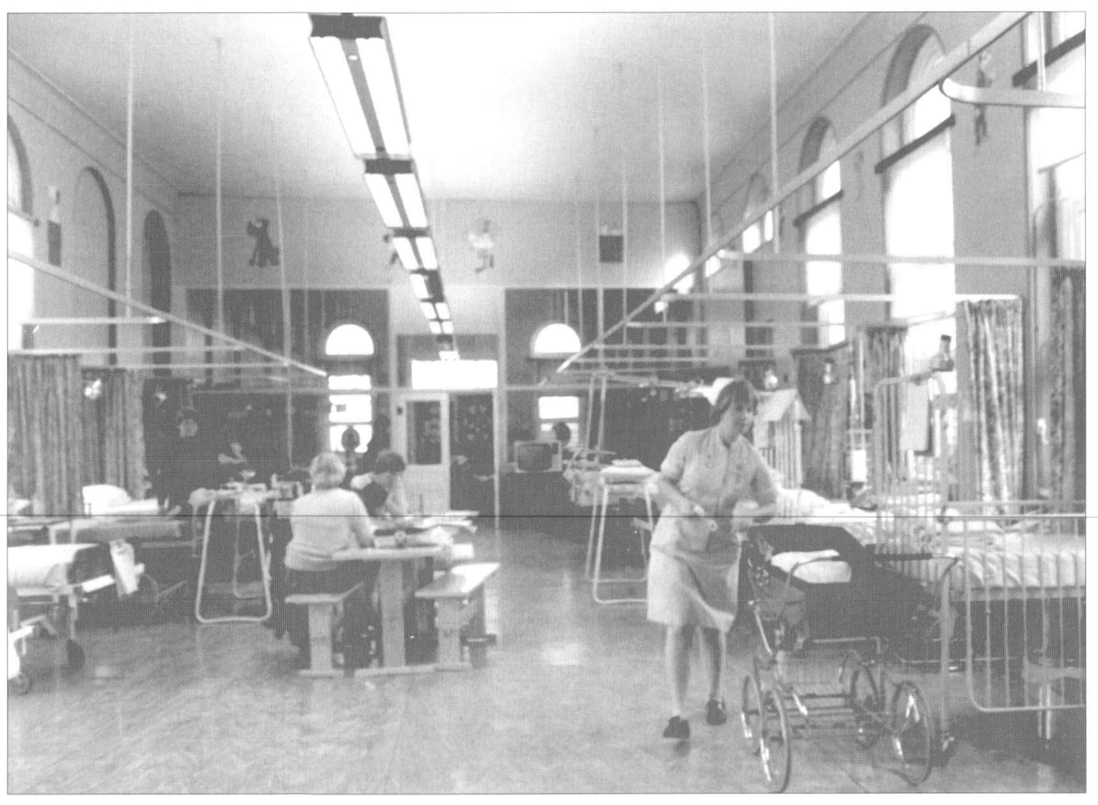

School classes in the centre of Liebert Ward in 1984. The Hospital School now has a separate suite of rooms, as well as giving bedside lessons.

Play area in Gartside Street out-patients in the 1950s

The Play and Preparation Service was set up at RMCH in 1986 - an innovation of the new Head of Nursing, Anne MacDonald.

Play area on Borchardt Ward with a Hospital Play Specialist. Play is now an integral part of care plans, allowing information to be given to children in a friendly way.

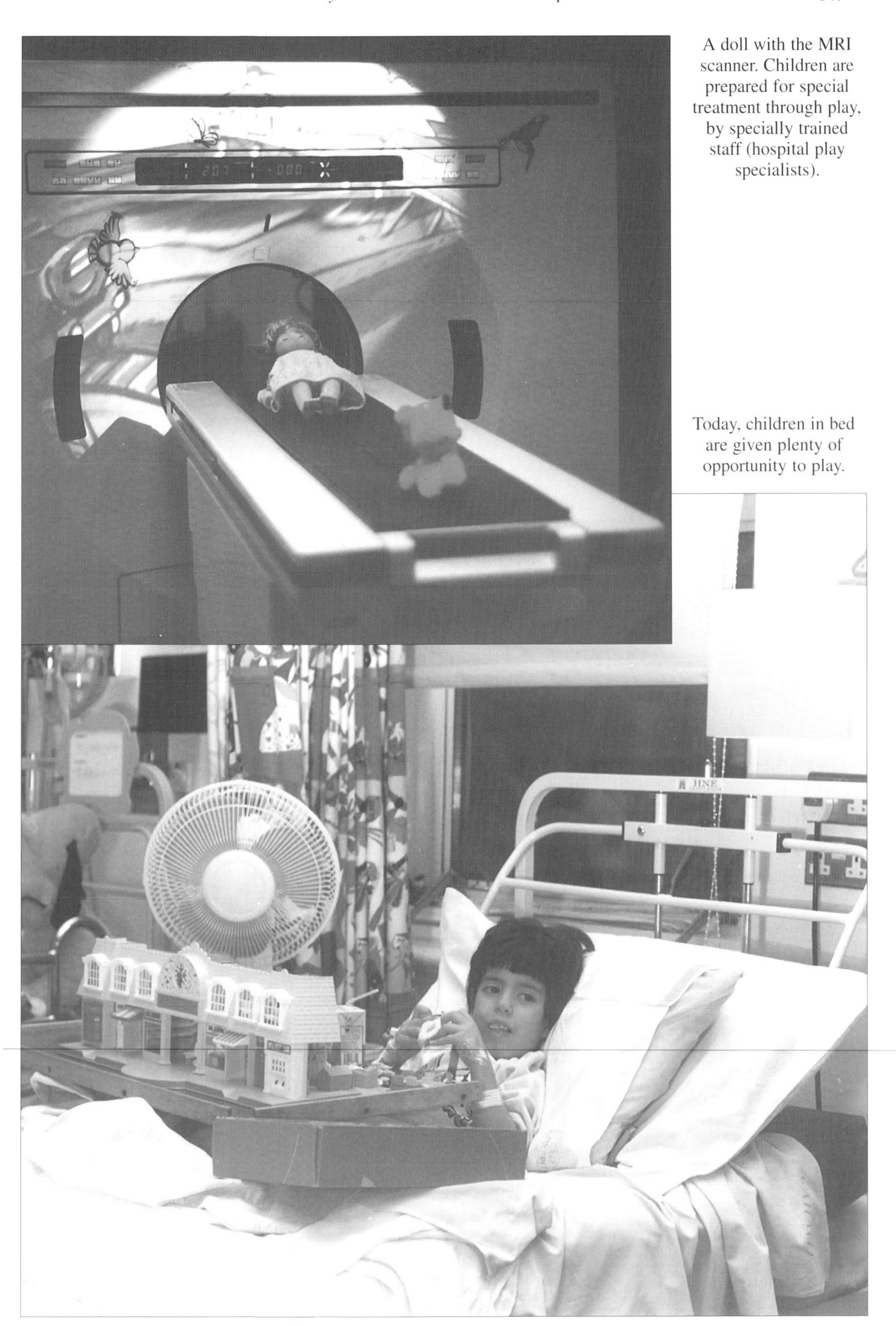

A doll with the MRI scanner. Children are prepared for special treatment through play, by specially trained staff (hospital play specialists).

Today, children in bed are given plenty of opportunity to play.

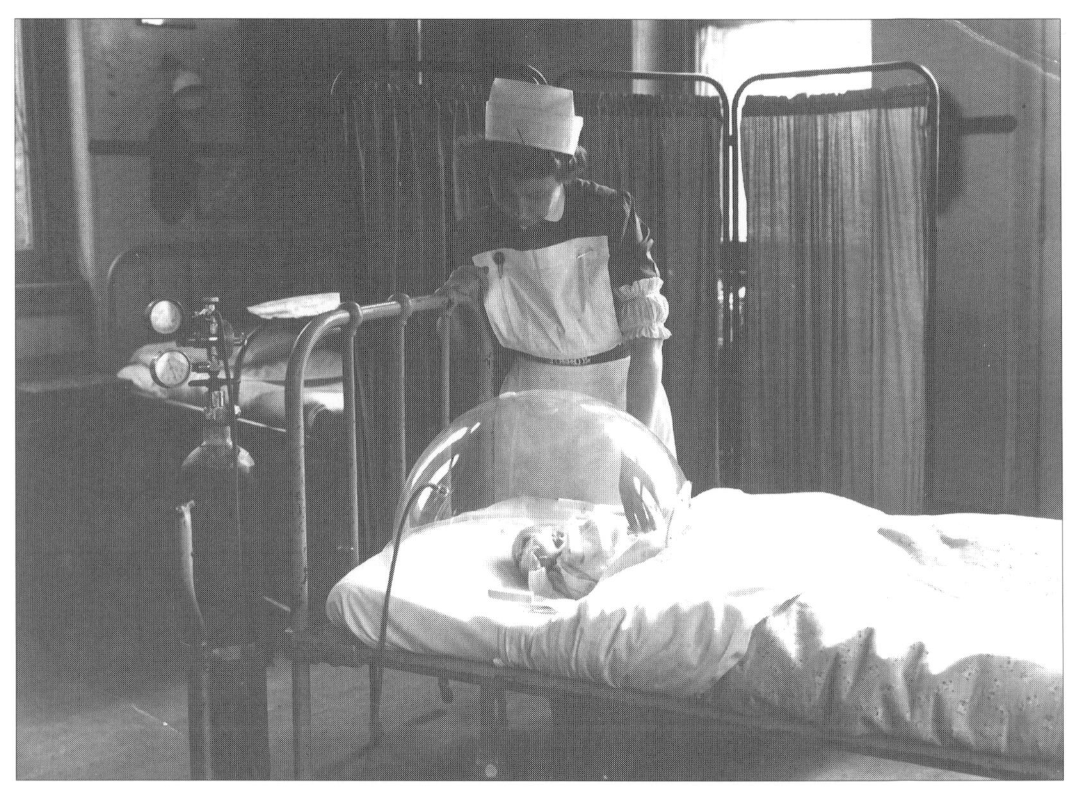

Sister Moon and 'Pendelbury Tent' 1950.

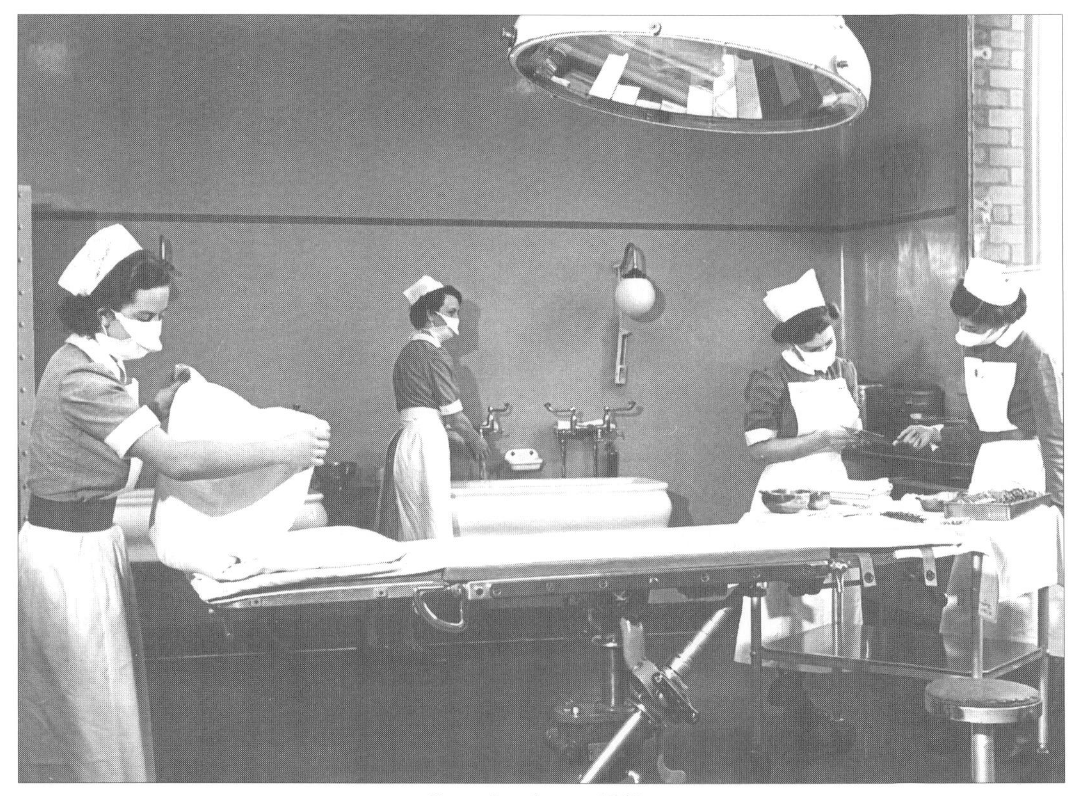

Operating theatre 1952.

CHAPTER 8

THE NATIONAL HEALTH SERVICE

The National Health Service did not just happen overnight. Long before the Second World War moves had begun in the direction of a more cohesive health service. This is described in great detail in John V. Pickstone's book *Medicine and Industrial Society*, 1985, Manchester University Press, in which he traces the pattern of hospital services in the North West through the 1930s up to their inheritance by the National Health Service.

The Dawson Report of 1918 had proposed coordination of preventative and curative services. Dawson proposed a movement away from local municipally run services and a change towards reflecting medical interests. The Report stated *"the best means in procuring health and curing disease should be available to every citizen by right and not by favour."* There were opposing arguments but the Dawson Report held sway. With the Local Government Act of 1929, the sick were placed under Public Health Committees, with provision to link voluntary and municipal hospitals. This was the beginning of change and by the mid-1930s a joint committee had been set up in Manchester.The annual report of Pendlebury, 1935 stated:

> *In conjunction with the other Voluntary Hospitals, the Board has confirmed their agreement with the foundation of a JOINT ADVISORY BOARD, comprised of representatives of Municipal Authorities, the University and the Voluntary Hospitals. The Chairman of the Board has been elected to serve on this committee, which is certain to prove of vital importance to all Manchester Hospitals and requires the hearty co-operation of all concerned.*

One object of this new committee was to be *"to secure for Manchester a thoroughly coordinated series of medical and surgical services that will compare with any in the country"* (Manchester Guardian 1935).

The Royal Manchester Children's Hospital was therefore able to claim a place for children in the very early days of the service in Manchester. Despite this, many members of the Board were jealous of their voluntary principle and wary of change. Mr James Sillavan, then Chairman of the Board of Governors, took a seat on this Joint Committee and represented the interests of the Hospital, the Duchess of York Hospital for Babies and Booth Hall Children's Hospital, as well as sick children city-wide.

A notable achievement of the committee, the Manchester Joint Hospitals Advisory Board, was the new orthopaedic block opened at the Manchester Royal Infirmary in 1939. The leading surgeon in this venture was Sir Harry Platt. He had already contributed in an advisory capacity to services at Royal Manchester Children's Hospital over many years and would have a far-reaching influence on children's services not only in Manchester, but throughout the United Kingdom and world-wide in the early years of the National Health Service.

It was through the Joint Board that proposals were submitted to establish a University Chair in Paediatrics and in 1942 The Royal Manchester Children's Hospital, as well as the Manchester Royal Infirmary (inclusive of St Mary's) recommended an Institute of Child Health (see Chapter 9).

The Beveridge Report of 1942 was the forerunner for a Government White Paper published in 1944. The opening statement was one of great nobility: *"Everybody, irrespective of means, age, sex or occupation, shall have equal opportunity to benefit from the best and most up to date medical and allied services available"*, and that the service would be *"comprehensive for all who wished to take advantage of it; that it would be free of charge and that it would promote good health, rather than the treatment of bad health".*

The National Health Service Bill, driven by the then Secretary of State, Aneurin Bevan, was launched on 5th July 1948. This was the beginning of one of the most significant chapters in the development of medicine and allied services anywhere and has become the envy of the world. Much work, however, had preceded during the years between 1942-48. How would the voluntary hospitals be incorporated into the system alongside public hospitals? The implications for Pendlebury, of course, were far-reaching. It was an extremely complicated situation where all interests needed to be addressed. It is difficult now to realise the enormity of the task faced by hospital boards. Pendlebury, alongside others, would need to consider the special character of their hospitals, the investment of their funds, yet continue to offer a service to patients - *"the same devoted care will always be bestowed on sick children who seek its aid."* But the problem of amalgamating local government services with the voluntary hospital services was immense.

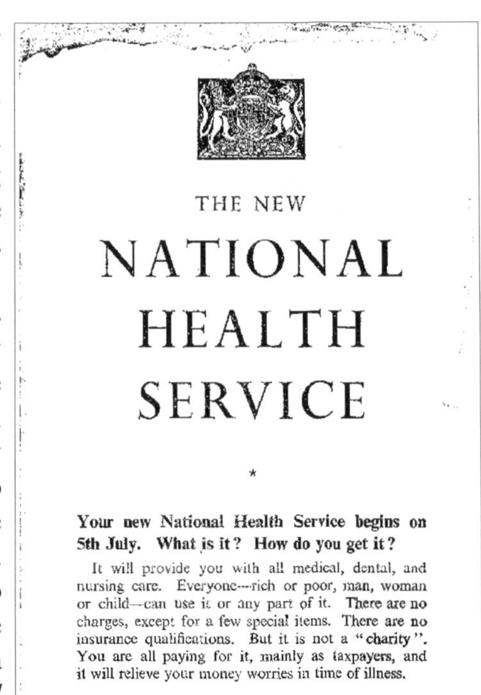
THE NEW

NATIONAL HEALTH SERVICE

*

Your new National Health Service begins on 5th July. What is it? How do you get it?

It will provide you with all medical, dental, and nursing care. Everyone—rich or poor, man, woman or child—can use it or any part of it. **There are no charges, except for a few special items. There are no insurance qualifications. But it is not a "charity". You are all paying for it, mainly as taxpayers, and it will relieve your money worries in time of illness.**

The leaflet announcing the NHS to the population of Britain, 1948.

At the establishment of the National Health Service, The Royal Manchester Children's Hospital in 1948 came under The Salford Hospital Management Committee of the Manchester Regional Hospital Board. This was to be the format for several years. The hospital was managed by the Royal Manchester Children's Hospital Committee, of which Mr Francis A. Willink, O.B.E., M.A. was Chairman. The Willink Research Unit is named after this man who devoted many hours of his life to the Children's Hospital. With the changes that were brought about by the restructuring of management within the National Health Service Mr Willink was the last link with the previous era of long serving trustees. This is not to demean in any way many who continue to support the hospital through our many charities both little and large.

A further re-organisation within the National Health Service took place in 1974. The Children's Hospital then came under the Salford Area Health Authority (Teaching), North Western Regional Health Authority, succeeding Salford Hospital Management Committee. Subsequently it was to become Salford District Health Authority (Teaching) and then Salford Health Authority NHS Trust in 1991. At the same time Salford Health Authority assumed the responsibility for Booth Hall Children's Hospital (see Chapter 11) and both Royal Manchester Children's Hospital and Booth Hall Children's Hospital in North Manchester were to be managed as a single unit for children's secondary services in Salford and North Manchester and for tertiary services within the North West and beyond.

On 1st April 1995 both children's hospitals, staff, services, buildings and equipment moved from the direct management of Salford and Trafford District Health Authority to become the responsibility of Manchester Children's Hospitals NHS Trust. The Trust was a new legal entity and managed by a newly-formed Trust Board of executive and non-executive directors.

The change to a National Health Service for local government hospitals and voluntary hospitals must have caused many difficulties. The Government was still prepared to allow subscribers to contribute to particular hospitals of their choice. Voluntary organisations were encouraged to continue their efforts on behalf of these hospitals.

At the same time medicine was changing rapidly too. The first half of the twentieth century saw great changes in the development of children's medicine but the second half was to see massive changes. In the aftermath of World War II there was an increased knowledge and understanding of antiseptic and aseptic techniques, and the advent of antibiotics and their development would enable medical frontiers to be pushed back further and further.

Doctors, not only in the adult hospitals but in children's hospitals, were beginning to specialise more and more, but parents were totally excluded from the hospitals where children were admitted, the opinion being that they brought in infection and only upset the children! Medical people felt that *"children in hospital needed care but were better off without their parents"*. This was also true of Pendlebury. Parents were excluded except for the weekly visits on Sunday afternoons.

The first years of the NHS were not only marked by great changes in medicine, but also by what became known as the "open visiting campaign" in paediatrics. The World Health Organisation, also initiated in 1948, supported a study of homeless refugee children. They appointed John Bowlby, a British psychiatrist who had an immense understanding of children, to carry out this research. His paperback book *Child Care and the Growth of Love*, published in 1952, was to revolutionise the perceived adult view of hospitalised children. The government set up a committee under Sir Harry Platt, the eminent orthopaedic surgeon at the Manchester Royal Infirmary with an interest at Pendlebury, to investigate the welfare of children in hospital. Their findings were published in 1959 and became described as 'The Platt Report'. Their recommendations would be the yardstick used to measure the quality of children's services for the future. It was not until 1990 that the Department of Health issued a new document that superceded the Platt Report, and even then its recommendations were incorporated within the new document, The Welfare of Children and Young People in Hospital, HMSO, 1990.

A portrait of Sir Harry Platt on his 90th birthday. He lived to 100.

The Platt Report inaugurated a changing culture for hospitalised children. Children, although valued at the time of the NHS, were kept separate from their parents; this was possibly a casualty of the progress in medicine. Armed with the Platt Report a group of mothers initiated the organisation Mothers Care for Children in Hospital, in London in 1961, backed by progressive paediatricians. The organisation formed a branch in Manchester in 1962. This pressure group was to become the greatest influence in promoting enlightened change in paediatrics in the Country. Dr George Komrower from Pendlebury, at the 1964 National Conference of the organisation held in Manchester, spoke significantly in support of mothers staying in hospital with their young sick children. The argument was strengthened at Pendlebury by the raising of monies to attach a purpose-built unit for mother/child accommodation to Ashby Ward in 1965. It was another 15 years, however, before the open visiting programme was fully implemented. Today it would be unthinkable not to have open visiting and parents staying with their sick child.

Mothers Care for Children in Hospital changed its name in 1965 to become The National Association for the Welfare of Children in Hospital. Pendlebury and Booth Hall Hospitals have always had a long history of co-operation with the Association and professionals have worked alongside parents to complement good practice. The name has changed again to that of Action for Sick Children, as the remit has widened (1991). The Department of Health uses this organisation to advise them on child policy, as their expertise on the needs of sick children is second to none. The Manchester Branch is still active and a representative from the group is asked to join all consultative meetings pertaining to services for children.

1974 was to see further re-organisation within the entire National Health Service. Regional Health Authorities were created to manage district management teams; consensus management was introduced, teaching hospitals which included Pendlebury were brought into a more unified structure, and community health councils were formed. Many Action for Sick Children (NAWCH) members were appointed to these councils and were able to continue to advance good practice and policies for children in this way.

As the start of National Health Service the pace of the hospital was indeed much slower. The average length of stay was about two weeks. Now the average length of stay can be as little as two days. A typical medical ward in 1948 would nurse children with acute rheumatism, chorea, Still's disease, bronchiectasis and varying forms of TB. Streptomycin was the new 'wonder drug' on trial. Children with infections such as pneumonia and croup were nursed in oxygen tents and steam tents. The nurse in attendance on these children was not to allow the cylinder to run out or the steam kettle to boil dry!

On the orthopaedic wards the children were usually long term and continued to be nursed on the open balconies in all weathers. There were no offices or clinic rooms and the central fireplaces were still being used on all the wards. Steam sterilizers were situated near the entrance to the wards and the 'Ward Maids' were resident. They ruled their domains!

Radiators were topped by lengths of cotton wool. "Fluffing up" with heat prior to making woolly balls for dressings was a task for any spare moments, as was cutting 'gauze' for placing in the autoclave, a responsibility of the Student Nurse or Theatre Night Sister. The supply of baby feed bottles was autoclaved for the following day.

Syringes were boiled in a pan on the 'kitchen stove' and blunt needles were sent off for re-sharpening. All medical wards had a feed kitchen and the designated 'Baby Nurse' made up the feeds for her own ward. Very few children were allowed to be up and about, there were no play rooms, and it was not until 1950 that school lessons commenced. Visiting daily for two hours began in the early fifties and there were four beds in the basement available to mothers should it be necessary.

Prayers were taken in the Chapel morning and evening, and there were separate dining rooms for Medical Staff, Sisters, Nurses and Domestics. The few parents who were able to stay in the early sixties took their meals with the domestics in the basement.

The middle 1950s saw a big increase in speciality work in paediatrics unknown before then. Pendlebury became recognised also for oncology, orthodontics and cardiac work, to name but a few. This was the era that also saw the disappearance of the central fireplaces on the wards. Gradually the verandahs were enclosed, and became play rooms, and offices for staff and cubicles for children were introduced.

There was only one operating theatre in Pendlebury at the start of the NHS in 1948. By the mid-fifties another theatre was installed. Then in 1962 the new Twin Operating Theatres were opened by HRH The Princess Royal, Princess Mary. As well as the new theatres, an Admission Unit was added and a new Pharmacy.

Mr F. A. Willink OBE MA, who at the time of the above developments was the Chairman of the Royal Manchester Children's Hospital Committee, referred in his report in 1962 to the 'Ten Year Plan for the Hospital Service'. This government plan would bring changes regarding the future of many hospitals, but it seemed that Pendlebury did not feel threatened by it. The hospital was expected to be included in the scheme for the extension of postgraduate teaching. A meeting had already been held in 1961 and included the following:

Mrs J. Boucock (Sister in Charge, Children's Clinic, St Marys)
Professor Wilfrid Gaisford
Dr A. Holzel
Dr D. M. Buscroft (Administrator for Staff, UMH)
Miss W. F. Morgan, Principal Matron
Dr G. M. Komrower

This was a Project Team on Paediatrics within Manchester and District. Under discussion was the possibility of having an Institute of Child Health with its headquarters and university team based on the Manchester site. There would be provision for 180 paediatric beds and all the supporting services. Their report was submitted to the Board of Governors of the United Manchester Hospitals. No action was taken at this time. When the Duchess of York Hospital for Babies in Burnage moved to Withington Hospital in 1987 further discussions regarding centralisation were again raised. Now in 1999, the decision has been taken to move the children's tertiary services to the Central Manchester Hospital Site, and planning for this new childrens hospital is well underway. Local paediatric services will remain in the district.

At the time of these first discussions in 1961 the situation at Pendlebury was one of a flourishing and prestigious paediatric establishment. Although the Zachary Merton Trustees had also built a convalescent home on site in 1936 the convalescent home at St Annes-on-Sea was continuing to offer a valuable service. Both Pendlebury and the Dispensary at Gartside Street were continuing to develop a comprehensive specialised service. The Hospital had 227 beds with various specialised units, and housed the Department of Child Health of the University of Manchester, which is now called the Gaisford Unit. It was dealing with some 4,500 in-patients and 24,000 out-patient attendances per year. The unit possessed its own specialist paediatric X-ray, Physiotherapy and Pathological departments. There were a number of laboratories for research and other projects and Pendlebury had its own School of Nursing with an annual intake of sixty student nurses.

One innovation that was to enlarge the Hospital's reputation was the special service for Developmental Medicine set up in 1965 by Dr R. I. MacKay and others. 1973 saw the opening of the Agnew Unit which would accommodate not only Developmental Medicine but also a Department of Child Psychiatry. The Pathology service increased; requests in 1946 numbered 20,000; by 1972 requests had risen to 60,000. A Neurological service was incorporated into the development of the Assessment Unit. The Department of Electro-encephalography was providing a service for all children attending hospitals of the Manchester Regional Hospital Board. The work of the Willink Biochemical Genetics Laboratory, another new innovation, had by 1973 achieved international acclaim under its directors, Dr G.M. Komrower and Dr I.B.

Sardharwalla, and today the work in this laboratory continues to be of international repute with leaders in the field such as Dr Ed Wraith and Dr Maurice Super.

Pendlebury is also a leading hospital in oncology, under the direction of Professor Tim Eden. The Children's Tumour register is based at the Hospital on the old Stancliffe Ward. This is an old free standing ward built in 1937 in the grounds near Ashby Ward to accommodate the increasing numbers of patients admitted. (Named after F.S.Stancliffe, a governor from 1929 to 1947 and Chairman of the Board 1943-47).

During the last twenty-five years there have been continual significant improvements and advances in medicine, so that now a very comprehensive range of health care is available to children from the cities of Manchester and Salford and the natural catchment area of places such as Bury, Rochdale, Bolton, Wigan, Stockport, Tameside, Oldham and Trafford.

When Manchester Children's Hospitals (Pendlebury and Booth Hall Children's Hospitals) obtained trust status in 1995, the Trust became responsible for the management of its own budget, hospital accommodation and services including the management of teaching and research facilities. After almost fifty years, under a wider NHS management structure, the Children's Hospital with Booth Hall was once again managing its own paediatric services, a very important circumstance in the treatment of children.

This brief resumé of the past 50 years means that many contributions by practitioners in all areas of the hospitals have received the barest mention. The story of paediatric services over the last fifty years has been one of tremendous success. Frontiers in treatments have been pushed back and there have been many dedicated members of the hospital and of its sister hospital, Booth Hall. Services have developed beyond recognition over these years, yet the core of the service has always remained the same; to deliver the best possible care for sick children and their families. The hospital has continued to be elevated by the involvement of both benefactors and people of learning and foresight. Many other individuals and organisations have continued to contribute to the hospital, such as the League of Friends, Students' Rag Fund, Women's Voluntary Service and Radio Lollipop. This continues to the present day.

The 50th Anniversary of the NHS coincided with many exciting developments in children's services. Children with very complex conditions can now be treated within the hospital, for example children requiring bone marrow transplantation. There is a high level of intensive, high dependency and transitional care available. A new neurosurgery operating theatre was built and opened in 1998. A very innovative experiment has been the opening of a 'Gene Shop' at Manchester Airport, with European Funding Initiative monies, and aimed at raising public awareness of genetics. The Willink Biochemical Genetics Unit at the hospital has a national and international reputation. In many areas of treatment Nurse Specialists have been appointed, such as in gastroenterology and the treatment of cystic fibrosis.

The first fifty years of the NHS has been an exciting time of development in child health services, and a great chapter in the history of Pendlebury. The Childrens Trust, amalgamating Pendlebury and Booth Hall Children's Hospitals, is a Specialist Trust, catering for a very wide spectrum of medical conditions, and with a national and international reputation for excellence. Its services will continue to develop to meet the needs of sick children and their families as we go into the new millennium.

The Bishop of Salford attending the Garden Party at Pendlebury to mark the 50th Anniversary of the National Health Service. All denominations of the clergy have been involved with Pendlebury since the earliest days: Rule XIII: Ministers of any denomination may visit patients at the request of parents and guardians, subject to the approval of Matron.

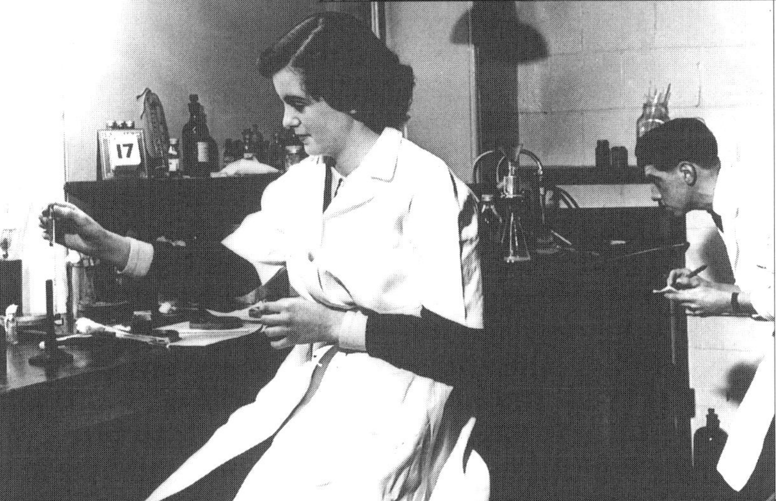

Pathology service 1948.

X Ray 1950s.

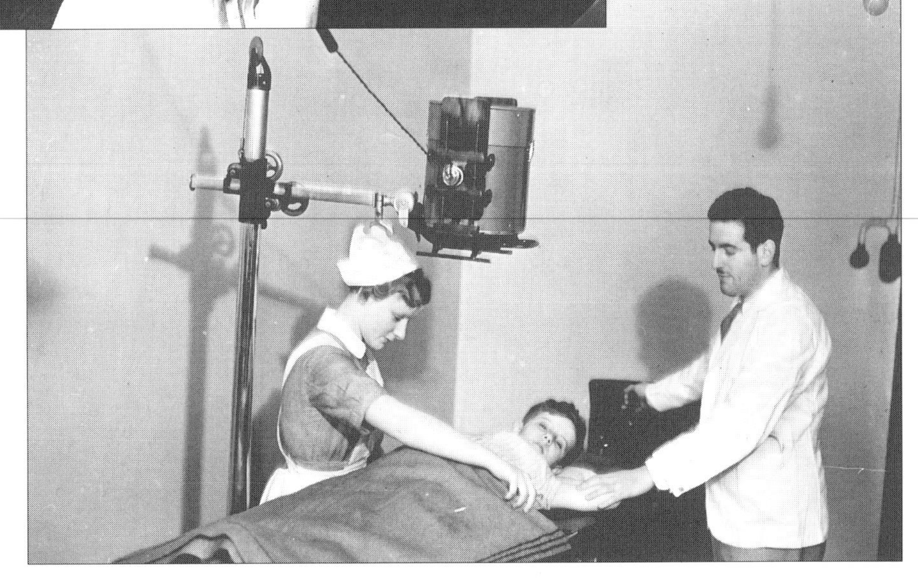

Watching the Coronation in 1953. The first television was donated in 1952.

1952. The Anglers' Society making a donation to the Hospital. Many groups, clubs and organisations have supported the Hospital generously over the years.

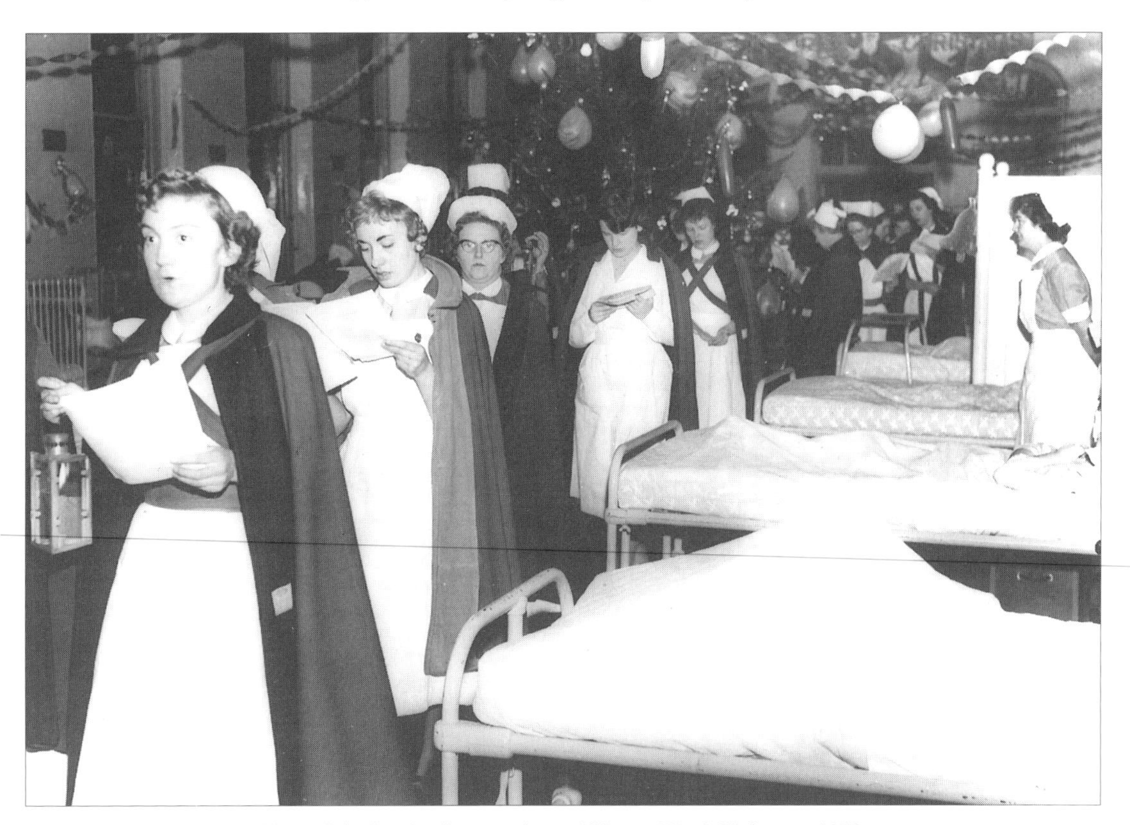

Sister Grindley leading carols on Sillavan Ward Christmas 1958.

Heywood Ward Christmas 1954. Sister Fran Floyd is holding a young patient.

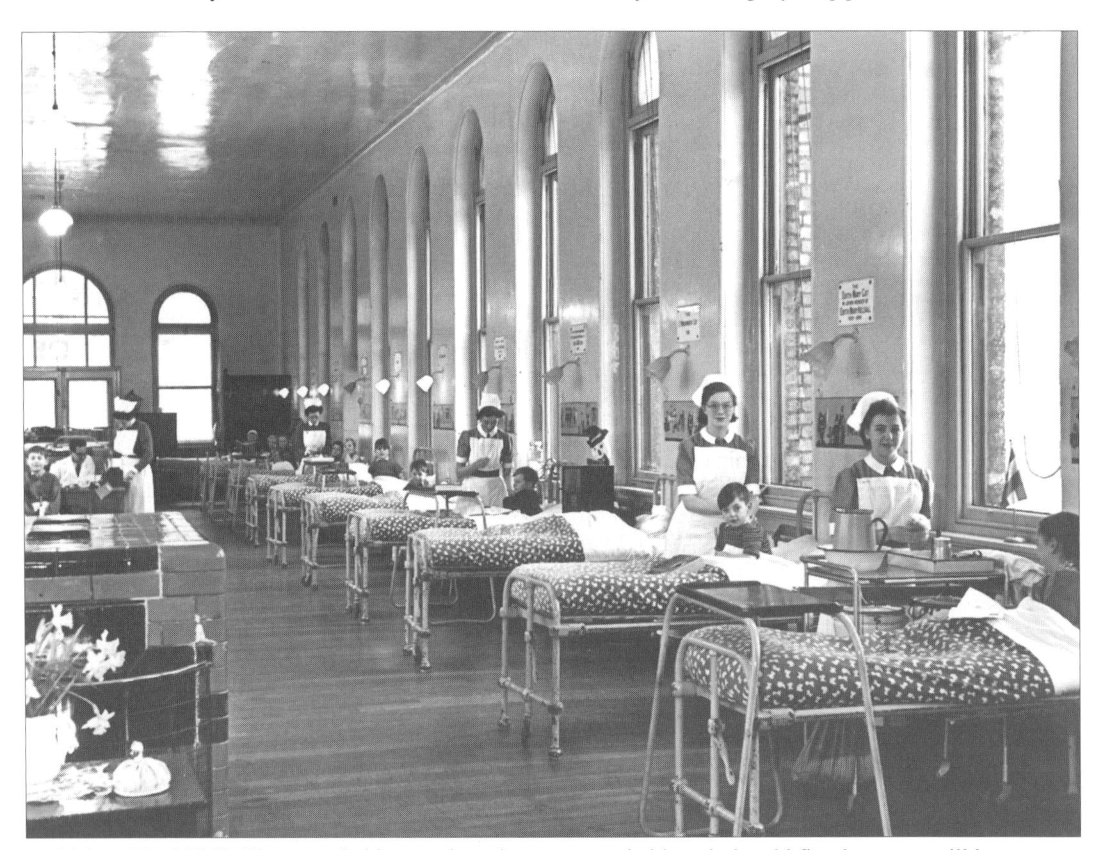

Liebert Ward 1952. The central chimneys have been removed although the old fireplaces can still be seen. The children are all 'tidily' in bed.

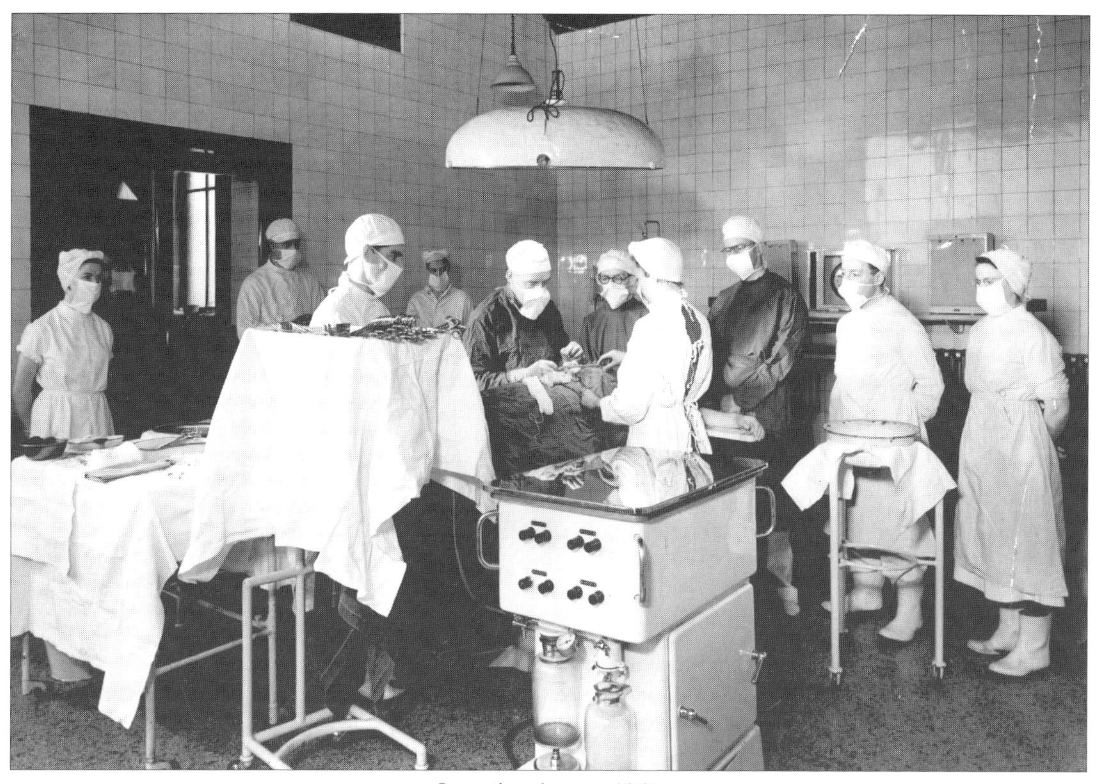

Operating theatres 1951.

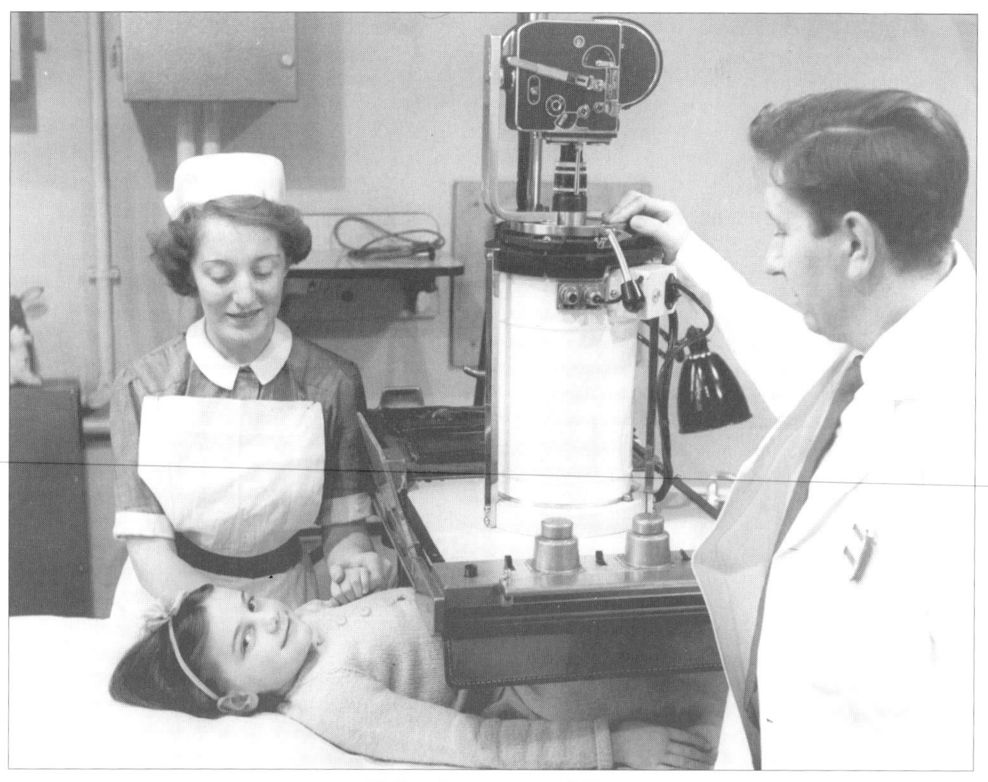

X-Ray Department 1958.

The new Twin Operating Theatres were opened in 1962 by HRH the Princess Royal.

The Agnew Unit, reception area. The Unit was opened by HRH Princess Margaret in 1973. The Unit was named after two former Presidents and benefactors of the Hospital, Sir William Agnew (1893-1910) and his son Sir George W. Agnew (1911-1920).

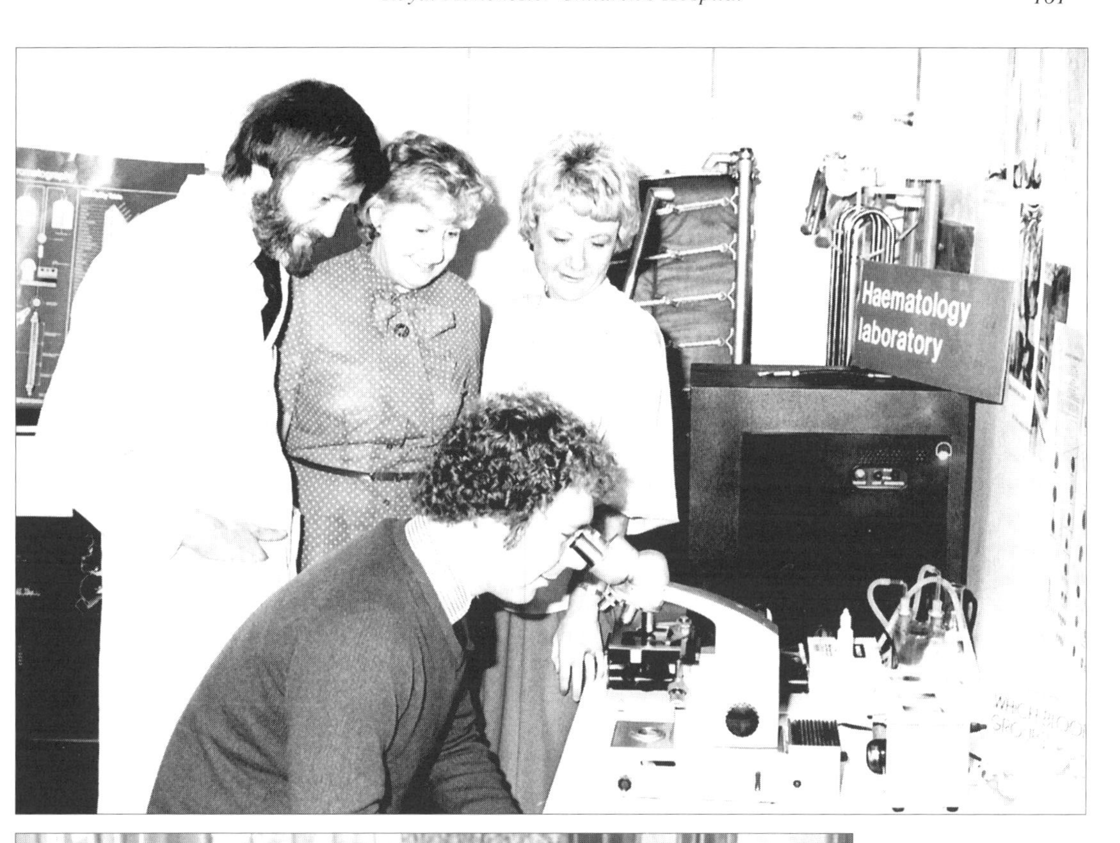

The 150th Anniversary of the Hospital was celebrated in 1979. The Hospital was opened to the public and here visitors are being shown equipment in the haematology laboratory.

Parents through the 1980s and 1990s have increasingly become a part of ward life.

Celebrating 50 years of the National Health Service. The procession from the Children's Trust is seen in the aisle of Manchester Cathedral 5th July 1998. Over 600 people attended the event organised by the Children's Trust.

Members of the Board of the Manchester Children's Hospitals Trust 1999.
L to R, standing: P. Brearley, V-Chairman, A. Burn, A. Larkin, P.A. Barnes
Seated: M. Guymer, R. Howard, Dr A. Sabberwal, Chairman, S. Smalley, R. Goodier

The first Manchester Children's Hospitals NHS Trust Chairman, Mr Tom Lavin, 1995.

A tiny patient from Kuwait with his proud father and the author looking on.

The Gene Shop at Manchester Airport 1997. Mr Stuart Smalley, Chief Executive, Dr A. Sabberwal, Chairman and Dr M. Super, Head of Regional Genetic Services. Genetic information is provided on a drop-in basis.

Dr Hugh T. Ashby

Prof Wilfrid Gaisford

Mr R. Ollerenshaw

Prof.John Davis

Prof. Robert Boyd

Prof. Ian Houston

Dr Aaron Holzel (Later Hon. Prof.)

Prof. Tim David

Prof. Tim Eden

CHAPTER 9
THE MANCHESTER PAEDIATRIC CLUB AND THE FUTURE OF PAEDIATRICS

It has always been a fundamental principle for professionals to group together, to promote an understanding of their own distinctive roles and to share information, in order to move forward. It took a long time in the history of modern medicine before paediatrics was to become a speciality in its own right. Indeed the Manchester Medical Society, which included Salford, took a long time to evolve, even though it was considered to be one of the oldest medical societies in the country.

The Literary and Philosophical Society in Manchester was started in 1781 and was to be the closest to a medical society for many years. Most of the twenty-four members were medical men and early papers were given by medical men. Dr Hull, an obstetrician, called for an association of the medical profession in 1834, at a meeting in Manchester. He envisaged a North of England Society with a library and reading rooms.

The British Paediatric Association claims the distinction of establishing paediatrics as an organised discipline in Britain and was founded in London in 1928 with the objectives of *"the advancement of the study of paediatrics and the promotion of friendship amongst paediatricians."* Before this time, and in many hospitals for a long time after, children were regarded and treated as mini-adults, with very few doctors specialising in their treatment. Dr. C. Paget Lapage of Pendlebury attended the second annual meeting of the British Paediatric Association in Buxton, but it was not until 1948 that paediatricians came together to form their own Manchester Paediatric Club. Many members of this club played an important part in the British Association which received Royal College status in 1996. There were at this time no less than seven Manchester and Salford paediatricians on the BPA Academic Board including Dr Frank Bamford, Professor Robert Boyd, Dr George Komrower, Dr John Dobbing and Dr Pat Morris Jones.

Diseases of childhood were not considered a worthy or even a lucrative aspect of medicine until the early twentieth century. Early pioneers such as Louis Borchardt and Henry Ashby were very influential within the Manchester and Salford areas, and the North West, in promoting the treatment of children as a branch of medicine in its own right. The Society for the Study of Children's Diseases was formed in London in 1900. This was the beginning of recognition by the medical profession of the study of childhood disease in this country.

The Department for the Diseases of Children was only instituted in 1913 in Manchester, well after the death of Henry Ashby. The department was under the direction of Dr C. Paget Lapage. The scope of this department was at this time very limited. Indeed the whole of the UK lagged behind both Germany and the U.S.

The initiation of a children's dispensary in Manchester and Salford in 1829 was through the industry of John Alexander and Walter Barton Stott - but the real development in paediatric medicine came through the enterprise of the two émigrees, Louis Borchardt from Germany and August Schoepf Merei from Hungary. Both had been specialists in children's diseases in their own countries prior to immigrating to Manchester, where their connections with wealthy merchants enabled them to pursue again their medical careers in child health. Merei was to work with James Whitehead, a surgeon at the Manchester Lying In Hospital; Borchardt was to succeed Dr Alexander at the Children's Dispensary. The untimely death of Merei in 1857 left the small children's unit he had founded without any expert in children's diseases, and although it was to continue, it never acquired the status of the Children's Dispensary.

The Children's Dispensary moved forward under the helm of Borchardt. The governors allowed Borchardt a free hand in medical staffing and management of the hospital. This caused problems and there were many quarrels during his twenty-five years of leadership. Yet it seems to have allowed the Children's Hospital to become firmly established, with an excellent reputation and as a centre for paediatric research. In the mid-fifties in the last century there was a new movement in setting up paediatric hospitals. There were many controversial issues surrounding childhood disease at this time, particularly in over-populated areas of industrial cities like Manchester and Salford. The very high mortality rate was not only due to lack of hygiene, and infectious diseases, but there was also the growing concern with 'baby farming' and infanticide. Early paediatrics was a very complex issue of disease and social issues.

Henry Ashby in 1879 took up the mantle of children's medicine and together with George Wright (1851-1920) wrote a combined work on Diseases of Children, which had a world-wide circulation and was still being used in the 1930s.

It was not until 1943 that there was any serious discussion about an Institute and Chair in Child Health, although the Medical School in Manchester had been running since 1874. The University was approached by the Joint Hospitals Advisory Board in Manchester, Salford and Trafford, and a subsequent conference was held in 1944. It was agreed a Chair could be established if the money was raised from outside sources. Donations were agreed amounting to £5,500 per annum over a period of five years; one grant of £1,000 per annum coming from the Royal Manchester Children's Hospital itself.

In November 1946 applications were invited for the Chair of Child Health and in April 1947 Professor W. F. Gaisford was appointed. Another very eminent refugee doctor, Aaron Holzel, was then to join Professor Gaisford in establishing the new academic Department of Paediatrics. He came from Prague, escaping to England after the occupation of Czechoslovakia in 1939, and brought considerable experience in child health. Holzel's interest was particularly in milk allergy, lactose intolerance, and cystic fibrosis. Gaisford's interests were particularly in B.C.G. vaccination, antibiotic delivery and the care of the new born. He is recognised in paediatric circles as the grandfather of paediatric oncology, and with Professor Colin Campbell he founded the Manchester Children's Tumour Registry.

The University Department of Child Health was established in three centres: at Royal Manchester Children's Hospital, Pendlebury; at Booth Hall Children's Hospital, North Manchester, and at St Mary's Hospital on the University site.

St Mary's had begun life as a "Lying in Charity", for the delivery of poor women in their own homes, in 1790. It was renamed St Mary's Hospital in 1854 and moved to Quay Street. Later there were two sites, High Street and Whitworth Street, where they received in-patients - women, and children under the age of 12 who required surgery. By 1928 St Mary's was taking in about 360 children a year and 1,300 babies.

An enormous contribution to child health was also made by the eminent women doctors, Dr Catherine Chisholm, who established the Duchess of York Hospital for Babies in Burnage, and Dr Sylvia Guthrie, who worked mainly at Booth Hall Children's Hospital. Professor Gaisford was able to gather around himself many imaginative appointments that would distinguish Manchester in its research and practice in paediatrics, which in turn would be the foundation for all the paediatric practice and research carried out at the children's hospitals in Manchester and Salford through the years of the National Health Service to today.

The membership of the Manchester Paediatric Club, founded in 1948, was to form the very heart of this aspect of medical science. The number of paediatricians was quite small and membership was limited to those with substantial clinical responsibility. The first President was to be a woman, Dr Chisholm, and the following made up the first membership, of whom five other members were women.

1948 - 1949

PRESIDENT - Dr Catherine Chisholm SECRETARY - Prof. W. Gaisford

TREASURER - Dr W. H. Patterson

EXECUTIVE COMMITTEE: Dr Hugh T. Ashby, Dr Sylvia K. Guthrie, Mr T. S. Heslop, Dr G. Komrower

---

Original Members

ASHBY Dr Hugh T.
BURBURY Dr W. M.
CAVANAGH Dr Florence
CHISHOLM Dr Catherine
DALTON Dr H. W.
EGAN Dr Margaret
FISHER Dr T. Norman
GAISFORD Prof. Wilfrid
GUTHRIE Dr Sylvia K.
HESLOP Mr T. Stewart
HOLZEL Dr A.
KOMROWER Dr G.
LANGLEY Dr F. A.
MACKAY Dr R. I.
PATERSON Dr Edith
PATTERSON Dr W. H.
THOMSON Dr M. L.
WARD Dr J. Forbes
WELLS Dr Nesta A. P.
WOLMAN Dr B.

Additional Members Elected January, 1949

ALLAN Dr J. D.
BURN Dr J. L.
GUTHKELCH Mr A. N.
JENKINS Dr E. M.
KANE Dr Winifred A.

Many of these names are well-known within Pendlebury. Professor Gaisford fought long and hard to achieve a separate paediatric examination in Final MB in Manchester. Dr George Komrower's interest in metabolic disease and biochemical genetics was the foundation for the Willinck Biochemical Genetics Unit, and he was President of the British Paediatric Association in 1979. Dr H.T. Ashby also went on to become President and was at the forefront of every move to improve the care of children in Manchester and Salford. Dr R.I. Mackay became well-known in the field of child assessment, and for his work at the the Agnew Unit, which opened in 1973.

The Section of Paediatrics of the Manchester Medical Society was inaugurated in 1964, when Dr Aaron Holzel was the first president with Dr G. V. Feldman the secretary.

Professor Gaisford held the Foundation Chair at the dawn of the National Health Service. Professor Holzel was awarded a personal Chair in Paediatrics in 1971 in honour of his enormous contribution, and Professor Emeritus on his retirement. Professor John Davis took the Chair in Paediatrics when Professor Gaisford retired after 17 years in 1965. Professor Davis moved to Cambridge in the seventies. Professor Ian Houston was awarded a Chair in Paediatrics in 1974, retiring in 1996. Professor Robert Boyd became Professor in Child Health from 1979 to 1996. At the same time Professor Tim David was awarded a Chair in Paediatrics in 1992 at Booth Hall Hospital and Professor Malcolm Chiswick was awarded an Honorary Chair in Neonatology at the St Mary's site. Further chairs in paediatric disciplines have been held by Professor Basil Marsden in Paediatric Pathology at R.M.C.H. and Professor John Dobbing in Experimental Pathology. A Chair is presently held by Professor "Tim" Eden within the R.M.C.H. and Christie Hospital sites in Paediatric Oncology, and Professor R. Harrington has a Chair in Child and Adolescent Psychiatry at R.M.C.H.

Alongside these prestigious chairs in child health have been many other eminent doctors, physicians and surgeons, pushing back the frontiers in paediatrics. They have enhanced the reputation of paediatrics in Manchester and Salford, and established Manchester University Medical School as a major centre for paediatrics in the region and far beyond.

Several specialist units have honoured staff in their names. The Gaisford teaching Unit was attached to the main corridor at Pendlebury. Almost all of the undergraduate clinical teaching was at Pendlebury at that time. In 1998 the unit was relocated into the central Manchester teaching complex and an extended facility in respiratory and cardiac paediatrics took its place, the Watson-Mann Unit named after Dr Geoffrey Watson (1959-85) and Dr Noel Mann (1970-84). The Jolleys Unit on Victoria Ward is named after Ambrose Jolleys, surgeon (1952-84), the father of paediatric surgery in this Country.

Today the children's services offer a very extensive range of health care on two sites, at Booth Hall Children's Hospital and Royal Manchester Children's Hospital, and links with St Mary's. Advanced teaching and research facilities are available and there are well-developed links with the University of Manchester Medical School. The very specialised areas at Pendlebury and Booth Hall include haematology and oncology, endocrinology, paediatric neurology, inherited metabolic disease and biochemical genetics, to name but a few.

Within the children's surgical services there is outstanding work. They are pre-eminent in the fields of oral surgery, plastic surgery, orthopaedics, cardiology and neurosurgery.

During the last fifty years of the National Health Service, and the Royal Manchester Children's Hospital, there has been an explosion in progress - so much has happened so rapidly that documenting this is a book in itself. The Children' Trust continues to lead these advances.

When the NHS was inaugurated in 1948, the average length of stay for children in hospital was three weeks, and parents were not allowed in except on visiting days - usually once a week for one hour. Nurses tell of the long queues of parents waiting to visit (by ticket only), turned out promptly when their hour was up, to leave wards full of crying children.

With the research carried out by the Robinsons and the committee set up by the Department of Health and chaired by Sir Harry Platt, the Welfare of Children in Hospital was studied and the results published in 1959. This led to an improvement in hospitalisation of children throughout the county and also within the Children's Hospital. Parents were encouraged to stay with their children; a parent accommodation unit was attached to Ashby Ward in 1965 with monies raised by charitable funds, and Action for Sick Children (formerly N.A.W.C.H.), an independent national charity, took up the challenge of implementing the Platt Report. A more enlightened approach with a better understanding of the emotional needs of children was established. The Children's Hospitals of Manchester and Salford now cultivate an informal and unstructured approach to the delivery of health care despite the implementation of new technical requirements.

Now, children spend less than two days in hospital on average, parents are welcome at all times, education is available and most paediatric units have established hospital play programmes for the emotional well-being of their patients. All are supported by specialist paediatric services including physiotherapy, radiology, pharmacy, nutrition and dietetics, and occupational therapy, plus the hospital's own specialist pathology service. With the coming together of the two children's hospitals, Royal Manchester Children's Hospital and Booth Hall Children's Hospital, other specialist services were brought together, including an accident and emergency service for children at Booth Hall.

Within the service now there are many doctors who are specialists in the various fields of paediatric medicine and surgery; many at the forefront of their profession with national and international reputations. One of the many in this category is the exciting metabolic programme. Very recently a Tandem Mass Spectrometer was donated through charitable funding, enabling the screening of all newborn babies within the North West, allowing a rapid diagnosis in inherited metabolic disease. A further aspect in maintaining a reputation as a world leader in paediatrics has been the key role of teaching, research and development. The hospital also contributes to a large teaching programme in paediatrics for medical students and young doctors.

The excellence of the service today and the continuing drive for improvement, are a testimony to the dedication and commitment of all who have served sick children in the hospital over the years. Most are not mentioned here by name but their contribution has been none the less and very many parents and children know the depth of gratitude they hold for their special doctor or nurse.

Many emminent men and women have contributed to the excellence of Pendlebury. None more so than Drs Geoffrey Watson and Noel Mann. The refurbished teaching unit was reopened by Sir Bobby Charlton as the Watson-Mann Unit in 1998. Mrs Mann, Dr Mann's widow, and Dr Watson are seen at the opening.

Dr Alan Shaw at his leaving party in 1998. He was a Consultant Anaesthetist at Pendlebury from 1967. His wife, Alex Susman, seen with him, is a haematology nurse specialist in the oncology department.

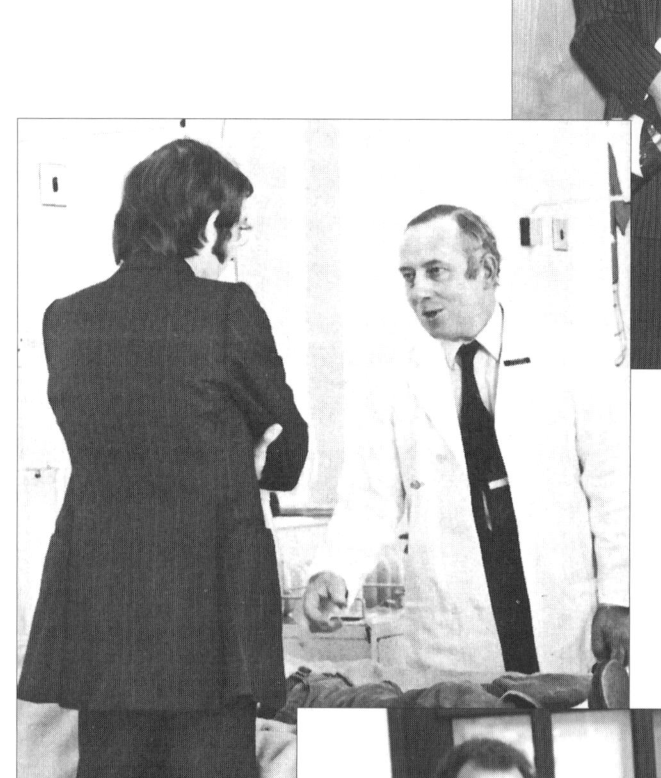

Dr John Davies, who followed Professor Gaisford as Professor of Paediatrics in 1965, is seen here with a young patient's father.

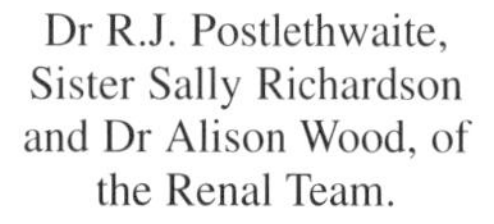

Dr R.J. Postlethwaite, Sister Sally Richardson and Dr Alison Wood, of the Renal Team.

Dr Richard Newton, first Medical Director of the Children's Trust, and a specialist in paediatric neurology.

Dr A Kelsey, Consultant Histopathologist, who became Clinical Director of the Pathology and Radiology Directorate when the new Trust was established in 1995.

Dr Gordon Gladman, cardiologist, and, with Dr Kay Hawkins, Postgraduate Tutor. There is a great emphasis on teaching and research in the Trust, and there are three academic 'chairs' within it.

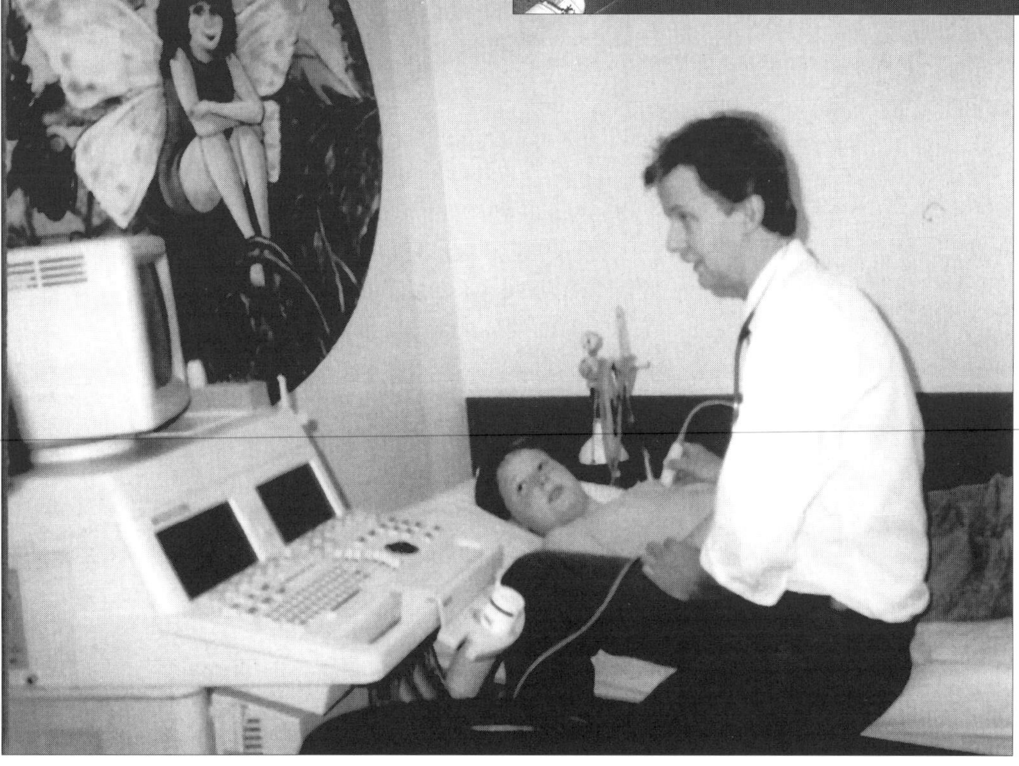

The Royal Manchester Children's Hospital, Pendlebury, and Booth Hall Children's Hospital, came together in April 1995 as the Manchester Children's Hospitals NHS Trust.

CHAPTER 10

COMING TOGETHER - THE CHILDREN'S TRUST
The Royal Manchester Children's Hospital and Booth Hall Children's Hospital
The Fate of the Duchess of York Hospital for Babies - Burnage, Manchester

During the fifty years of the National Health Service, reorganisation has been carried out several times and this has had its effect on the services for children in the Greater Manchester and Salford areas. At one time there were nearly 1000 paediatric beds in the area.

In 1973, the Royal Manchester Children's Hospital was managed by Salford Hospital Management Committee; Booth Hall Children's Hospital and Duchess of York Hospital for Babies was taken on by the Manchester Area Health Authority. Another reorganisation in 1991 led to Booth Hall Children's Hospital being transferred to the management of Salford Health Authority, along with the Royal Manchester Children's Hospital.

When the opportunity to take Trust status in their own right arose, the two children's hospitals applied for this in the new reorganisation. This was granted April 1995, and at last the services for children were once again a discrete entity responsible for their own budget and able to pursue a high level of care without interference from adult services.

A very short history of both Booth Hall Children's Hospital and the Duchess of York Hospital for Babies will be addressed in this chapter.

BOOTH HALL CHILDREN'S HOSPITAL

The history of Booth Hall Children's Hospital is very different from that of Pendlebury. The hospital is on the site of Booth Hall, built by Humphrey Booth in the early 1600s, and situated about four miles north of Manchester. The original house was demolished in 1907 and the new hospital built in 1908.

The New Booth Hall Infirmary of the Prestwich Poor Law Union was built on 34 acres of ground overlooking Boggart Hole Clough. It cost £70,000 and provided beds for 750 patients. The hospital continued to care for the poor of the Prestwich Union until the outbreak of war in 1914. Then the Prestwich Poor Law Unions and the Manchester Board of Guardians combined to create a separate Children's Hospital in 1915.

Manchester Corporation appropriated Booth Hall Children's Hospital in 1931 and it remained, together with Monsall and Crumpsall, directly responsible to the Department of Health, via the Medical Officer, until the advent of the National Health Service.

The hospital in 1929 contained 750 beds for children (97th Annual Meeting British Medical Association, July 1929), of which 204 were 'open-air beds'. There were separate beds in cubicles into which all newly-admitted patients were placed for a period of quarantine. Booth Hall was the first hospital in the north of England to install sunlight treatment for orthopaedic cases, and milk was supplied from their own farm near Blackburn, which practically eliminated outbreaks of gastro-enteritis in the infant wards.

Booth Hall, before the National Health Service, treated such diseases as tuberculosis, bronchitis, measles, chicken pox, whooping cough, scabies and ringworm. Booth Hall Children's Hospital admitted children of the very poor many of whom were hospitalised for long periods of time, frequently up to ten weeks or more. An interesting difference at the time between here and the Children's Hospital, was the way in which children undergoing tonsillectomies were treated. At Pendlebury, almost all the children were treated in the outpatient department, and discharged an hour or two after surgery; Booth Hall, on the other hand, offered tonsillectomy with a three day stay in hospital, at the price of one guinea.

A separate unit for the treatment of children with burns and scalds was opened in 1953, and was the first of its kind in the country. Another area in which Booth Hall was to lead,as early as 1952, was in the increase in visiting hours for parents of sick children. Visiting was allowed every day for one hour, and if a child was seriously ill, for two hours daily. It was not until the pressures from parent groups such as Action for Sick Children (N.A.W.C.H.) in the 1960s that other hospitals for children moved in this same direction.

Booth Hall has played a major part in the development of health care services for children in Greater Manchester and the North West. Perhaps one of the greatest contributions has been the demonstration of the appropriateness of designated accident and emergency services for children.

Many larger than life personalities have added to the history of Booth Hall over the years. Dr W. H. Patterson's long association in charge of the hospital was of great significance in the development of paediatric services, as was Professor Aaron Holzel's influence. Other names include Mr Ambrose Jolleys (who also worked at R.M.C.H.), Mr Frank Robinson, plastic surgeon, and Dr N. S. Gordon, the neurologist. Mr Jolley is considered by many to be the first truly paediatric surgeon here in Manchester and Salford. And a history of Booth Hall would be incomplete without mention of Miss Huck, a very formidable matron who retired in 1956. Her personality made her a character in her own right.

Dr Basil Wolman was also an inaugural member of the Paediatric Club and very well known for his paediatric practice in Booth Hall. Alderman Onions completed 21 years of service as Chairman of Booth Hall and Monsall Hospitals upon his retirement in 1969.

Five other characters that must be mentioned are the 'ponies'. Two ponies, Jack and Jill, who had drawn Cinderella's coach at the Palace Theatre, Manchester in 1946, were given to Booth Hall Hospital to give rides to the children. However, when Jill gave birth to a foal named Ginger, Jack was so jealous that the partnership broke up. Jill and Ginger continued the rides for children in the wagonette. When they came to pensioning off, two palomino ponies, Brandy and Bubbles, another gift to the hospital, took the place of Jill (aged 30) and Ginger (aged 23) in 1969. Unfortunately, a fire in the stables in March 1971 caused the death of the ponies and this loss ended the children's pony rides.

Booth Hall was in the forefront of nurse training, providing the approved training for Registered Sick Children's Nurses (R.S.C.N.) It was an approved centre for children's probationer nurse training as far back as 1929.

Booth Hall open air pavilions, built to accommodate 200 children, were opened by HRH Princess Mary in 1927.
Each child was in a separate open air cubicle.

King George VI and Queen Elizabeth visiting Booth Hall Children's Hospital in 1941.

Princess Michael of Kent opening the Renal Dialysis Unit at Booth Hall in 1980.

The Princess Royal visited Booth Hall in 1989 and opened the new Paediatric Intensive Care Unit. She is seen with the Unit General Manager, Alyson Jones.

Ward 12 Booth Hall Children's Hospital 1928 (Courtesy Mrs Winterbottom).

Annual Nurses' Sports Day at Booth Hall Children's Hospital in the 1930s.

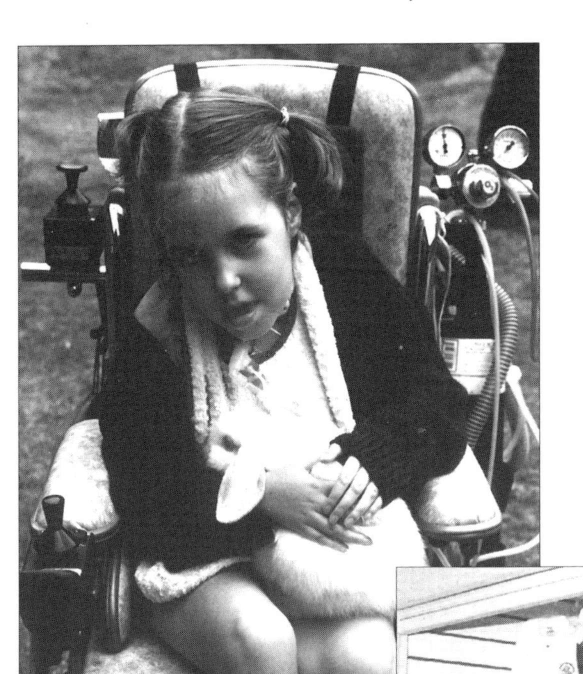

Transitional care at Booth Hall Children's Hospital. This is a new approach to care between hospital and home.
Amanda with the ward's pet rabbit.

Booby Bear's Gift Shop at Booth Hall Children's Hospital.
The Paediatric Intensive Care Unit, the Accident and Emergency Unit, and the new Out-Patients department, have all been built with money raised by charities.

A gardener at Booth Hall. The gardens at Pendlebury and Booth Hall have always been an important part of the hospital environment.

Ponies Jill and her son Ginger gave endless entertainment to children at Booth Hall.

THE DUCHESS OF YORK HOSPITAL FOR BABIES

This was the youngest of all the Manchester hospitals. Medical women in Manchester were anxious to provide more treatment for small infants than was available, and wished to set up a small hospital of 12 beds. This they did in 1914 in Chorlton-on-Medlock with the encouragement of Margaret Ashton, Chairman of the Maternity and Child Welfare Group. Here they opened 12 cots. The following year, 1915, the hospital moved to Slade Lane in Levenshulme where 30 cots were established. In 1920 they removed to Cringle Hall, the Burnage site where there were 50 cots.

The first Resident Medical Officer was a Dr Dorothea Baird. But the real driving force behind the Duchess of York Hospital for Babies was Dr Catherine Chisholm, Manchester's first woman graduate in medicine in 1904. She was a brilliant student but was unable to obtain a post in a hospital in Manchester, so she worked in London for some years, returning to Manchester as a G.P. She had a particular interest in the problems of nutrition in babies and she studied rickets in children aged less than two years. Dr Duncan Macaulay, himself a notable paediatrician, said of Dr Chisholm *"Whose energy, vision and determination created the Hospital, sustained it through two world wars and a prolonged economic depression, and handed it with a great reputation to the National Health Service"*. During the Second World War Dr Chisholm evacuated the hospital to Calderstones, except for 17 infants too ill to move. The hospital suffered minor damage but a Mr McCrea FRCS, a surgeon there since 1923, and who also worked at Pendlebury, was sadly killed in an air raid.

Dr Chisholm retired in 1947 and died in 1952. At this time there were over 1,000 admissions per year and the hospital was recognised as a training school for the Register of Sick Children's Nurses in association with Booth Hall Children's Hospital. The name of the hospital was changed from Manchester Babies' Hospital to Duchess of York Hospital for

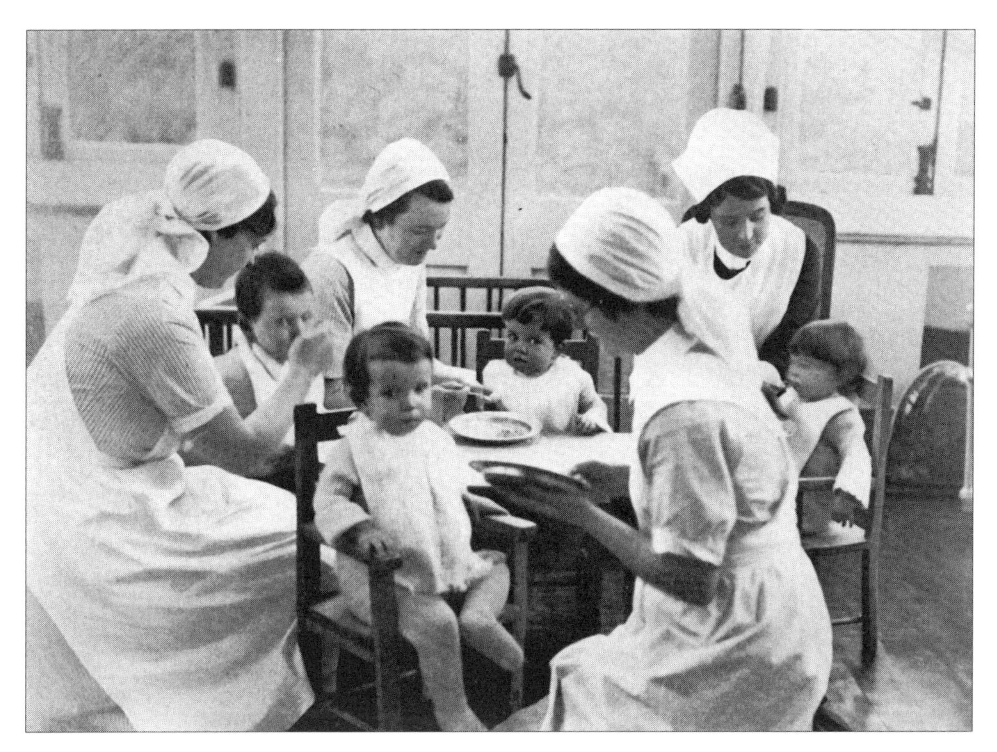

Nurses and patients at the Duchess of York Hospital. One of the earliest child centred environments with child-sized furniture.

Babies in 1935 after a visit by HRH The Duchess of York, now HRH Queen Elizabeth, The Queen Mother.

During the 1980s the Management Committee from South Manchester Health Authority felt that the hospital in its present form was no longer viable as a stand-alone unit, and a new unit for children with 60 beds was attached to the Withington Hospital. The Cringle Hall site was closed. This new unit, still under the name of the Duchess of York Hospital, has continued to provide a valuable service for children and remains part of the paediatric training for both doctors and nurses.

Within the Greater Manchester area, all three children's hospitals, together with the Unit at St Mary's Hospital, have had a great influence on paediatrics nationally and internationally. Paediatricians from these four institutions have maintained a high profile and together with the University given paediatrics here a high reputation within the medical world. Alongside this progress for doctors was the very large role all the units played in promoting a high quality nurse training for sick children.

Dr Catherine Chisholm, the first President of Manchester Paediatric Club and founder of the Duchess of York Hospital for Babies. She was the first woman to be accepted as a medical student at the University of Manchester.

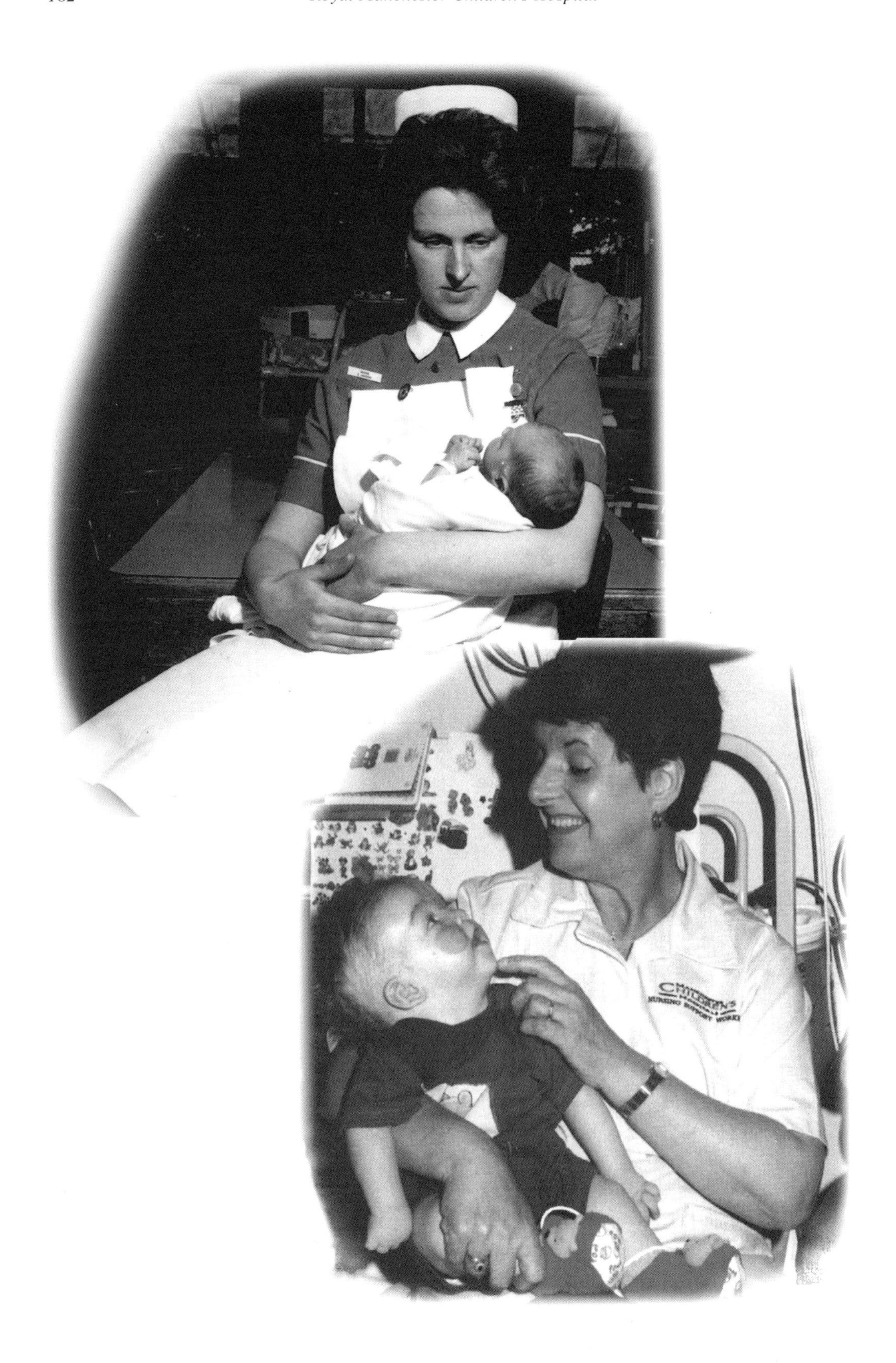
CHILDREN'S

CHAPTER 11

LOOKING BACK - LOOKING FORWARD

THE OBJECTS OF THE INSTITUTION ARE :

1. **The Medical and Surgical Treatment of Poor Children.**
2. **The Attainment and Diffusion of Knowledge Regarding the Diseases of Children.**
3. **The Training of Nurses.** 1946

Our mission statement will remain foremost in our minds:

Together we will provide the
best possible healthcare
for children 1999

Much wonderful work has gone on within the walls of the two hospitals which now form the Children's Trust, although I have concentrated on the Royal Manchester Children's Hospital, the oldest paediatric establishment in the Country. A history of Booth Hall Children's Hospital is available elsewhere.

The details of advances in medical technology are beyond this history, particularly over the last fifty years, with paediatrics very much to the forefront. The importance of paediatrics was underlined with the granting of the charter to the Royal College of Paediatrics in 1996 and many of the staff at the Royal Manchester Children's Hospital have helped to create the present advanced care available to children.

The overwhelming problems of poor housing, lack of hygiene, poverty and illness for children, seen at the beginning of this history, have been reformed. The hospital has changed from a charitable institution for the *"worthy sick poor"* into an all purpose medical establishment. So, too, has changed the way in which families view their children's hospitals.

Perhaps the most important advances in paediatrics have been the advent of immunisation and antiseptic surgery, and later from just before the Second World War, and increasingly from the late 40s onwards, the discovery of antibiotics. Today, parents want their children with any serious illness to go to 'their' hospital, - 'the hospital that cures their child'.

The history of the Royal Manchester Children's Hospital mirrors and follows developments in other western countries. The first book on paediatrics was published in 1765 in Germany. The first survey on childhood diseases in English came in 1784 written by Michael Underwood. Slowly and laboriously the path of children's medicine was carved out. With discoveries in science came advances in the treatment of disease and alongside these progress in nursing. But paediatric progress is not merely a matter of impersonal scientific advances, it is a story of human endeavour. Gone now are the days when the patients stayed in bed, wearing their scarlet or blue bed jackets. Gone too are the days of prescribed visiting times. Today the ward patterns reflect the needs of families and their sick children.

Glancing back, one's mind is caught by the vision of so many who had the tenacity to continue in the face of public indifference, and alongside the ever present necessity for funding, to cure sick children in pioneering times. They cannot be too highly commended.

By the outbreak of the Second World War the hospital was a thriving, bustling institution. There were 322 beds within the hospital, and there was the Zachary Merton Home and the seaside home at Lytham St Annes. Patients remained for an average of 19 days, with 2300 admissions and over 1,300 operations. There was a large ear, nose and throat department, a dental department, X-ray department, pathology department, massage, gymnastic department and artificial sunlight (physiotherapy), speech clinic and psychology clinic. The first almoner, Miss R. R. Turner, was appointed in 1941, the beginning of the Social Work Department.

The developments post-war and during the last fifty years have been dramatic. The Hospital, with its sister hospital Booth Hall, remains a centre of excellence in paediatrics in the North West. Important links with the University provide the structure for research, development and training. The Hospital is divided into directorates which include many paediatric specialities within the North West region. The Hospital houses a Research Centre, which is one of the finest in the UK, with research in haematology and oncology, child and adolescent psychiatry, nephrology, endocrinology, gastroenterology, paediatric neurology, inherited metabolic disease and biochemical genetics, as well as in nursing, remedial therapies and meeting parents' needs.

So to the future - what does the future hold for paediatric services in Manchester and Salford? No doubt there will be change. It has already been agreed that because of the very nature of specialisation within paediatrics there needs to be services for children available in their own community and in their local district general hospital, but with a specialist hospital available for paediatric intensive care and other specialist services for children and young people. This hospital, and its sister hospital Booth Hall, are to be relocated. It was nearly fifty years from the opening of the first tiny dispensary for children to the new and exciting building in 1873 at Pendlebury. Now, in 1999, it is planned to move into a new 'build', linked to the long established Royal Infirmary of Manchester dating back to 1752.

The services for children will continue to develop over the years to come but in moving to its new location it is important that none of its hard won ethos is lost. Whatever the dramas of paediatric progress in the future, it should not be forgotten that the Manchester Children's Services story all began in an ordinary house at 25 Back King Street on 14th January 1829. The future for children who are sick will be brighter and full of optimism because of the many who have had faith enough to make our children their main priority, in the past, in the present and in the future.

133 Artist's impression of the new hospital

A&E	Dr.L.P.Duane	Otolaryngology	Mr. M.P. Rothera		Dr. M.J. Newbould
Paediatrics	Dr. E.M. Baildam		Mr. D.J. Willatt	Med. Microbiology	Dr. D. Sanyal
	Dr. M. Bradbury		Mr. A.P. Zarod	Radiology	Dr. B. Barry (Paed)
	Dr. A.N. Campbell	Traumatic and	Mr. J.B. Day		Dr. D. Hughes
	Dr. R.H.A. Campbell	Orthopaedic Surgery	Prof C.S.B Galasko (Hon)		(Neuroradiologist)
	Dr. M.A. Cleary		Mr. P.R. Kay		Dr. Sinclair Forbes
	Dr. P.E. Clayton (Hon)		Mr. T.H. Meadows		
	Dr. J.M. Couriel		Mr. J.B. Williamson	(Neuroradiologist)	
	Prof T.J. David (Hon)		Mr. I. Trail		Dr. I.W. Turnbull
	Dr. S. Davidson	Ophthalmology	Mrs. J.L. Noble		
	Dr. C.I. Ewing	Urology	Mr. K.J. 0'Flynn	(Neuroradiologist)	
	Dr. H. Jaques	Plastic Surgery	Mr. P.J Davenport		Dr. J.M. Weller
	Dr. G. Hambleton		Mr. K.W. Dunn		(Neuroradiologist)
	Dr. M.A. Lewis	Cardio-thoracic Surgery	Mr. R.A.M. Lawson		Dr. B.P.M.Wilson (Paed)
	Dr I.A. McKinlay (Hon)	Neurosurgery	Miss. C.M. Bannister		Dr. N.B. Wright (Paed)
	Dr. V. Miller		Mr. R.A. Cowie	Anaesthetics	Dr. P Ashford
	Dr. L.R. Patel (Hon)		Mr. J.R.S Leggate		Dr. M. Baxandall
	Dr. R.J. Postlethwaite		Mr. A. Sofat		Dr. O.R. Dearlove
	Dr. D.A. Price (Hon)		Mr. G.C. Victoratos		Dr. A.G. Griffiths
	Dr. M.J. Robinson		Mr. C.G.H. West		Dr. W.D. Lord
	Dr. H.C. Smith	Paediatric Neurology	Dr. M.A. Clarke		Dr. G.H. Meakin (Hon)
	Dr. A.G. Thomas		Dr. R.W. Newton		Dr. T. Montague
	Dr. J.H. Walter		Dr. I. Hughes		Dr. D. Patel
	Dr. N.J.A. Webb		Dr. T.R. Martland		Dr. R. Perkins
	Dr. J.E. Wraith		Dr. P.1. Tomlin		Dr. A. Razak
Cardiology	Dr. E.J. Ladusans	Child/Adolescent Psychiatry	Dr. D. Firth		Dr. D. N. Robinson
	Dr. R.J. Patel (Paed)		Dr. J.M. Green (Hon)		Dr. A. Sharples
	Dr. G. Gladman		Prof R.C.Harrington (Hon)		Dr. R.W.M. Walker
Rheumatology	Dr. A.L. Herrick (Hon)		Dr. H. Lloyd		Dr. Y.Y Youssef
Medical Oncology	Dr. B.M.D. Brennan		Dr. A. Thapar (Hon)	Paed. Intensive Care	Dr. D. Stewart
	Prof 0.B. Eden		Dr. M. Kelsall		Dr. R.W. Yates
	Dr. L.S. Lashford (Hon)	Oral Surgery	Mr. I.D. Campbell		Dr. K. Hawkins
Clinical Genetics	Dr. D. Donnai		Mr. R.E. Lloyd		
	Prof R. Harris (Hon)		Mr. P.R. White	ASSOCIATE SPECIALISTS	
	Dr. B.A. Kerr	Orthodontics	Mr. J. Brady	Otolaryngology	Dr. M.H. Fathy
	Dr M. Super		Mr. W.H.J.P. Bogues	Mental Illness	Dr. E. Jones
General Surgery	Mr. R.W.G. Johnson		Mr. M.J.F. Read	(Forensic and Ch. Adol., Paed. Oncol.)	
(Major interest in Renal Transplantation)			Prof W.C. Shaw (Hon)	Oral Surgery	Mr. G.G. Ball
Paediatric Surgery	Mr. A. Bianchi	Chemical Pathology	Dr. G.M. Addison		
	Mr. J.C. Bowen	Haematology	Dr. R.J. Stevens		
	Mr J. Bruce		Dr. A.M. Will		
	Mr. A.P. Dickson		Dr. R. F. Wynn		
	Miss. C.M. Doig (Hon)	Histopathology	Dr. A.M. Kelsey		
	Mr. D.C.S. Gough		Dr. L. Moore		

LIST OF CONSULTANTS OF THE CHILDREN'S TRUST, 1998

Clinical Directorates

Medical Directorate

Clinical Director – Dr. John Walter
Service Manager – Mrs Joanne Shaw

Our Medical Directorate provides a wide range of services across both our hospitals. These include:

Ambulatory Paediatrics - this service aims to reduce the number of children who require admission to hospital and provides continuity of care in the home environment
Bone Marrow Transplantation - we are one of the top three centres in the U.K.
Cardiology and Cardiac Surgery
Cardiothoracic Surgery
Child and Adolescent Psychiatry
Child Protection and Social Paediatrics
Clinical Psychology
Cystic Fibrosis
Dermatology including Atopic Eczema
Developmental Paediatrics
Diabetes
Emergency Medicine
Endocrinology and Growth Disorders
Gastroenterology
General Paediatrics
Genetics:

- Biochemical: this provides pre and postnatal diagnosis and treatment for inherited metabolic disease
- Clinical: this provides accurate diagnosis both pre and postnatally of genetic disorders such as Cystic Fibrosis

Pathology and Radiology Directorate

Clinical Director – Dr. Anna Kelsey
Service Manager – Mr Alan Milford

Our Pathology and Radiology Directorate provides specialist paediatric diagnostic services including:

Chemical Pathology
Haematology and Blood Transfusion
Histopathology
Microbiology
Radiological Imaging

Haematology and Haemophilia – our Haemophilia Centre is the second largest in the U.K.
High Dependency Care
Intensive Care – we have one of the largest specialist intensive care centres in the U.K.
Neurology
Oncology – we are a renown Cancer Centre and the third largest paediatric centre in the U.K.
Respiratory Medicine
Rheumatology
Transitional Care Unit – this unit looks after children who require long term specialist care before moving into a more natural setting either at home or in the community.

Surgical Directorate

Clinical Director – Mr. James Bruce
Service Manager – Mrs Freda Williams

Our Surgical Directorate also provides a wide range of services across both our hospitals. These include:

Anaesthesia
Burns – a specialist service supported by a specialist Plastic Surgery Service and an After Burns Clinic
Dental Specialties comprising:

- Dentistry
- Oral and Maxillo-Facial Surgery
- Orthodontics

Ear, Nose and Throat Surgery
Neonatal Surgery – surgery on children one month old and under
Nephrology – including Renal Transplantation
Neurosurgery
Ophthalmology
Orthopaedics and Trauma – this includes specialist surgery or rare and complex conditions such as curvature of the spine and other complex spinal abnormalities
Plastic Surgery – includes Cleft Lip and Palate Surgery
Urology.

Professions Allied to Medicine

Clinical Director – Mr. John Lockwood
Service Manager – Mrs Linda Thompson

Our Directorate of Professions Allied to Medicine provides therapeutic services to our patients including:

Audiology
Chiropody
Medical Illustrations
Nutrition and Dietetics
Occupational Therapy
Pharmaceutical Services
Physiotherapy
Speech and Language Therapy

Freda Williams, Services Manager for the Surgical Directorate, with, below, a nurse and patient in the Directorate.

Manchester Children's Hospitals NHS Trust **1996/97 Activity**

Purchaser	Elective	mergency	Day Case	New	Follow up
BOLTON & WIGAN	593	750	793	841	3666
BURY & ROCHDALE	536	2258	996	1996	7882
CALDERDALE AND KIRLEES	18	29	10	21	99
CHESHIRE NORTH	15	18	23	39	153
CHESHIRE SOUTH	74	152	286	51	400
EAST LANCS	352	342	580	246	1567
ECR	108	140	90	104	429
GPFH	1678	28	717	4424	16059
MANCHESTER	1088	3760	1461	4311	12503
MORECAMBE BAY	135	92	200	64	383
NORTH DERBYSHIRE	27	46	84	8	56
NORTH WEST LANCS	196	181	431	100	658
OVERSEAS/PRIVATE	14	14	4	13	23
PRIVATE	52	9	43	19	64
REGIONAL HEALTH AUTHORITY					27
SALFORD & TRAFFORD	1203	3459	1072	4279	12394
SOUTH LANCS	112	124	338	76	410
STOCKPORT	158	339	383	135	869
WEST PENNINE	667	1096	903	1166	5287
	7026	**12837**	**8414**	**1166**	**5287**

APPENDIX 1: MILESTONES AT A GLANCE

1828	Meeting to investigate setting up of a Dispensary for children.
1829	General Dispensary for Children opened at 25 Back King St (Ridgefield).
1829	Daniel Grant donated £42 to the new Dispensary for Children.
1832	Outbreak of cholera - implications for service.
1850	Dispensary moved to North Parade.
1853	Dr Merei opened second Dispensary for Children in Stevenson Square, with 2 beds.
1854	Ragged & Industrious School opens in Salford.
1853	Dr Louis Borchardt appointed to Dispensary for Children (6 beds opened).
1857	Death of Dr Merei. Service moved to Cheetham.
1858	Dispensary for Children moved to 16 Bridge Street.
1868	First Medical Officer in Manchester.
1868	Out Patient Department in Gartside Street opened near to Dispensary for Children.
1870	Purchase of 6 acres of land in Pendlebury.
1873	Opening of new hospital at Pendlebury, with 3 wards and 80 beds.
1875	Grand Bazaar at Free Trade Hall. Building completed to 6 wards.
1877	Grace Neill appointed Lady Superintendent.
1879	Borchardt Ward named after Dr Borchardt, who had completed 25 years of service.
1879	Letter of congratulations on the hospital from Florence Nightingale.
1879	Dr Henry Ashby appointed Hon. Physician.
1883	Death of Dr Borchardt.
1889	Dr Henry Ashby and G A Wright published '*Diseases in Children*'.
1890	Nurse Training programme in place.
1897	Convalescent Home at St Annes, built by Sir William Agnew at his own expense.
1904	David Lewis Manchester Epileptic Colony opened.
1906	Verandah erected outside Holden Ward for open air treatments.
1907	Gartside St Outpatients Hospital rebuilt with monies from estate of Godfrey Ermen.
	Death of Dr Henry Ashby. His son, Dr Hugh T Ashby at Gartside Street.
1911	National Insurance Act.
1914	Outbreak of First World War. Members of staff enrolled for military duties.
	Duchess of York Hospital for Babies opened in Chorlton.
1915	First Physiotherapist employed at RMCH.
	Booth Hall opened as a children's hospital.
1918	First World War ends.
1919	Founding of the General Nursing Council.
1920	Duchess of York Hospital moves to Burnage.
1922	General Nursing Council's approval of Nurse Training Courses at Pendlebury.
1923	Royal Charter granted - becomes the Royal Manchester Children's Hospital.
1924	Colwyn House opened as a new Nurses' Home.
1927	Miss Annie Sommerfield appointed as pathologist.
1928	Discovery of Penicillin. Vitimin C isolated.
1929	Centenary of the Hospital.
1930	Wall Street Crash and world wide depression. Purchase of the 5 acre wood estate.
1935	Delayed Centenary celebrations. Centenary Book published. Typhoid outbreak.
1936	Zachery Merton Convalescent Home built. Iron gates and lodge erected.
1938	Commencement of neurosurgery. Appointment of Mr G F Rowbotham.
	Introduction of speech therapy and child psychiatry. Clinic for psychology.

1938/9	Mr R Ollerenshaw, President orthopaedic section of the Royal Society of Medicine.
1939	Outbreak of Second World War.
1940	Hospital damaged by bombing. Penicillin developed as antibiotic.
1941	Social Work commenced.
1942	William Beveridge Report.
1945	End of Second World War.
1946	Formation of the League of Friends.
1947	First Chair in Paediatrics in Manchester - Professor Wilfrid Gaisford at RMCH.
1948	World Health Organisation founded. Formation of Manchester Paediatric Club.
1949	Daily visiting for one hour introduced. Introduction of penicillin and streptomycin.
1957	Miss J I Jackson appointed Senior Nursing Officer.
1959	Publication of Platt Report on Welfare of Children in Hospital.
1962	HRH Princess Mary, Princess Royal opens new operating theatres.
1963	New pharmacy.
1964	Paediatrics invited into Manchester Medical Society.
1965	Opening of Mother & Child units at RMCH.
1970	Closure of St Anne's Convalescent Home.
1973	Agnew Unit opened by HRH Princess Margaret, Countess of Snowdon.
1976	Publication of Court Report.
1983	Wallness Gamma Camera Unit opened by HRH Duchess of Gloucester.
1990	Welfare of Children & Young People in Hospital published by HMSO.
1991	Closure of Gartside Street Outpatients Dept. Transferred to Colwyn House.
	RMCH and Booth Hall come under single management.
1995	Manchester Children's Hospital NHS Trust created.
	HRH Duchess of Kent opens Magnetic Resonnance Scanner.
1996	British Paediatric Association becomes a Royal College.
	Gene Shop opens at Manchester Airport, through the European Funding Initiative.
1997	Play Services Department open a Computer Club for patients.
	Children's inter-hospital bus service commences.
1998	Celebrations to mark the 50th Anniversary of the National Health Service.
	Opening of Transitional Care Unit, Watson Mann Unit and new operating theatre.

APPENDIX 2 HISTORY OF EPONYMOUS DEPARTMENTS

ASHBY WARD	Named in 1947 to commemorate the unbroken association with the hospital of Dr Hugh T. Ashby, Honorary Physician, and his father, Dr Henry Ashby, for over 65 years.
SILLAVAN WARD	Named in 1947 after James Sillavan for 25 years a member of the Board of Governors. Past Chairman and Honorary Secretary to the Board 1927-1947.

Ashby and Sillavan wards were originally the dormitories in the Zachary Merton Convalescent Home built by generous donation of the Trustees of Zachary Merton Estate in 1936. The Nurse Training School was also here until 1947.

BORCHARDT WARD	Named after Dr Louis Borchardt, Honorary Physician 1854-1883.
VICTORIA WARD	Originally the Nurses' Home. It was altered to a medical ward in 1902 and named in memory of the late Queen Victoria.
HOLDEN WARD	Originally named South Ward. This was altered in 1899 after the receipt of £10,000 from the trustees of the late James Holden of Rochdale. Now no longer extant. Used as High Dependency Unit.
WRIGLEY WARD	Originally named North Ward. This was altered to Wrigley in 1881 after a bequest of £10,000 from the late Thomas Wrigley of Bury.
HEYWOOD WARD	Named after Oliver Heywood, a Vice-President of the hospital from 1860 until 1865, and President from 1865 until his death in 1892.
LIEBERT WARD	Named after Bernhard Liebert who gave £3,000 to the building fund in 1872.
STANCLIFFE WARD	F. S. Stancliffe was a member of the Board of Governors 1929-1947, Chairman of the Dispensary Committee 1936, and Chairman of the Board 1943-47. Opened in 1937 and extended in 1974. No longer used for clinical practice. Occupied by National Children's Tumour Registry.
WILLINK UNIT	Named after Mr F. A. Willink, a member of the Board of Governors in 1947 and later Chairman of the Hospital Management Committee.
AGNEW UNIT	No longer present - subsumed within Mackay-Gordon Centre. Father and son, Sir William and Sir George Agnew Bt., were Presidents of the hospital in succession from 1893 to 1920: Father 1893-1911, Son 1911-1920. Sir William Agnew built at his own expense the convalescent home at Lytham St Annes which closed in 1970.
MACKAY-GORDON CENTRE	Dr "Bob" Mackay, Paediatrician, and Dr Neil Gordon, Paediatric Neurologist, consultants to the hospital 1950s-1970s.
WATSON-MANN UNIT	Dr Geoffrey Watson, Paediatrician/Cardiologist 1959-1985. Dr Noel Mann, Paediatrician/Respiratory Disorders (CF) 1970-1984.
JOLLEYS UNIT	On Victoria Ward Ambrose Jolleys, Surgeon 1952-1984, ex-President of British Association of Paediatric Surgeons.
KOMROWER METABOLIC UNIT	On Ashby Ward Dr George Komrower early worker in inherited metabolic disorders. Ex-President of British Paediatric Association. Consultant Paediatrician 1950-1974.
GAISFORD TEACHING UNIT	Wilfred Gaisford, first Professor in Child Health at University of Manchester 1947-1968. Founder of Manchester Paediatric Club now merged with Paediatric Section, Manchester Medical Society.
JAFFE RENAL UNIT	Dr Joe Jaffe, local G.P. - charitable work with Wallness organisation for support to children's renal services.
LEDBROOKE HOUSE	Named after Samuel Ledbrooke, a local solicitor. He was Chairman of the Hospital League of Friends for many years in the 1970s/80s.
WALLNESS OUT-PATIENTS	Wallness Road, Salford. Charitable group supporting renal services for over 25 years. This building, previously the Colwyn Nurses' Home, named after Lord Colwyn, President of the Hospital 1921-1946.

APPENDIX 3: BIBLIOGRAPHY AND REFERENCES

Annual General Report 1997 — Thomas Coram Foundation
Boomtown Manchester 1800-1850 — A Brookes & Bryan Haworth — Portico Library 1993
The Story of Booth Hall Hospital — R. Hargreaves — Ross Anderson Pub. 1987
The British Paediatric Association 1928-1988 J O Forfar, A Jackson, B Laurence Land & Unwin 1989
The British Paediatric Association 1928-1952 H C Cameron — Metcalfe & Cooper 1955
British Paediatric Association 1952-1968 Victor Neale — Pitman 1970
Bye Laws — The Royal Manchester Children's Hospital Annual Reports
Cambridge Illustrated History of Medicine — ed. Roy Porter — CUP 1996
Care of Young Babies — J Gibbons — Churchill 1940
A Centre of Intelligence — C Field & J Pickstone — John Rylands Library 1992
Centuries of Childhood — P Aries — Pimlico 1960
Child Care and the Growth of Love — John Bowlby — Penguin 1952
Children and Industry — M Cruikshank — Manchester UP 1981
Children in Hospital — R Landsdown — Oxford Medical 1996
Diseases of Children — H Ashby & G A Wright — Longmans 1899
Grace Neill the Story of of a Noble Woman JOC Neill — N M Peryen NZ 1961
Hospital Centenary Gift Book — R Ollerenshaw — Harrap 1935
A History of Lancashire — J J Bagley — Phillimore 1982
The Life and Times of a Voluntary Hospital — H G Calwell — Brough Cox,Dun Belfast 1973
Manchester, this Good Old Town — A Brookes & Bryan Haworth — Carnegie 1997
Manchester — A Kidd — Keele UP 1993
Royal Manchester School of Nursing — Prospectus 1970
Some Manchester Doctors — WJ Elwood & AF Tuxford — Manchester UP 1984
Manchester in the Victorian Age — G S Messenger — Manchester UP 1985
The Book of Manchester and Salford — Prof A H Burgess — Faulkner & Sons 1929
Medicine in the Making of Modern Britain 1700-1920 — C Lawrence — Routledge 1994
Medicine and Industrial Society — J V Pickstone — Manchester U P 1985
A Medical Tour Through The Whole Island of Great Britain — Louis Appleby — Faber 1994
The Moral and Physical Conditions of the Working Classes Employed in Cotton Manufacture in Manchester — Dr James Phillips-Kay — James Ridgeway 1832
In the Name of the Child: Health and Welfare 1880-1940 — Routledge 1992
Notes on Nursing (1859) — Florence Nightingale — Duckworth 1970
Nursing Children Psychology, Research & Practice — Muller Harris Watley Lippencott — Harper Row1986
The Other Side of Paediatrics — June Jolly — Macmillan 1981
Paediatric Nursing — M Duncombe & B Weller — Ballière Tindall Cox 1974
Paediatric Surgery E D Strathdee & D G Young Modern Practical Nursing — Heineman 1971
Pupils With Problems — DFE 1994
Small and Special; the Development of Hospitals for Children in Victorian Britain — EMR Lomax — Welcome Institute 1996
A Social History of English Working Classes — E Hopkins — Hodder & Stoughton 1979
Staying This Dreadful State of Things — PVA Garrod 1997 — History of Medicine Manchester
Surgery and Society in Peace and War — Roger Cooter — Manchester University 1993
The Welfare of Children and Young People in Hospital — HMSO 1990
The Yorkhill Story — Edna Robertson — Glasgow U P 1972

Manchester Evening News
Manchester Guardian
Salford Local History Archives
The Royal Manchester Children's Hospital Medical Library Giving for Living Centre
Rylands Library, Manchester University
Department of History of Medicine, Science and Technology Maths Tower
Notes on the Duchess of York Hospital — Dr Duncan Macaulay
Notes on Pendlebury for Nurse Training — Kay Worsley Cox
NHS 50th Anniversary Resource Pack — D O H 1998
Action for Sick Children 1962-1998
The Royal Manchester Children's Hospital Annual Reports from 1829-1998
Information also from interviews with present and past staff and questionaires to retired 'Pendlebury' nurses.

The University of Salford

School of Nursing

The School of Nursing is one of the schools within the Faculty of Health Care and Social Work. The School had its origins in the National Health Service in the form of the Northern College of Nursing, Midwifery and Health Studies. The College amalgamated with the University of Salford in 1996 when all nurse education moved into the Higher Education Sector.

The School of Nursing currently provides a wide variety of education and training at a number of levels for nurses. We offer a portfolio of courses at Diploma, Bachelor and Masters levels, and these offer educational opportunities for nurses at different career stages and, therefore, with differing professional needs. Some of our courses lead to professional qualifications together with an academic award, while others provide only an academic award.

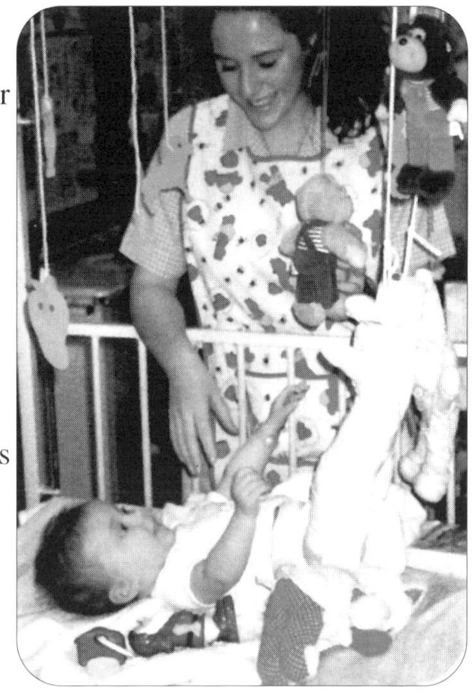

We also offer a wide range of opportunities for qualified children's nurses, leading to specialist practitioner or the Higher Award.

For further information about opportunities for nurses, phone for a prospectus on:
0161 295 2718/2783/2763,
or visit our web site at:
http:/www.salford.uk/nursing/

This book has been sponsored by the ROYAL MANCHESTER CHILDREN'S HOSPITAL LEAGUE OF FRIENDS

Over fifty years ago a group of people began visiting the Hospital, helping to improve the comfort and happiness of the children. This work continued after the War and the League of Friends at Royal Manchester Children's Hospital was founded in 1956.

We are not professional fund-raisers, just ordinary people interested in the welfare of the patients and the work of the hospital. Anyone who shares our interest and has a little spare time is welcome to join and help us.

Over the years, groups have worked together in Swinton, Salford and Manchester and further afield in Lancashire and Cheshire. Many sections of the community have contributed; businesses, shopkeepers and the general public, all unfailing in their support and generosity. Each summer until 1996, all groups got together to organise our major event of the year, the Annual Garden Party. This was held in the hospital grounds and attracted large crowds with the 'Tombola' and 'Grand Draw' being especially popular.

Garden Party 1960

The League of Friends was the first charity in the hospital; other charities initially sponsored by the League include the Bone Marrow Trust and Radio Lollipop. Proceeds from Garden Parties, amounting to several thousand pounds, have gone to give these charities their initial financial impetus.

The aim of the League of Friends remains to improve the comfort and welfare of patients, parents and staff, by providing extra requirements and amenities as well as equipment essential to the day to day running of the hospital which may not be otherwise obtainable.

One of our recent purchases has been to provide the ball pool and safe climbing frame in our Out Patients department along with other improvements to make out patient visits much less daunting than previously. Now the children who have to make repeated visits find the surroundings more welcoming and this can only help both the patients and their families.

In addition to individual purchases there are continuing costs including the provision of toys and decorations at Christmas, a taxi service for parents in distress and maintenance of the fish tanks.

There is a lot of satisfaction to be gained from knowing you are helping to speed the recovery of sick children and make their time in hospital happier. Members of the League of Friends are immensely proud of their long association with this great hospital and would like to take this opportunity to offer our grateful thanks to everyone who has contributed in any way, however large or small, to the work of the League of Friends over the years.

Thank you.